SPACES OF PEACE, SECURITY AND DEVELOPMENT

Series Editors: **John Heathershaw**, University of Exeter, UK, **Shahar Hameiri**, University of Queensland, Australia, **Jana Hönke**, University of Bayreuth, Germany, and **Sara Koopman**, Kent State University, USA

Volumes in this cutting-edge series move away from purely abstract debates about concepts and focus instead on fieldwork-based studies of specific places and peoples to demonstrate how particular spatial histories and geographic configurations can foster or hinder peace, security and development.

Available now

Shaping Peacebuilding in Colombia
International Frames and Spatial Transformation
By **Catalina Montoya Londoño**

Unarmed Civilian Protection
A New Paradigm for Protection and Human Security
Edited by **Ellen Furnari**, **Randy Janzen** and **Rosemary Kabaki**

Navigating the Local
Politics of Peacebuilding in Lebanese Municipalities
By **Hanna Leonardsson**

Precarious Urbanism
Displacement, Belonging and the Reconstruction of Somali Cities
By **Jutta Bakonyi** and **Peter Chonka**

Post-Liberal Statebuilding in Central Asia
Imaginaries, Discourses and Practices of Social Ordering
By **Philipp Lottholz**

Doing Fieldwork in Areas of International Intervention
A Guide to Research in Violent and Closed Contexts
Edited by **Berit Bliesemann de Guevara** and **Morten Bøås**

Surviving Everyday Life
The Securityscapes of Threatened People in Kyrgyzstan
Edited by **Marc von Boemcken**, **Nina Bagdasarova**, **Aksana Ismailbekova** and **Conrad Schetter**

For more information about the series and to
find out how to submit a proposal visit
**bristoluniversitypress.co.uk/
spaces-of-peace-security-and-development**

SPACES OF PEACE, SECURITY AND DEVELOPMENT

Forthcoming

Memory Politics after Mass Violence
Attributing Roles in the Memoryscape
By **Timothy Williams**

Development as Entanglement
An Ethnographic History of Ethiopia's Agrarian Paradox
By **Teferi Abate Adem**

International Advisory Board

Rita Abrahamsen, University of Ottawa, Canada
John Agnew, University of California, Los Angeles, US
Alima Bissenova, Nazarbayev University, Kazakhstan
Annika Björkdahl, Lund University, Sweden
Berit Bliesemann de Guevara, Aberystwyth University, UK
Susanne Buckley-Zistel, Philipps University Marburg, Germany
Toby Carroll, City University of Hong Kong
Mick Dumper, University of Exeter, UK
Azra Hromadžić, Syracuse University, US
Lee Jones, Queen Mary University of London, UK
Louisa Lombard, Yale University, US
Virginie Mamadouh, University of Amsterdam, Netherlands
Nick Megoran, Newcastle University, UK
Markus-Michael Müller, Free University of Berlin, Germany
Daniel Neep, Georgetown University, US
Diana Ojeda, Xavierian University, Colombia
Jenny Peterson, The University of British Columbia, Canada
Madeleine Reeves, The University of Manchester, UK
Conrad Schetter, Bonn International Center for Conflict Studies, Germany
Ricardo Soares de Olivera, University of Oxford, UK
Diana Suhardiman, International Water Management Institute, Laos
Arlene Tickner, Del Rosario University, Colombia
Jacqui True, Monash University, Australia
Sofía Zaragocín, Universidad San Francisco de Quito, Ecuador

For more information about the series and to
find out how to submit a proposal visit
**bristoluniversitypress.co.uk/
spaces-of-peace-security-and-development**

GENDER AND CITIZENSHIP IN TRANSITIONAL JUSTICE

Everyday Experiences of Reparation and Reintegration in Colombia

Sanne Weber

First published in Great Britain in 2025 by

Bristol University Press
University of Bristol
1-9 Old Park Hill
Bristol
BS2 8BB
UK
t: +44 (0)117 374 6645
e: bup-info@bristol.ac.uk

Details of international sales and distribution partners are available at bristoluniversitypress.co.uk

© Bristol University Press 2025

British Library Cataloguing in Publication Data
A catalogue record for this book is available from the British Library

ISBN 978-1-5292-3412-1 hardcover
ISBN 978-1-5292-3413-8 paperback
ISBN 978-1-5292-3414-5 ePub
ISBN 978-1-5292-3415-2 ePdf

The right of Sanne Weber to be identified as author of this work has been asserted by her in accordance with the Copyright, Designs and Patents Act 1988.

All rights reserved: no part of this publication may be reproduced, stored in a retrieval system, or transmitted in any form or by any means, electronic, mechanical, photocopying, recording, or otherwise without the prior permission of Bristol University Press.

Every reasonable effort has been made to obtain permission to reproduce copyrighted material. If, however, anyone knows of an oversight, please contact the publisher.

The statements and opinions contained within this publication are solely those of the author and not of the University of Bristol or Bristol University Press. The University of Bristol and Bristol University Press disclaim responsibility for any injury to persons or property resulting from any material published in this publication.

Bristol University Press works to counter discrimination on grounds of gender, race, disability, age and sexuality.

Cover design: blu inc, Bristol
Front cover image: Sanne Weber

Contents

List of Figures and Table		vi
List of Abbreviations		vii
Notes on the Author		viii
Acknowledgements		ix
Introduction: Reparation, Reintegration and Transformation		1
1	Gender, Violence and Reconciliation in Colombia	17
2	Tales of Machismo and Motherhood: Gendered Changes across War and Peace	49
3	Between Victimization and Agency: Gendered Victim–Perpetrator Dichotomies	77
4	Gendering Reconciliation? The 'Differential Perspective' of Reparation and Reintegration	100
5	Gradations of Citizenship: Of Radical Agrarian Citizens and Transitional Justice Bureaucracies	129
6	Overcoming Obstacles to Citizenship: Imagining Post-Conflict Gender Equality	146
Conclusion: From Victimhood to Citizenship		165
Appendix: Checklist for Ethics in Research on Gender and Conflict		179
References		201
Index		232

List of Figures and Table

Figures

1.1	Map of Chibolo within the Magdalena department and Colombia	32
1.2	Map of Fonseca within the department of La Guajira and Colombia	34
1.3	House in La Pola	36
1.4	House in La Palizua	37
1.5	Houses in Pondores	38
2.1	Woman milking a cow	54
2.2	Cooking on wood fire	63
2.3	Women as veterinarians	72
4.1	The farm as a family business	110
4.2	The importance of the animals	110
6.1	The need for basic services	147
6.2	The need for basic services	148
6.3	The need for basic services	148
6.4	Chickens project	150
6.5	Tailoring projects	151

Table

A.1	Ethics checklist for research on gender and conflict	180

List of Abbreviations

ACR	High Council for Reintegration
ANUC	National Association of Tenant Farmers
ARN	Agency for Reincorporation and Normalization
AUC	United Self-Defence Forces of Colombia
CEV	Colombian Commission for the Clarification of Truth, Coexistence and Reconciliation
CJYC	Corporación Jurídica Yira Castro
DDR	disarmament, demobilization and reintegration
ELN	National Liberation Army
ETCR	territorial space for training and reincorporation
EU	European Union
FARC	Revolutionary Armed Forces of Colombia
IDDRS	Integrated Disarmament Demobilization and Reintegration Standards
IDPs	internally displaced persons
JEP	Special Jurisdiction for Peace
JPL	Justice and Peace Law
LRU	Land Restitution Unit
NAP	national action plan
NCHM	National Centre for Historical Memory
NGO	non-governmental organization
NPU	National Protection Unit
PDET	territorial rural development plans
TJ	transitional justice
TRC	Truth and Reconciliation Commission
UN	United Nations
UNDP	United Nations Development Programme
UNFAO	United Nations Food and Agriculture Organization
UP	Patriotic Union
VU	Victims' Unit
WPS	Women, Peace and Security

Notes on the Author

Sanne Weber is a research fellow at the International Development Department of the University of Birmingham. She obtained her PhD at the Centre for Trust, Peace and Social Relations at Coventry University. Her research explores how conflict affects gender relations. She uses ethnographic, participatory and creative research methods to understand whether and how transitional justice and other post-conflict justice and reconstruction mechanisms are capable of transforming gendered and other structural inequalities. She has worked primarily in Latin America, particularly in Colombia and Guatemala. She has also worked as a researcher and senior programme officer on gender and transitional justice for human rights and development organizations in Guatemala and Europe.

Acknowledgements

This book is the result of many years of reading, writing and talking to many people who have been essential for how my thinking has developed. First of all, a very special thank you goes to the women and men in La Pola, La Palizua and Pondores, who have been so generous with their time and have opened their homes and communities to me. I only hope that this research has also been somehow meaningful for them. This book is dedicated to them. A big thank you too to all the other people who collaborated with my research in Colombia, from state institutions and civil society organizations, as well as academics and practitioners who supported me with connections or information, like Lina Céspedes-Báez, Donny Meertens and Martha Lucía Gutiérrez. A special thank you to the Corporación Yira Castro, for enabling contact with the communities in Chibolo.

Secondly, I would like to thank my PhD supervisors, EJ Milne, Michaelina Jakala and Rosalind Searle, for guiding me and giving me the trust and freedom to find my own path. A very special thank you to EJ, for inspiring and guiding my thinking about methods and participation, and being such a great mentor even in difficult times. A big thank you to Paul Jackson too, who supported me during my postdoctoral work, and still does. Thanks to the Instituto Pensar at the Javeriana University in Bogotá for welcoming me as a visiting researcher in 2019. I am indebted to Coventry University, the University of Birmingham, the Leverhulme Trust, the Fran Trust and the Society for Latin American Studies for financially enabling my research. Finally, I am very grateful to Bristol University Press and the anonymous reviewers for their enthusiasm for this book and their suggestions for finalizing the manuscript, and especially to Zoe Forbes and her support with preparing it.

During my research, I have made many friends for life who have supported me both academically and through drinks, coffee and friendship. Tatiana Sanchez Parra, Adriana Rudling and Justina Pinkeviciute: thank you for your immense support in many ways. Mijke de Waardt and Floortje van Toll, whom I met in Valledupar of all places, were of great moral support during fieldwork, and have become good friends back home too. I would like to thank Julia Zulver and Francy Carranza for all the interesting conversations and ongoing and future collaborations. Charlie Rumsby, Becca Weber, Eve Buck-Matthews and Pascal Bodemeijer were great friends who helped me to readapt to the UK after fieldwork. All of you have been a great feminist support network! I would also like to thank Sayra van den Berg, Raquel da Silva, Laura S. Martin, Sandra Rios Oyola, Merisa Thompson, Nic Cheeseman and other colleagues at the University of Birmingham for reviewing chapters of this book and other pieces of writing that contributed to it. There are many others who contributed to this research through conversations over coffee or beers, like Nury Martínez, Cielo Piñeros, Gwen Burnyeat, Kiran Stallone, Pryscill Anctil, Janieke Drent, Hanna Bertelman, Silke Gatermann, Raúl Castro, Megan Janetsky and Dáire McGill.

Intellectually, my work was inspired by many scholars. Particularly, I want to mention Brinton Lykes and Linda Tuhiwai Smith for their inspiring work on research methods and ethics, Kimberly Theidon and Erin Baines for their wonderful ethnographic work which helped me to find my own voice, Mo Hume, who writes so eloquently about gender and violence in Latin America and has been very supportive to me, and, finally, the authors developing transformative justice ideas, like Wendy Lambourne, Simon Robins and Paul Gready, who helped me to think creatively about transitional justice. A big thank you also to Impunity Watch, for inspiring my academic work in the first place and helping me to connect my academic research to the 'real world'.

My friends in the Netherlands and Europe, who helped me to remember there are other things in life than work, are too many to mention. A thank you to Wouter for his support in the final stretch of writing this book. Finally, I could not have written this book without my fantastic family, who were always there to support when things were difficult, or to celebrate my achievements.

Introduction: Reparation, Reintegration and Transformation

> 'There is peace, but we continue to suffer, so we don't know what peace really means.'
>
> Josefa, Chibolo IDP community leader

This is what community leader Josefa[1] exclaimed in 2017 when I visited her in her community of former internally displaced persons (IDPs) in Chibolo, on the Caribbean coast of Colombia, where I had been researching the gendered dynamics of Colombia's Victims' Law of reparations and land restitution since 2015. This Law provides survivors of Colombia's conflict with individual and collective reparations and the rare measure of land restitution, thus aiming to address the situation of the millions of IDPs resulting from Colombia's conflict. Together with Josefa and her husband, I watched the historic handshake between *Fuerzas Armadas Revolucionarias de Colombia* (Revolutionary Armed Forces of Colombia [FARC]) leader Timochenko and President Santos, after signing the peace accord on victims' rights in September 2015. This agreement paved the way for the final peace agreement signed in December of the following year, which brought an end to over 50 years of armed conflict between the Colombian state and the FARC. Various other guerrilla movements, as well as the paramilitary, had already demobilized, while other guerrilla and criminal groups remained active. Although the peace deal with the former FARC guerrillas would not directly change the situation of Josefa and her community, who had been displaced by paramilitary groups, its signing did instil hopes for a better future, and for a government that would finally guarantee a dignified life for all of its citizens, including in remote and rural parts of Colombia.

The historic 2016 peace agreement led to the disarmament, demobilization and reintegration (DDR) of the FARC. This DDR process has received much attention nationally and internationally, not only for involving one of the oldest guerrilla movements worldwide but also for adopting a

---

[1] All names of participants are pseudonyms to protect their anonymity.

collective and rural approach, and for its connection to yet another ambitious transitional justice (TJ) package by the Colombian government. Since 2018, I have studied the FARC's reintegration process in the collective reincorporation zone in La Guajira. Examining the experiences of those affected by conflict in relation to both these post-conflict processes has allowed me to better understand what peace – or at least the process of building it – looks like in practice, not only for survivors but also for former combatants. It is these lived experiences of peace, justice and reconciliation processes that I describe in this book, with a particular focus on contrasting them with the expectations raised by TJ and DDR laws and policies. The expectations and needs of the participants in my research can be best described by two words which they uttered over and over again: *salir adelante*, or moving forward. *Salir adelante* can also mean to 'move on', which is what TJ processes can help people to do.

I analyse these questions through a gendered lens. In a patriarchal society like Colombia, and in a region known to be particularly *machista* like the Caribbean coast, *salir adelante* has particular gendered dynamics. Women encounter distinct obstacles to defining and developing their own life projects and realizing their hopes and dreams. They are often limited by societal gendered norms and expectations which limit their access to many, mostly public, spheres of life. Likewise, men can also be trapped in rigid notions of masculinity which limit their active involvement in family life and make them more prone to participate in and become victims of violence. Post-conflict peace and reconciliation mechanisms can, at least in theory, play a role in transforming gendered norms and provide support for women and men to fulfil their envisioned roles in life, alongside their families and communities. Literature over the past decades has examined the gendered impacts of conflict and how TJ and other peacebuilding mechanisms can address them (Enloe 2000; Cockburn 2007; Buckley-Zistel and Zolkos 2012; O'Rourke 2013). In this book, I contribute empirical data to make sure that the implementation of gendered TJ policies responds to the everyday realities on the ground.

This book shows and explains the problematic gap between theory and practice of gendered TJ and DDR. Using Colombia as a case study, I ask: what are the gendered dynamics of reparation and reintegration laws and policies on the ground and do they effectively transform structural gender inequality, thus enabling communities to '*salir adelante*' or move forward? I show that in their current state, in Colombia, these fail to understand gender in a complex and relational way. Instead, they often reinforce victim and perpetrator binaries rather than treat women as agents, undermining gender equality and ultimately holistic and sustainable peace. As a result, the peace that is being established in Colombia is not actually the peace that the protagonists of this book had envisioned. To overcome this, I offer a new approach to TJ and DDR practice that centres gendered citizenship, which allows women to become more equal actors in private and public spheres, enabling them to transform their own lives and communities.

Although the main focus of this book is on gender, it is not a book about sexual violence, which is often the subject of 'gender-sensitive' TJ. Rather than focusing on experiences of violence, I aim instead to examine the structures of gender inequality, to explore how these are experienced and how they can be transformed. Following a long tradition of feminist research, I believe that looking at everyday experiences at the community level is crucial for understanding the impacts of inequalities and strategies for transformation. Zooming in on these localized and gendered everyday experiences is one of the contributions this book makes to peace studies. It does so by using a feminist ethnographic approach, which is combined with participatory visual research to ensure that the study is more meaningful for the participants and to avoid speaking *for* the research participants as a White European researcher. This approach, which is explained in more detail in the next chapter, enabled participants to show me their everyday lives in ways that I might not have otherwise considered. In fact, many of the images included in this book are produced by the participants themselves.

In this way, the book not only contributes rich and novel empirical data on the gendered dimensions of peacebuilding and TJ, analysed from the perspectives of both victims and those seen as perpetrators, but it also provides new methodological insights into 'doing' and researching peace. Throughout the book, I will discuss the ethical and practical challenges and benefits of a more participatory approach to conducting research with people who have been affected by conflict, especially with women and on sensitive issues. The book also deals with the ways in which participation can facilitate better inclusion of marginalized communities in peacebuilding processes. Based on the experiences, ideas and images of the protagonists in this book, I engage with and push TJ theory forward by proposing ways to ensure that peace can actually transform structural inequalities, particularly gendered ones, to help men, and especially women, to move forward – *salir adelante*.

Transitional justice and disarmament, demobilization and reintegration

This book examines the experiences of two different post-conflict tools for building peace and reconciliation: reparations for conflict survivors and reintegration processes for armed actors. Both these processes have the potential to make tangible impacts on the lives of people affected by conflict, and both have increasingly attempted to incorporate a gendered perspective. TJ refers to a set of measures aimed at addressing serious human rights abuses in states that are transitioning away from authoritarianism and conflict towards democracy and peace. It consists of various elements, generally implemented through separate mechanisms. Processes of truth telling, generally non-judicial truth commissions, aim to create a broader historical perspective, promote individual healing and help societies overcome their traumatic past (Hayner 2001; Mani 2002). Criminal justice processes, ranging from national and international tribunals to hybrid courts, are perceived as necessary to make a break between past and present (Mani 2002; Teitel 2003). Reparations are meant to offer redress to survivors of human rights violations. According to the United Nations (UN), comprehensive reparations should include restitution, compensation, rehabilitation, satisfaction and guarantees of non-repetition, combining material, financial and symbolic, and both individual and collective reparations (United Nations General Assembly 2005). Reparations are generally implemented by governments through administrative programmes, like the one created through Colombia's Victims' Law. Although guarantees of non-repetition are often understood to be part of reparations, they are also treated as a separate area which includes institutional, constitutional and legal reform, processes of vetting and lustration of those responsible for human rights violations and DDR processes (Teitel 2001). Although this means that, in a way, the two processes at the heart of this book can both be seen as part of TJ, there are also tensions between them, as I will describe further on.

This book engages with two central debates in the TJ field. One of these is the centrality of victimhood in TJ practice and research. Yet the focus on victimhood is problematic, as it tends to create rigid binaries between innocent victims and guilty perpetrators, ignoring a 'grey zone' of those implicated in violence to different degrees, including complicit bystanders (Levi 2013; Moffett 2016). This book will illustrate, through a gendered lens, that, for many people, a victim identity is not helpful for transitioning towards a life that is no longer defined by conflict experiences, while for others it can be a way of avoiding responsibility for violence. As a result, I prefer to use the term survivors, in an attempt to uphold the agency that most survivors have displayed in very challenging circumstances. In some instances, though, I use the term victims, as it is hard to ignore when writing about the Victims' Law, whose many institutions and mechanisms make explicit reference to victimhood. In this book, I show that the centrality of victimhood is an obstacle to *salir adelante*, and to the active citizenship that can help people to move forward.

The second critique of TJ that I engage with is its scope for transformation. TJ has long prioritized legal-institutional reforms over socio-economic transformation. It tends to focus on the most serious human rights violations, specifically in the form of direct violence and civil and political rights violations, while paying less attention to the social and economic impacts of conflict (Miller 2008). TJ thus tends to promote what Galtung (1969) defines as negative peace, or the absence of direct violence, generally falling short of facilitating positive peace or the absence of structural violence – structures of economic, geographical, gender and ethnic inequality (Farmer 1996; Evans 2016). These criticisms have led to proposals for transformative justice, which prioritizes the transformation of the structural inequalities which lie at the heart of conflicts (Lambourne 2009; Gready et al 2010; Gready and Robins 2014). Although these proposals in turn have been critiqued for being too vague, too broad and requiring a timeframe that goes beyond the lifespan of TJ institutions (De Greiff 2009; Waldorf 2012), I am interested in exploring how TJ could be made more transformative, especially in relation to gendered inequalities. It is increasingly argued that reparations could play a role in such transformations. Transformative reparations should go beyond returning victims and survivors to the status quo ante, instead including aspects of redistributive justice which contribute to addressing underlying structures of socio-economic inequality, for example, through development measures and social services (Uprimny Yepes 2009). This idea has been applied to the transformation of gender inequalities too. The 'Cotton Field' decision of the Inter-American Court of Human Rights, for instance, has indicated that in conditions where violations were committed in a context of structural discrimination, reparations should aim to transform this pre-existing situation (Rubio-Marín and Sandoval 2011). Otherwise, reparations risk returning women to the situation of structural discrimination they suffered before the conflict (Durbach and Chappell 2014; Lemaitre and Sandvik 2014). I argue that a gendered process of citizenship building can aid such transformations.

As described, DDR can be seen as an element of guarantees of non-repetition. However, it is also considered a field of practice and study in and of itself. Since the late 1980s, over 60 DDR processes have been initiated, mostly in the aftermath of conflict but sometimes also as part of peace processes to support the reintegration of former combatants into civilian life (Muggah and O'Donnell 2015). By 2000, it was described by the then UN Secretary-General as 'vital to stability in a post-conflict situation' (Humphreys and Weinstein 2007, 532). DDR aims to disband armed factions by offering economic alternatives and incentives to ex-combatants. It also seeks to generate their trust in democratic institutions and facilitate social trust between ex-combatants and communities (Humphreys and Weinstein 2007). DDR programmes generally take place in different phases. An initial phase of disarmament includes weapon surrender (often in exchange for cash or other goods). This is followed by demobilization, which involves assembling troops and dismantling command structures. Reinsertion support often takes place in demobilization camps, through material, social and economic assistance that supports ex-combatants in transitioning to civilian life. The longer-term reintegration process which follows entails the insertion of former members of armed groups as civilians in a post-conflict society (Ball and Van de Goor 2006; Bowd and Özerdem 2013).

Reintegration, often the weakest link in DDR, is a complex and long-term process without a clearly defined timeframe or end date, consisting of three interrelated political, economic and social spheres (Knight and Özerdem 2004; Ball and Van de Goor 2006; Waldorf 2009). Within these, social reintegration is hardest to measure, since it involves rebuilding civilian identities, social relationships and trust between groups, issues which are not so easily quantified (Bowd and Özerdem 2013; Friedman 2018). Returning 'home' is often fraught with difficulties, since communities and families are not always willing to receive ex-combatants, who tend to be regarded with suspicion, fear or stigma (Bowd and Özerdem 2013). The initially more security-focused emphasis on individual ex-combatants has now given way to a broader goal of building the conditions for sustainable peace, through promoting reconciliation and rebuilding the livelihoods of ex-combatants. This has led to a stronger involvement of and support for the communities where ex-combatants reintegrate, to increase the success of longer-term reintegration (Humphreys and Weinstein 2007; Muggah 2010; Willems and Van Leeuwen 2014; Kaplan and Nussio 2018).

In spite of both being essential elements of peacebuilding, there are clear tensions between TJ and DDR, which explain why both policy areas, as well as research into them, have long developed separately (Sriram and Herman 2009). First of all, TJ mechanisms are mainly concerned with redressing the needs of survivors, whereas DDR principally occupies itself with former combatants. Unsurprisingly, these approaches may compete for funding among the same donor pools, while security concerns mean that DDR processes tend to be more generously supported than TJ processes (Sriram and Herman 2009; Waldorf 2009). This frequently leads to a perception of perpetrators of crimes being privileged over victims. For example, ex-combatants in Uganda received material and psychosocial support, while IDPs received little financial or other support when returning to their land (Sriram and Herman 2009; P. Clark 2014). This can lead to grievances and resentment among community members, which can in turn produce distrust towards ex-combatants or towards the government (Theidon 2007b; Bowd and Özerdem 2013; Sriram and Herman 2009). As I will show in Chapter 3, a similar pattern can be seen in Colombia.

Tensions also relate to the different goals emphasized by DDR and TJ. Whereas DDR processes aim to produce security and peace through the disbandment of armed groups, TJ mechanisms aim to promote accountability for past violence. These two goals can conflict, as the prospect of criminal prosecutions may deter combatants from participating in peace processes (Sriram and Herman 2009). Nevertheless, the TJ field increasingly values a broader approach to peacebuilding in which retributive justice may give way to more restorative approaches to justice. The South African Truth and Reconciliation Commission (TRC) in fact promoted amnesties in return for truth telling, assuming this would better help society heal than retributive justice. Amnesties are also common in DDR processes, including various of the DDR processes implemented in Colombia. They are often contingent upon ex-combatants taking part in non-judicial TJ measures such as truth telling, reparations or restorative justice approaches like rituals and ceremonial cleansings (Sriram and Herman 2009; Bowd and Özerdem 2013). The connections between TJ and DDR have also been recognized by the UN's 2006 adoption of an integrated approach to DDR (P. Clark 2014). Colombia's approach to DDR is a good example of this, as the next chapter will describe in more detail.

That TJ and DDR are indeed compatible can be explained by their similar long-term goals, with both processes ultimately promoting security, peace and reconciliation (Sriram and Herman 2009; P. Clark 2014). In fact, together they form part of what MacKenzie (2012, 139) describes as a post-conflict formula: 'peace accord + disarmament + transitional justice = healing, forgiveness and harmony'. An essential step for achieving this is rebuilding trust between those affected by conflict and the state, as well as community members (Waldorf 2009). In this sense, DDR, and especially reintegration, is closely connected to reparations, which are regarded as an instrument for reintegrating survivors as equal citizens and rights holders in a political community, thereby re-establishing trust in state institutions (De Greiff 2009; Roht-Arriaza and Orlovsky 2009; Laplante 2015). Thus, as reparations promote the integration of survivors as equals in society, reintegration aims to do the same for ex-combatants (Rodríguez López, Andreouli and Howarth 2015; Wiegink, Sprenkels and Sørensen 2019). Both reintegration and reparations are thus in a way processes of 'social engineering' (Muggah 2010; McMullin 2013) that provide opportunities to negotiate and (re)construct identities, helping individuals transition from their position as victim or perpetrator towards a civilian life. In this way, both processes are connected to citizenship building. This book will zoom in on reparation and reintegration processes, and analyse their connection to the promotion of citizenship practices.

I argue that citizenship is a way to give TJ a concrete goal which can help to overcome victim–perpetrator binaries and gender inequality. There have been many debates about what citizenship exactly entails. First and foremost, citizenship is a legal category, which includes people as equals in a political community. It is often related to nationality, or to birth lineage, and is considered by different authors as a status, a standing or an identification (Cohen 2009). Citizenship entails rights and obligations, and thus requires individuals to actively demand their citizenship rights according to the rules of a shared political community, based on a sense of political autonomy

(Mouffe 1992; Taylor 2004). Citizenship can thus be understood as a practice which is constructed, involving civic duties of participation (Mouffe 1992; Jelin 1996; Kabeer 2012). It is a mechanism for making claims, including to the state (Lazar 2013b). Citizenship is therefore both a process and an outcome (Lister 2003). I am mostly interested in the process, in the actual practice of citizenship. A difference can exist between the status and practice of citizenship: those who fulfil the expected actions related to citizenship may not necessarily have a citizenship status, for example, in the case of refugees (Cohen 2009). Vice versa, some people, including women, may have formal citizenship rights but lack the possibilities or knowledge to exercise these (Bareiro 1997; Kent 2016). Economic or social alienation prevents many people, even in democratic states, to exercise their citizenship rights. The same goes for structures of gender inequality that marginalize women (Yuval-Davis 1997; Hearn and Biricik 2016). Citizenship is not a linear process but rather exists in gradations, as will be apparent from examples in this book. The practice of citizenship can be lost (Bareiro 1997; Rosaldo 2013), for example, through the disarticulation of forms of social organization caused by conflict, as described in Chapter 2. The central function of citizenship is, however, to make citizens equal (Cohen 2009). Citizenship as a practice is an important instrument to make demands on the state for basic rights and inclusion. As such, it helps to overcome the passivity frequently inherent in victimhood discourses and identities. In this book, I describe how TJ and DDR in Colombia tend to reinforce passivity and dependency, and how promoting active citizenship could instead help those affected by conflict to transform their lives. In analysing this question, I take a gendered approach.

Gendering peace and conflict: advances and pitfalls

Over the last few decades, there has been much attention on the different impacts of conflict on women and their active role in conflict and peace. The surge in academic interest in these areas was fuelled in part by the recognition of large-scale sexual violence in the conflict in the former Yugoslavia and the Rwandan genocide, and the ground-breaking jurisprudence related to sexual violence that was developed by the resulting international criminal tribunals. Attention for gender in peacebuilding policies has been mainstreamed into what is now known as the Women, Peace and Security (WPS) Agenda, which aims for women to be protected from (sexual) violence and to become peacebuilders and agents for change. However, the WPS debate reflects a wider tendency within TJ and peacebuilding to understand gender solely as women, and mostly heterosexual women at that. By addressing only one part of gendered power relations, excluding LGBTQ women and masculinities, the WPS agenda's effectiveness in transforming gendered inequalities is limited (Hagen 2016; Wright 2020).

Gendered attention in TJ practice – less so in research – has predominantly focused on sexual violence against women, which is considered to be *the* gendered war experience (Theidon 2007a). Such 'hypes' (Hilhorst and Douma 2018), which attract extremely high levels of media, political, humanitarian or academic attention for particular periods of time, can increase awareness. Hypes can, however, also have their pitfalls, as the strong attention on the different manifestations of sexual violence has diminished attention and resources for its prevention, as well as for other gender-based crimes (Meger 2016). Albeit a devastating, long-unrecognized crime, sexual violence is not the only crime women experience in the context of conflict, whereas not all women experience sexual violence as the most traumatizing conflict experience. Nevertheless, this 'conceptual myopia' (Bueno-Hansen 2015, 110) obscures other experiences women might have had, such as socio-economic difficulties or the loss of a child (Franke 2006; Crosby and Lykes 2011; Berry 2018). Inviting women to break the silence about sexual violence is important to address the crime, but, at the same time, it can expose women to judgment, stigmatization or even rejection by their communities and families, who consider them impure and promiscuous. Furthermore, the way in which defence lawyers in criminal trials interrogate sexual violence survivors can make witnessing a disempowering and even retraumatizing experience, which risks essentializing women as victims with no agency (Mertus 2004). Addressing women merely as potential sexual violence victims, moreover, reinforces stereotypes about women's sexualized vulnerability, maintaining the understanding that rape equals social death for women, and thus upholding patriarchal ideas about the need for male protection (Žarkov 2007; Otto 2010). In this way, 'gender-sensitive' TJ processes have too often resulted in an 'add women and stir' approach which fails to address the wider social and economic inequalities and deeply embedded gendered power relations between men and women prior to, during and after the conflict (Ní Aoláin 2006; Buckley-Zistel and Zolkos 2012; Swaine 2018).

The prioritization of sexual violence diverts attention away from women's resistance, resilience and agency, both during conflict and post-conflict periods (Kent 2014; Baines 2015; Björkdahl and Mannergren Selimovic 2015). This diminishes possibilities for women to become political agents in the post-conflict context. Although the WPS agenda was important for emphasizing women's roles as peacebuilders, frequently, this peacemaker narrative relies on the assumption that women are natural peacemakers because they are mothers, with innate caring and nurturing capacities (Cockburn 2001; Sjoberg 2016). Although women themselves sometimes use this representation to legitimize their role as political actors (Berry 2018), it risks reinforcing patriarchal notions which maintain the idea that women are those principally responsible for reproductive tasks. The expectation of being peacemakers and rebuilding communities that are still characterized by patriarchal relationships can place an additional burden on women, especially if they are not supported by actions that transform the underlying gender inequality that caused violence against them in the first place.

Beyond violent men and vulnerable women

The idea that all women are peaceful is far from true. In the last decade, research on women's active roles in political violence has increased considerably. This shift in focus is important, since women constitute significant parts of armed factions, especially in guerrilla groups and liberation movements (Goldstein 2001; Alison 2004). In media and policy accounts, female fighters are often regarded with particular curiosity and fascination. They are, however, frequently portrayed in stereotypical ways. On the one hand, female combatants tend to be represented as victims of forced recruitment or (sexual) violence by armed groups, or as bush wives, camp followers or sex slaves (Coulter 2009; MacKenzie 2009). Alternatively, they are often believed to have joined armed groups for personal reasons, for example, following male family members or escaping (sexual) violence, whereas men's desire to take up arms tends to be presented as politically or ideologically motivated. Women are therefore presented as somehow less responsible, as instrumentalized by others (Gonzales Vaillant et al 2012; Henshaw 2016; Eggert 2018). On the other hand, female combatants are portrayed as even more violent than men because they transgress traditional notions of women's peacefulness and innocence. This leads to a portrayal of deviance and exceptionality, calling into question their 'womanhood' (Alison 2004; Sjoberg and Gentry 2007). Eventually, both these representations uphold gendered stereotypes of women's inherent innocence and peacefulness. Yet, like men, women make conscious decisions to join armed groups and commit violent acts, even including sexual violence (Cohen 2013; Sjoberg 2016). They should therefore be considered as political actors, individuals with agency and ideological stances who are equally capable of committing violent acts, which they need to be held accountable for. At the same time, they might have specific needs and experiences which need addressing.

This was long not the case in post-conflict programmes. For example, DDR programmes have tended to focus mostly on male combatants, who are seen as the 'real' combatants and thus a greater security risk. Women were often excluded for having played support roles, or were prevented from handing in their arms by male soldiers or commanders. In certain circumstances, women have preferred to abstain from participating in DDR to avoid the stigma of association with armed groups (Coulter 2009; MacKenzie 2009; Jennings 2009). Women's inability to participate in DDR has had detrimental effects. Communities have treated female ex-fighters as pariahs who have disrupted traditional gender norms. Stigma tends to be even stronger when women return with children conceived during conflict, making communities regard them as promiscuous and impure (Coulter 2009; Vastapuu 2018).

UN Security Council Resolution 1325 was the first to highlight the particular needs of women in DDR, albeit without offering specific guidance. The Integrated Disarmament Demobilization and Reintegration Standards (IDDRS), adopted in 2006, include a gender module that provides more detail about potential gender-sensitive DDR measures. Among others, it lists the need for female-specific health support, childcare, the need to combat negative gender stereotypes and the provision of skills and leadership training for women (UN IAWG, 2006). Although the IDDRS have been updated in recent years, as of 2023, the module on gender was still under revision. Unfortunately, programmes addressing female-specific needs have often reinforced gender stereotypes. Liberia's DDR programme, for example, offered women training on tailoring and hairdressing skills, while Sri Lanka's programme encouraged women to marry and have children (Jennings 2009; Friedman 2018). Most programmes fail to incorporate measures to overcome structural obstacles to reintegration, such as labour market discrimination, childcare needs or social attitudes (Specht and Attree 2006; Dietrich Ortega 2009; Hauge 2020). Chapter 4 will show that this tendency holds true for Colombia as well.

The other aspect that is often overlooked in 'gendered' approaches to peacebuilding is men's experience of conflict. It is increasingly recognized that men are not only perpetrators of gender-based violence but also victims, including of sexual violence. Male sexual violence has been insufficiently studied, as its victims fall outside of the imagined 'rape victim identity' (Simić 2015). Sexual violence is not only intended to emasculate men through its association with homosexuality but also acts as a means of instilling subordination between men of different warring groups (Jones 2006; Žarkov 2007; Schulz 2019). Sexual violence is also a method of socializing soldiers into aggressive masculinities, and used as a tool for establishing internal hierarchies of dominant and subordinated masculinities (Boesten 2014; Bueno-Hansen 2015). Silence in relation to these different modes of sexual violence is hard to break due to the shame and stigma attached to it (J.N. Clark 2014). This means that male survivors do not always receive the support or recognition that might be afforded to women.

This book will not address sexual violence against men, but it does engage with the need to transform (militarized) masculinities. The conflict-era militarized male role is often understood to include protecting women, children and nation (Enloe 2002). This role becomes irrelevant when the conflict is over, causing men to feel a sense of loss of masculine status and power, which is compounded by the perceived gains that women have made during conflict, and the emasculating effects of major social changes such as poverty, unemployment and crime (Cleaver 2002; Myrttinen, Khattab and Naujoks 2017). The result is often referred to as a crisis of masculinities (Thomson 2002). This crisis leads some men to reassert their hegemonic masculinity in the post-conflict era, sometimes using violence against women to re-establish gendered social norms, in a patriarchal backlash (Pankhurst 2008; Berry 2018). It is therefore not surprising that levels of domestic violence among families of ex-combatants tend to be high (Tabak 2011). Violence against women in post-conflict societies can be just as significant as during periods of conflict. It is often perceived to have intensified, although it is not always clear whether this is indeed the case, or whether reports about it simply increase because of changed norms and heightened awareness (Swaine 2018).

At the same time, male ex-combatants may have their own conflict-related traumas and can find the experience of demobilization and the loss of their fighter identity an emasculating process (Specht 2013; Bulmer and Eichler 2017). Alcohol abuse tends to be high among war veterans (Goldstein 2001). The consequences of demobilization thus produce a complex picture, in which men – like women – can be perpetrators and victims of violence at the same time. TJ processes and DDR mechanisms, however, often fail to incorporate strategies to address the violence men suffer (Hauge 2020). Nor do they prioritize the transformation of harmful and militarized masculinities into more peaceful and supportive ways of being men, or promote changes in society that make young men less attracted to joining armed groups as a way to gain masculine status (Theidon 2009; Ní Aoláin, Haynes and Cahn 2011; Duriesmith 2014).

Transformative gender justice

Too often, the incorporation of gendered perspectives in TJ processes or DDR programmes translates into centralizing the (sexual) violence that women suffer, without recognizing women's social, economic and political agency, nor men's experiences and the ways in which masculinities impact and are impacted by conflict. This approach overlooks the underlying gender inequalities, and the socially constructed roles men and women are expected to enact in public and private spheres, which have been detrimental to both women and men. This book explores the ways in which reparation and reintegration programmes can engage with those gendered structures so that societies genuinely transform. To transform means to actually *change* the social system which causes gendered and other inequalities, rather than aiming to *reform* it, which would mean to solve problems but leave the system intact (Collins 2019). I use transformative gender justice as an approach. Although the term gender justice is often used by researchers and activists, what the concept actually entails remains vague, and it is often limited to a focus on women's rights (Goetz 2007; Vergel Tovar 2011). I understand it as a process that aims to transform underlying structures of gender inequality to guarantee men and women a future in which they have equal possibilities and opportunities. Merely addressing the symptoms of inequalities is not sufficient for this.

An approach that is useful for thinking about transformative gender justice and devising ways of putting it into practice is Nancy Fraser's model of trivalent justice, which argues for 'justice against structures' of inequality (Fraser 2008, 49). In order to be transformative, justice should entail the realization of three interconnected elements: recognition, redistribution and representation. Although not originally developed to specifically address gendered inequalities, the model has been applied to transformative reparations for sexual violence (Williams and Palmer 2016) and to broader ideas of gender justice (O'Reilly 2017). *Recognition* refers to the need to recognize, value and validate women's conflict experiences beyond victimization, instead recognizing agency in order to strengthen women's societal status and create scope for their social and political activism. It is thus essential to transform ideas and imaginaries that keep intact structures of gender inequality. It is important to add here that men's gendered experiences should also be recognized. *Redistribution* should promote equitable access to economic resources for men and women. Beyond material resources, redistribution also entails generating equality by addressing male and female roles and tasks, including in the household. It thus addresses the socio-economic dimensions of women's oppression. *Representation* should encompass the active participation of women and girls in peacebuilding processes (*internal representation*) as well as in national, political and economic life (*external representation*) (Williams and Palmer 2016). It addresses women's marginalization from decision-making spaces, and their unequal opportunities to be political actors in the public sphere. The three Rs are thus interrelated, running across the public and private spheres.

A concept that is crucial in this understanding of gender justice is agency. Agency can be described as the capacity to consent, dissent or negotiate (Kabeer 2012) in order to make a difference to the pre-existing state of affairs (Giddens 1984). Agency can vary from reactive to proactive, and be exercised in formal, or political, and informal spaces, including in women's everyday lives (Björkdahl and Mannergren Selimovic 2015). It is often understood to be liberatory but can in fact also be repressive, as it depends on each context and the relationships in it (Baines 2017). Agency is thus not a black and white concept, with agency and passivity as two extremes, but should rather be seen as a scale, a complex and situated phenomenon, which can consist of sweeping actions but also of small acts or the refusal to act; it is not constant but a capacity that can be developed (O'Reilly 2017;

Hume and Wilding 2019). Agency is constrained by deeper structures of (gendered) power relations, which can fluctuate over time and place and across social and political contexts. This means that agency should not be seen merely as an individual phenomenon or capacity, as is common in (neo) liberal understandings of it as a solution for combating poverty, stressing individual responsibility and empowerment, which disregards the need for social change to overcome the systems of oppression that undermine agency (Wilson 2008). Agency is a relational concept, situated in particular socio-cultural contexts which define to what extent agency is possible. It can therefore coexist with vulnerability, even though agency and vulnerability are often presented as two opposites (O'Reilly 2017; Kreft and Schulz 2022).

Agency is a crucial component of citizenship, a concept that is too often overlooked in TJ and peacebuilding. As I explained earlier, both reparations and reintegration are connected to citizenship, aiming to integrate survivors and perpetrators as equal citizens in society and to build relationships of trust between citizens and the state. Furthermore, citizenship is a way of making rights claims to improve the situation of those who were affected by conflict (Lazar 2013b). Citizenship is also a useful analytical tool to analyse women's subordination, and it has been a crucial concept in struggles for women's emancipation in and beyond Latin America, to promote their active participation and agency in all spheres of life (Lister 1997; Molyneux 2007; Turner 2016). In this book, I argue that transformative gender justice could be more effective if it promotes equal and active citizenship. I will explain and unpack the connection between reparation, reintegration, gendered transformation and citizenship. I show specifically how the current practice of TJ and DDR does not help to promote agency and citizenship, and instead risks undermining it, making people dependent on well-intentioned but little impactful 'women's projects' that eventually maintain inequality. Instead, I argue that building active citizenship practices, and promoting the socio-economic and gendered changes required for women to have equal citizenship, is a more effective and sustainable way to transform gender inequality, by giving women the tools to demand their rights, to change their futures, to *salir adelante*.

The structure of this book

This book will unpack the question of whether TJ and DDR processes contribute to transforming gender inequalities, using Colombia as a case study. Colombia's TJ and DDR mechanisms have received a great deal of international acclaim and interest from policy makers and researchers. Yet what is often missing is the analysis of the effects of their implementation on the ground, at a community level. The relationship, and frequent mismatch, between theory and practice of gendered post-conflict mechanisms is what

INTRODUCTION

I study in this book. In doing this, I examine what transformative gender justice looks like, and how it is or could be better connected to processes of citizenship building. In this way, the book expands TJ theory by connecting it to citizenship studies as a lens to examine processes of gendered agency and transformation. The next chapter contextually situates the research in this book. It identifies the root causes and main (gendered) effects of the decades-long armed conflict in Colombia. I give a historical overview of TJ and DDR processes in Colombia, and how these have come to be seen as global examples of how to 'do' peacebuilding. The chapter also introduces the locations on Colombia's Caribbean coast where my research took place, describing the methodology used and ethical challenges encountered in the research process. Ethical questions are further reflected upon throughout the book, and they are discussed in detail in the Appendix.

In Chapter 2, I move on to the book's core empirical contributions. I describe gender roles before, during and after Colombia's conflict. Rather than understanding 'gender' solely through the lens of sexual violence, I instead focus on the everyday experiences of conflict and post-conflict lives, and how these are defined by structures of gender inequality. I describe how conflict disrupted traditional gender relations, both for IDPs and combatants, producing emancipatory experiences for women in both groups, as well as changes in models of masculinities. Such changes could be steps toward post-conflict gender equality. Unfortunately, I also identify the continuities of structural gendered inequalities and traditional female roles in the post-agreement situation. To set up the book's main argument, I specifically analyse women's participation in community structures during and after conflict, as well as their own organizational spaces. Such organizational processes could provide building blocks for active citizenship.

Chapter 3 engages with the politics of victimhood in TJ, providing a gendered analysis. I illustrate how the often-critiqued dichotomy between victims and perpetrators actually plays out in communities that were affected by conflict. I uncover how victim hierarchies are performed in different ways and with diverse goals by both victims and perpetrators. The emphasis on sexual violence during the conflict in Colombia risks excluding other gendered narratives of conflict, especially those of agency. Their *recognition* could in fact be an important tool for transforming gender inequality through building active citizenship. Drawing on insights from social identity theory, I suggest how citizenship as an overarching identity could replace victim and perpetrator identities which hamper genuine transformation and reconciliation.

In Chapter 4, I deconstruct the ways in which gender is conceptualized in TJ and DDR in Colombia, and how essentialized understandings of gender risk neglecting structural gendered inequalities in the public and especially the private sphere. I show the effects of the strategy commonly used by both state institutions and accompanying civil society and international organizations, of offering 'women's projects' to promote gender equality. These activities do not necessarily respond to the needs of women, nor do they provide the *redistribution* aimed for in Fraser's trivalent justice. Instead, they tend to create exhaustion and frustration because these projects fail to become successful and sustainable. I show how well-intended efforts at gender trainings and 'women's projects' can actually have counterproductive effects, by weakening women's organizational efforts and hampering their agency. This eventually weakens practices of active citizenship, and fails to train women with political skills to demand their rights based on their own needs.

Chapters 5 and 6 bring together the preceding critiques of 'gendered' TJ and DDR with women's post-conflict future and the role that agency and active citizenship play in this. Chapter 5 describes how both IDPs and ex-combatants express a feeling of being second-class citizens, while, at the same time, they seem to have lost previous practices of active and radical citizenship. The chapter explains some crucial elements of Colombia's reparation and reintegration processes which reinforce the weakening of citizenship practices. Chapter 6 describes women's hopes for the future, and the importance of education, work and organizational processes among women to achieve these goals. It contrasts women's dreams with their stark realities, in which the 'baby boom' among former FARC guerrillas and the spike in adolescent mothers in former IDP communities have meant that motherhood and oppressive masculinities remain key obstacles to a stronger practice of active citizenship for women. It finishes by zooming in on the importance of organization, a key theme throughout this book and connected to *representation*, as a crucial element for enabling reparations and reintegration to be more effective at transforming gender inequality and promoting women's citizenship. Practices of active citizenship could make women less dependent on their families or on projects provided by the state or international organizations. Economic and political independence could in turn help to transform gender inequality.

The Conclusion draws the book to a close by bringing together the arguments made in the previous chapters, discussing how reparations and reintegration, as part of wider peacebuilding approaches, can fare better at promoting post-conflict gender equality by redefining an active and gender-equal practice of post-conflict citizenship for both men and women. I draw on Nancy Fraser's model of trivalent justice to map out how, instead of 'adding women', the building of a practice of active citizenship could help to transform gendered inequalities at different levels. Citizenship should therefore be central to gender justice. In this way, the book uses its rich empirical insights, with a central place for women's experiences, to contribute to feminist peace and conflict studies and gendered TJ theory, outlining concrete steps to make gender-sensitive TJ in fact gender-transformative.

1

Gender, Violence and Reconciliation in Colombia

Colombia is a country of extremes: geographical extremes with the country being divided by mountain ranges; extremes in terms of the unequal division of social and economic resources between population groups and between rural and urban areas; and political extremes, enjoying the longest-running democracy in Latin America while also facing one of the world's most protracted conflicts. Colombia's approaches to dealing with conflict and peacebuilding can also be characterized as somewhat extreme, albeit in a positive way for most observers, as the country has repeatedly innovated ways to resolve conflict, address the harms suffered by survivors and demobilize armed groups. This book shows that the implementation of such peacebuilding and reconciliation policies unfortunately tends to leave much to desire, as they change the everyday reality of those who experienced conflict often far less than their ambitious wording would suggest. In this chapter, I explain the socio-economic and political roots of Colombia's conflict, how different transitional justice (TJ) and other peacebuilding mechanisms have tried to address its harms and how they have tried to incorporate a gender perspective. I then introduce the locations where my empirical research took place, and explain the methods used for it and the ethical dilemmas I encountered.

Conflict, peace and reconciliation?

Colombia has a history of violence and unrest since its independence, with different periods of violent struggle starting with the end of the 19th century. Violence has historically functioned as a tool to effect political change and gain control over resources (Tate 2007). In spite of this violence, Colombia has had relatively stable economic growth from the 1940s onwards (Richani 2002). Nevertheless, a large part of its population has little or no access to resources and social services, with growth principally visible in the major cities but lagging in the rural areas, suggesting the existence of 'two Colombias' (Pearce 1990; Hylton 2006). The countryside itself is also characterized by strong inequality, with a small elite of very rich landowners and cattle ranchers owning large areas of land, in contrast to a large group of landless peasants. As a result, peasants have repeatedly occupied abandoned lands to achieve a means of subsistence, which was often responded to with violence (Reyes Posada 1987; Richani 2002). Even when land titles where granted after successful occupation, basic state services generally remained absent (Steele 2017).

Colombia's political system has historically been based on the exclusion of poor urban and rural population groups from political power, which was divided between two strong parties: Conservatives and Liberals. In the 1960s, this exclusion, combined with the persisting land inequality, sparked loosely organized armed self-defence groups which waged armed struggles against large landowners to eventually formalize into guerrilla groups (Pearce 1990; Chernick 2003). The strongest group was the Marxist-oriented FARC, formed officially in 1964 but formalized in 1966. Consisting mostly of peasants and active mainly in rural areas, it aimed to defend peasants from landowners and the state (Centro Nacional De Memoria Histórica 2014; González González 2014). At its height around 2002, the FARC consisted of over 18,000 combatants (Arias Ortíz and Prieto Herrera 2020). This makes it the largest ever guerrilla movement in Latin America. Moreover, it had the highest percentage of female members – approximately 30 per cent – although women never made it to top leadership positions (Pearce 1990; Richani 2002; Herrera and Porch 2008). The smaller Cuban-inspired *Ejército de Liberación Nacional* (National Liberation Army [ELN]) was founded in 1964 and had a more working-class membership and a lower representation of women. Nearly defeated in 1973, it managed to regain ground and is still active (Richani 2002). Colombia's historically weak state presence, especially in the peripheral regions, enabled the emergence of these, and other, smaller guerrilla groups. These groups filled this void and functioned as a de facto state, levying 'protection taxes', imparting justice and providing other basic services (Chernick 2003; Hylton 2006; Centro Nacional De Memoria Histórica 2014).

Conflict dynamics changed when Colombia became a major player in the global drug trade in the 1980s (Chernick 2003; Mantilla 2011). Drugs provided a source of income for the guerrilla movements, complementing the resources they had historically generated through kidnappings and extortion of businesspeople and landowners (Mantilla 2011; González González 2014). This enabled the professionalization and expansion of the guerrilla armies. The 1980s also saw the discovery of large oil, gold and coal resources, which enabled the guerrilla groups, mainly ELN and FARC, to 'tax' multinational companies and control territory and markets. As a result, their original communist ideology gave way, especially in terms of the public perception of these groups, to economic motivations pursued through criminal activity (Richani 2002; Centro Nacional De Memoria Histórica 2014).

The drug boom and professionalization of the guerrilla movements had another impact: the expansion of paramilitary groups in the 1980s, promoted and financed by large landowners and narcotraffickers who felt threatened. From the mid-20th century onwards, paramilitary groups have been active in Colombia, officially sanctioned through different decrees in the 1960s and 1970s (Taussig 2003; Civico 2016). This enabled the army to rely on the paramilitary to do the 'dirty work' to prevent the return of the guerrillas and extend its power to spaces normally outside of its control (Gutiérrez and Barón 2005; González González 2014; Civico 2016). Initially a network of separate units protecting landowners, these paramilitary groups became increasingly organized, uniting in 1997 in the *Autodefensas Unidas de Colombia* (United Self-Defence Forces of Colombia [AUC]). The AUC, especially strong in the north of Colombia, developed into a well-trained and professional military force, at its peak in the early 2000s consisting of 30,000 members. Estimates of the percentage of women in these groups range between 2 and 12 per cent (Richani 2002; Tate 2007). Towards the end of the 1990s, the AUC were responsible for 40 per cent of all massacres, which often led to displacement, and almost 80 per cent of other human rights violations, mainly targeting the peasant population. The FARC, instead, was more notorious for kidnappings (Steele 2017).

The AUC financed their operations in similar ways as the guerrillas, taxing indiscriminately and controlling drug trafficking and other lucrative economic sectors as gold and cattle ranching. They also became a political power, claiming to control 35 per cent of the national Congress in 2002. They co-opted over 1,000 local and national politicians by offering them support in return for influence in the so-called '*parapolítica*' scandal (García-Godos 2013; Grupo de Memoria Histórica 2013; González González 2014). The paramilitary's ability to infiltrate Colombian society in the political, economic and social sphere, blurring the line between the paramilitary and the state, is known as 'paramilitarism' (Taussig 2003; Theidon 2009). Colombian society and media were accomplices to this, as guerrilla violence was generally met with considerably more protest than paramilitary violence, which was largely received with silence and indifference. Likewise, the FARC's involvement in drug trafficking is much more central in public discourse than that of the paramilitary, even though many paramilitary leaders are serving prison sentences in the United States because of it (Centro Nacional De Memoria Histórica 2014; Civico 2016; Tate 2018).

The battles between these different armed groups and the state led to extreme levels of violence at different times. Although the total number of victims is unknown because of the lack of a unified register, according to the Colombian Commission for the Clarification of Truth, Coexistence and Reconciliation (CEV, after its Spanish acronym), it is estimated that over 450,000 people died as a result of the conflict between 1985 and 2018, and over 100,000 people forcibly disappeared between 1985 and 2016 (90 per cent of them civilians). Over 50,000 people were kidnapped between 1990 and 2018, approximately 70 per cent by the guerrillas (Comisión de la Verdad 2022b). The CEV also identified 32,446 cases of sexual violence, over 90 per cent of them committed against women, most of them young women and in rural areas (Comisión de la Verdad 2022a). Forced displacement occurred throughout the conflict. It increased considerably in the first half of the 1990s, with a peak in the early 2000s (Steele 2017). It became a key tool for gaining access to land. Around 5.5 million hectares of land were dispossessed, representing about 10.8 per cent of the land used for agriculture and livestock in Colombia (Grupo de Memoria Histórica 2010). The high degree of informality in land tenure, with less than half of Colombian peasants possessing formal land titles, facilitated displacement and land grabbing (Meertens 2019). Over 7 million people were displaced, and it is estimated that around 4.7 million of them were forced out from 1996 onwards, coinciding with the most intense years of paramilitary activity (Grupo de Memoria Histórica 2013; Gutiérrez Sanín 2019). Displacement has gendered impacts. Women tend to form the majority of displaced persons. Displacement often reinforces their poverty and marginalization, as they face discrimination in the labour market. This makes them more vulnerable to labour and sexual exploitation. Intra-family violence also tends to be higher among displaced households (Meertens 2010).

Between 1985 and 2001, five presidents initiated peace negotiations with the guerrilla groups – none of these processes, like the negotiations with the paramilitaries following in the early 2000s, involved female negotiators (Paarlberg-Kvam 2019). The demobilization of several smaller guerrilla groups in the 1990s led to amnesties combined with educational assistance, healthcare, vocational training and job support. Demobilized ex-combatants were also allowed to participate in politics and in a constitutional assembly, which led to the 1991 Constitution (Chernick 2003; Steele 2017; Carranza-Franco 2019). These early disarmament, demobilization and reintegration (DDR) processes did not have a gender perspective (Londoño Fernández and Nieto Valdivieso 2007). Peace negotiations were held with the FARC in the early 1980s, even leading to a two-year truce between 1985 and 1987. Despite the formation of the political party *Unión Patriótica* (Patriotic Union, UP) by the FARC in 1985, signalling its willingness to participate in electoral politics, peace negotiations failed. The surprisingly successful UP was practically decimated after thousands of its members were killed by state and paramilitary groups or driven into exile (Pearce 1990; Chernick 2003; Steele 2017). Renewed attempts to negotiate with the FARC were initiated in 1998, when the guerrillas managed to negotiate a zone free from government presence in El Caguán, an area the size of Switzerland in the south of the country. This peace process fractured in 2002, as the FARC used the free zone to expand their illegal practices (Steele 2017). The 9/11 terrorist attacks changed the international legal and political discourse, with the United States government labelling the FARC as a terrorist group (Centro Nacional De Memoria Histórica 2014). This discourse resonated with then President Alvaro Uribe, who outright denied the existence of an armed conflict. Although Uribe did attempt to negotiate with the FARC, these negotiations quickly failed, not least because of Uribe's strong aversion to the group. He accused the FARC of killing his father, and portrayed them as terrorists and criminals (Gómez-Suárez 2016). Uribe and his Defence Minister – and later president – Juan Manuel Santos strengthened the military campaign against the FARC which would eventually facilitate peace negotiations (Carlin, McCoy and Subotic 2019).

The Justice and Peace Law

Paramilitary violence had spiralled out of control by the early 2000s, making their disbandment urgent. Uribe's close ties and similar ideological position with these groups underscored his desire to guarantee them favourable demobilization conditions. The AUC began a process of demobilization from November 2003 onwards, while negotiations about the terms of their reintegration continued, as they refused to be extradited to the United States on drug trafficking charges (Guembe and Olea 2006). Eventually, in 2005 the Justice and Peace Law (JPL, Law 975) was approved, creating a process of DDR of armed groups, including both the AUC – collectively – and individual members of guerrilla movements. Those demobilizing without pending criminal prosecutions or those accused of minor crimes were pardoned and able to return to their places of origin, where they received economic, health and social benefits (Guembe and Olea 2006; García-Godos 2013). The remaining demobilized individuals were subjected to the JPL, which for the first time in Colombia connected TJ and DDR by providing reduced prison sentences of five to eight years in return for collaboration in truth telling and reparations. By 2010, over 54,000 people had demobilized, mostly through collective demobilizations. This number was much higher than the estimated number of AUC members, because many narcotraffickers also joined the demobilization process, benefiting from the support packages and lenient prison sentences (Steele 2017; Arias Ortíz and Prieto Herrera 2020).

The JPL received strong criticism because of its lenient prison sentences and lack of protection of survivors' rights (Laplante and Theidon 2006; Steele 2017). Although it can be considered as a step forward compared to the previous blanket amnesties granted to demobilized guerrillas, its achievements in terms of justice are meagre. By May 2021, only 89 cases had reached a verdict (Fiscalía General de la Nación 2021). The May 2008 extradition of 14 paramilitary leaders to the United States on drug trafficking charges undermined the public perception of the JPL's legitimacy, especially because of suspicions that the extradition aimed to prevent further information about the *parapolítica* corruption scandal coming to light (Centro de Memoria Histórica 2012; García-Godos 2013). Furthermore, few demobilized paramilitaries made confessions about the full scope of their responsibility, including their role in the massive displacement, or the economic and political links between the paramilitary, the drugs sector and third actors (Centro de Memoria Histórica 2012). Although a Reparations Fund was created as part of the JPL, it was very ineffective, while the accompanying process of conciliation with the perpetrators implied an additional emotional burden for the victims (García-Godos 2013; O'Rourke 2013). Furthermore, reparations under the JPL are only for those victims involved in the specific cases. In 2008, the state therefore created a parallel administrative reparations programme. Its gendered track record was not impressive, however. Women formed only 13.62 per cent of the beneficiaries of the reparations implemented between 2009 and 2011, even though they comprised 87 per cent of claimants. Only 0.1 per cent of reparations were paid to survivors of sexual violence (O'Rourke 2013; Salcedo López 2013). This programme was replaced by the 2011 Victims' Law, discussed later.

In 2012, the JPL was modified to prioritize the investigation of the most responsible paramilitary leaders and specific crimes, including sexual violence. Nevertheless, as of August 2015, only five sentences included gender-based crimes, progress which was, moreover, largely made thanks to women's rights organizations (Chaparro Moreno 2009; O'Rourke 2013; Corporación Humanas 2015). Gender was insufficiently considered in other ways too, such as in the failure to transform militarized masculinities of demobilized combatants, resulting in many instances of domestic violence in ex-combatants' households. There was no adequate attention on the specific needs of female combatants either, with the first gender strategy adopted only in 2010 (Theidon 2009; Tabak 2011; Avoine and Tillman 2015; Flisi 2016). As a result of stigmatization and the lack of economic opportunities in an increasingly technical and specialized labour market, many demobilized paramilitary found it hard to find viable economic alternatives, and turned to crime once more, joining new paramilitary organizations. These groups, whose methods and many of their leaders remained the same, continue to commit human rights violations in the ongoing struggle over land and natural resources. By 2011, they consisted of approximately 13,000 members (García-Godos 2013; Civico 2016; Arias Ortíz and Prieto Herrera 2020).

The Victims' Law

The meagre results of the JPL resulted in the 2011 adoption of Law 1448 of Victims and Land Restitution (known as the Victims' Law). It is widely recognized to be one of the most ambitious and complex reparation programmes worldwide, as it combines land restitution for the thousands of people who were displaced and dispossessed after 1991, with humanitarian assistance and individual and collective reparations for all victims of conflict-related acts by the guerrilla movements, paramilitary or state after 1985. The law entered into force in January 2012, creating a complex system of pre-existing and new TJ bodies, including newly trained land restitution judges and magistrates, national and regional offices of the Unit for the Attention and Reparation of Victims (Victims' Unit [VU]), the Land Restitution Unit (LRU) and the National Centre for Historical Memory (NCHM). The Victims' Law also created different municipal and departmental committees and participation spaces to coordinate local and regional reparation plans in coordination with survivors' representatives, and establishes that separate policies will be developed for victims of Indigenous, Afro-Colombian, Roma or other minority-ethnic backgrounds. The Law has a differential focus. Its article 13 explains its aim to counter the vulnerability of certain groups of victims due to their age, gender, sexual orientation and disability, to protect their rights and enable their participation. This has, however, mainly resulted in isolated programmes and projects for women, rather than a more structural transformation of gendered and other inequalities, as I will show in detail in Chapter 4.

The Victims' Law shows considerable advances compared to the Justice and Peace process, especially in relation to reparations. Land restitution was a historical claim of internally displaced persons (IDPs). The Law includes crucial regulations to protect its beneficiaries, including the use of alternative evidence such as testimonies and social maps to prove claimants' link to the land, and their assumed lack of consent to abandon or sell the land, placing the burden to prove that they acquired the land in good faith on opposing parties (Meertens 2019). In terms of gender, its goal of allocating land titles to men *and* women has real transformative potential. Actual implementation of this will be discussed in Chapter 4. Nevertheless, there are also several challenges, including the safety of land claimants, which might be an even greater concern for women and their organizations, as conservative groups in Colombia's patriarchal society regard their public demands of land restitution and reparation as transgressing gender roles (Lemaitre and Sandvik 2014; Meertens 2019). Another major concern is the pace of restitution. Institutional capacities have proved insufficient to meet the demand for land restitution, due, among other reasons, to insufficient financial and human resources, and the overly legalistic and case-to-case approach to restitution

(Gutiérrez Sanín 2019; Meertens 2019). As of November 2017, only 19 per cent of land claims had been included in the registry of abandoned land (Ruiz González, Parada Hernández and Peña Huertas 2019). By May 2021, after ten years of the Law's functioning, 6,365 land restitution sentences had been reached, benefiting just over 100,000 persons (Unidad de Restitución de Tierras 2021), a small proportion of the millions of IDPs. Furthermore, there is no effective system to monitor and follow up on the implementation of the land restitution sentences, which involve a plethora of local- and national-level institutions to make restitution sustainable and provide decent living conditions for beneficiaries (Meertens 2019).

The reparation measures provided by the Victims' Law are considered complex and integral, including individual and collective, and material and symbolic, reparations. Nevertheless, most effort has so far been made in terms of economic compensation, with the rehabilitation measures slow to take off. This undermines the transformative impact of reparations, as compensation by itself has not proven sufficient to structurally transform the lives of survivors, 97.6 per cent of whom live below the poverty line (Portilla Benavides and Correa 2015). Collective reparations, which can have a transformative potential through more development-oriented measures, also face implementation challenges. In 2021, only 28 collective reparation plans had been fully implemented, with only 200 out of 768 collective projects moving forward (Sandoval, Martínez-Carrillo and Cruz-Rodríguez 2022). Although the VU has attended to many more victims than the previous reparation programme, the high number of registered victims requires a well-oiled machine, with highly trained staff, sufficient funding for institutional functioning and reparations and smooth cooperation between the different implementing institutions. Even under President Santos, a more serious political and financial commitment was needed to make this ambitious reparation effort live up to its expectations (Portilla Benavides and Correa 2015; Sikkink et al 2015). The election of President Duque in 2018, a protégé of former president Uribe, halted much of the slow progress with the Victims' Law.

Peace with the FARC: justice, reparations and reincorporation

In 2012, a new peace process started between the FARC and the government. The FARC had lost political legitimacy as a result of continued engagement in drug trafficking and kidnappings. It had also been weakened militarily in the first decade of the 2000s (Steele 2017). Although the FARC had not been defeated, they knew they were unable to take power. Newly elected President Santos, who as Uribe's Defence Minister had led the military campaign against the FARC, decided to make peace his main goal. The FARC considered a negotiated settlement an 'honourable way out' (Centro

Nacional De Memoria Histórica 2014; Nasi 2018; Zambrano Quintero 2019). Almost four years of negotiations led to the signing of several partial agreements and a final peace agreement on issues including victims' rights, the drug problem, political participation, integral agrarian development, DDR and security guarantees. Nevertheless, Colombian citizens showed themselves relatively indifferent about the peace process – especially in urban areas which were less affected by the conflict (Guardiola Rivera 2014). The Santos government had lost popularity as the peace negotiations dragged on, while ex-president Uribe, popular with the military and conservative groups in society, started a strong campaign against peace, criticizing the government's leniency towards the guerrillas (Gómez-Suárez 2016). These issues, combined with bad weather conditions in the coastal areas and a low turnout (37 per cent), especially among overly confident yes voters, resulted in the peace agreement's unexpected defeat in the October 2016 plebiscite. Gender played a crucial role in the loss of the plebiscite, as will be discussed in the next section. A new, revised and amended accord was presented and approved by Congress by the end of November 2016. Nevertheless, violence is ongoing in Colombia, resulting from the ongoing presence of paramilitary groups, the ELN and groups of FARC dissidents. It is therefore better to speak of a post-accord than a post-conflict situation (Koopman 2020).

The final peace accord provided for the strengthening of the Victims' Law on the basis of a participatory process of discussions and consultations with survivors and other stakeholders. Nevertheless, according to an interviewee who monitors the implementation of the peace agreement, the suggestions made to strengthen the Law were dismissed by the government, which argued that the suggested initiatives were already part of the Law. She therefore described reparations as the 'ugly duckling' of the peace process, which is no longer prioritized (Interview, 7 May 2019). The accord also created a 'Comprehensive System of Truth, Justice, Reparation and Non-Repetition', consisting of the CEV, which published a very comprehensive and well-received report in 2022, about which I explain more in the next section, a Unit for the Search of Disappeared Persons and a Special Jurisdiction for Peace (JEP, after its Spanish acronym). The JEP deals with ten 'macro cases' of human rights violations, divided among regions, groups of victims and specific crimes. Alternative sanctions of between five and eight years for those most responsible for political crimes among the state and the FARC will entail restriction of freedom but not prison, and will have reparatory content, such as the construction of development or infrastructural projects. They are delivered on the condition of participation in truth and reparation efforts (De Gamboa Tapias and Díaz Pabón 2018; Sandoval, Martínez-Carrillo and Cruz-Rodríguez 2022). If responsibility is not recognized, or late, prison sentences will be applied. Through the JEP, the FARC will contribute to the reparation of the conflict's survivors, through resources and restorative and reparatory acts such as declarations of responsibility and projects to strengthen the social fabric of communities. Special sanctions will be connected to the rural development plans included in the peace agreement, and to already-existing collective reparation plans. This connects DDR with TJ. Both special sanctions and reparations will be designed in a participatory process between the JEP, the victims and the perpetrators of the cases, although it is still uncertain which victims will participate and how, as the macro cases involve large numbers of survivors (Sandoval, Martínez-Carrillo and Cruz-Rodríguez 2022).

The DDR process negotiated by the FARC has a collective and rural focus, to maintain the unity of the group, in contrast to previous demobilization processes. The FARC insisted on calling it reincorporation rather than reintegration,[1] signalling their intention to remain a political force for transformation rather than individually reintegrating in an unchanged society. The process was originally organized in 26 rural reincorporation zones, some of which were later closed. In these zones, ex-combatants live, study and receive support and collective productive projects that are meant to guarantee their economic sustainability. Communities close by are also meant to receive some support, connecting DDR with social and economic development (Carranza-Franco 2019; McFee and Rettberg 2019; Zambrano Quintero 2019). The process is accompanied by the Agency for Reincorporation and Normalization (ARN, after its acronym in Spanish), which is the new name for the previously existing High Council for Reintegration (ACR). The ARN manages both individual reintegration and collective reincorporation processes.

The FARC complied with its part of the demobilization, with over 12,000 demobilized combatants and militia members formally registered as demobilized, 23 per cent of them women, and over 7,000 of them moving into the reincorporation zones. They handed in over 8,000 arms (Zambrano Quintero 2019; Arias Ortíz and Prieto Herrera 2020). The government has, however, been slow to implement its promises, starting with the tardy preparation of the reincorporation zones, and the even slower provision of productive projects and other forms of support. On the political level, the FARC has turned into a political party, initially maintaining its old acronym, this time standing for Common Alternative Revolutionary Force (*Fuerza Alternativa Revolucionaria del Común*). Yet the first few disappointing election results showed that maintaining the old, tainted acronym – and leadership – was not wise, and the name was changed to *Comunes* or

---

[1] Throughout this book, I use these terms interchangeably, since, in spite of the FARC's decision to call their specific process 'reincorporation', the internationally used name for these processes is reintegration.

'Commons' in January 2021. Women make up 23 per cent of the party leadership (Zambrano Quintero 2019).

Another crucial element of the peace accord is the creation of a Land Fund, which is supposed to donate three million hectares of unused or unexploited lands, land seized in judicial processes and other lands obtained by the state to landless agrarian workers, prioritizing female-headed households and IDPs. Together with the adoption of 'territorial rural development plans' (PDETs, after their acronym in Spanish), which will incorporate collective reparation plans, this responds to the FARC's historical struggle for social and land equality. The level of victimization and affectation by conflict form a key selection criterion for the implementation of these PDETs. Yet although this makes reparation part of development, it does not necessarily make development part of reparations, since the accord does not state that all heavily conflict-affected areas will receive a PDET. As a result, of the two locations where my research took place, only La Guajira will receive a PDET. Nevertheless, four years after the signing of the peace accords, PDET implementation was not yet evident here, nor in most other locations, due in part to the low budget dedicated to the PDETs by the Duque government (Sandoval, Martínez-Carrillo and Cruz-Rodríguez 2022). This responds to a tendency in Colombia where overly ambitious laws suffer serious implementation gaps.

Gendering peace and justice

Gender has played an important role in the peace process with the FARC. The peace agreement was hailed for its comprehensive gender perspective, and it was the first in the world to explicitly mention LGBTQ rights (Cairo et al 2018). This attention on gender was, however, not a given. Initially, the peace negotiations were strongly male dominated, with only a few women involved on the FARC side, most of them not as full negotiators. As a result, the first points in the agreement did not have a gender perspective. Women's organizations mobilized to increase women's involvement in the process. In October 2013, they organized a National Summit of Women for Peace, which collected over 800 proposals for peace with an intersectional perspective. This led the government and FARC to integrate more women in their negotiating teams, and, in 2014, they created the Gender Subcommission. The goal of this Subcommission was to adopt a comprehensive gender perspective, going beyond 'adding women' and instead aiming for equality, stressing women's agency and including an LGBTQ perspective. The Subcommission held various meetings with women's and LGBTQ groups in Havana, leading to the incorporation of over a hundred measures with a gender perspective in the agreement (Céspedes-Báez 2018; Thylin 2018; Corredor 2021, 2022). Nevertheless, the creation of the Gender Subcommission did not necessarily lead to a greater gender perspective in the other subcommissions of the negotiating parties. The Subcommission on the End of the Conflict, which dealt with reintegration, for instance, only had one woman on board. This can perhaps explain the lack of a strong gender perspective in the reincorporation process, which I will discuss in more detail in Chapter 4. The members of the Gender Subcommission felt somewhat separate from the main negotiations. They felt that gender was generally seen as 'low politics'. This low priority, however, also had advantages, as the proposed gender measures received little resistance, leading to the comprehensive gender perspective of the final agreement (Corredor 2022).

Nevertheless, the inclusion of LGBTQ rights, as well as the increasing attention on gender and women's rights, were met with a societal backlash. Conservative forces – including the Evangelical churches, retired military officers as well as conservative and right-wing politicians – started protesting against what they called a 'gender ideology' that they perceived in the peace agreement. These groups opposed the idea of gender as a social and cultural construct, and argued that the agreement's LGBTQ-inclusive gender perspective threatened traditional values such as the importance of the nuclear family (Gómez-Suárez 2016; Bueno-Hansen 2018). This conservative anti-gender discourse played an important part in the defeat of the accords in the 2016 plebiscite and in fact proved to be the tipping point for the win of the 'no' vote (Koopman 2020; Corredor 2021). In the renegotiated version of the peace accords, the language about gender was toned down, referring more explicitly to men and women, heterosexual relations and focusing more specifically on sexual violence against women. Furthermore, in their introduction, the accords explicitly mention the family as the cornerstone of society (Céspedes-Báez 2018; Paarlberg-Kvam 2019; Gutiérrez and Murphy 2022). Nevertheless, the spirit of the gender perspective remained intact and many of the changes were semantic rather than substantive, for example, replacing 'sexual diversity' with 'LGBTI rights' (Corredor 2021). Although a representative of an LGBTQ rights organization agreed that the practical impact of the changes was limited, she considered the symbolic impact significant, because the fact that changes were made suggests that conservative forces won the gender battle. She believed that, as a result, politicians are now more careful and hesitant to include a progressive gender perspective in policies (Interview, 21 May 2019). A women's organization's representative had a different view:

'When we started with the accord, we talked about gender. Afterwards, with the … pedagogy against the accord, it was adjusted. So in the adaptation of the accord, a differentiation was made between gender, which includes specifically the LGBTI population, and women's rights specifically. ... For us, that was very important, because we didn't get stuck in the gender theme, but we were included specifically.' (Interview, 21 May 2019)

Her comment shows the ongoing divisions between the LGBTQ and women's movements, with parts of the latter still largely lacking an intersectional approach (Koopman 2020) and focusing on a limited number of specific women's rather than gender issues.

More detailed information about the gender perspective in Colombia's reparation and reintegration programmes is provided in the following chapters. It is important to note, however, that Colombian TJ actors have showed a specific pattern in dealing with 'gender', understanding it mostly as 'women'. As will become apparent in Chapter 3, women's organizations maintain a strong focus on sexual violence as *the* gendered crime (Céspedes-Báez 2018). This has contributed to a 'hyper-attention' to and 'fetishization of' sexual violence, turning it into a so-called 'hype' (Lemaitre and Sandvik 2014; Meger 2016; Hilhorst and Douma 2018), as described in the Introduction. The Constitutional Court has historically played an important role in putting gender and women's needs on the public agenda. Its Writ 092 of 2008, for example, specifically emphasized displaced women's delicate situation and their increased risk of suffering sexual violence and exploitation, forced work and the forced recruitment of their children, urging the government to create programmes to protect and assist them. These programmes were later incorporated into the Victims' Law (Meertens 2019). Other Constitutional Court judgments have also called for the protection of women from sexual violence and justice for their cases (Lemaitre and Sandvik 2014). These judgments have thus in a way contributed to the sexual violence hype in Colombia, which risks neglecting other gendered harms and needs of women and men. Instead, women need to comply with a script centred around sexual violence, in order to make claims to the state (Céspedes-Báez 2020). As a result, the 'gender' perspective in most TJ policies has long been limited to mentions or projects for women, without actually ensuring their meaningful participation or the transformation of gender inequalities. This tendency will be further unpacked in the following chapters.

Over five years since the signing of the peace agreement, its implementation is moving forwards, but more slowly than many people had expected. Gender is one of the areas which has faced most obstacles, especially in relation to mainstreaming it in rural development measures and the PDET process, in guaranteeing security for women participating in politics and in the PDET and other reconstruction processes, and in protecting the rights of LGBTQ women. Implementation fares a bit better in relation to reincorporation and TJ measures (Echavarría Álvarez et al 2021; Fajardo

2021). Nevertheless, this book shows that studying implementation at a community level, focusing on lived experiences, shows a different picture to the often quantitative forms of measurement undertaken by the most recent evaluations. Within the TJ aspects of the agreement, an important milestone has been the publication of the report of the CEV in the summer of 2022, in separate lengthy chapters released gradually. The report included a specific chapter on women and the LGBTQ population. Based on over 10,000 testimonies, it includes sections on the effects of displacement, sexual and reproductive violence and other crimes; violence and persecution of LGBTQ persons; the connection between violence and masculinities; as well as attention on agency and resistances. Specific recommendations include social and economic justice for women; the development of a national action plan (NAP) on WPS; reparations and justice for women, especially for sexual violence; and the promotion of education about gender equality (Comisión de la Verdad 2022a). A Committee has been installed to monitor and evaluate the recommendations, which newly elected President Petro has pledged to implement. The JEP is an area of more concern in terms of gender. So far, its ten 'macro cases' have not focused explicitly on gender or sexual violence. Women's organizations have lobbied for a macro case on sexual violence, but so far it seems more likely that this crime will be included in macro cases of other crimes, such as kidnappings or disappearances (Castrillón Palacio 2022).

In the summer of 2022, a new phase started for Colombia, when former M19 guerrilla and mayor of Bogotá Gustavo Petro took power as Colombia's new president, with Afro-Colombian grassroots leader Francia Márquez as his vice-president. This sparked renewed hope for the implementation of the peace agreement, efforts to end violence and the creation of a more equal and inclusive society. Petro's win marks the first time Colombians elected an explicitly left-wing president. His campaign strongly focused on peace and environmental protection. Already within his first 100 days in office, Petro managed to adopt a 'total peace' law, which paves the way for peace negotiations with the ELN guerrillas and other remaining armed and rebel groups through a special commission consisting of the High Commissioner for Peace, the Minister of Defence and the head of intelligence services. Through this law, the government also aims to strengthen regional infrastructures and dialogues for peace. Furthermore, the government has made efforts to strengthen the institutions implementing the peace agreement, including the points on rural development (Burnyeat and Gómez-Suárez 2022). Although these are promising developments, the Colombian context continues to be characterized by strong societal polarization, with conservative groups and economic elites reluctant to give up privileges, and societal support threatened by inflation and insecurity.

Researching the gendered impacts of conflict and transition on the Caribbean coast

I was interested in analysing these ambitious reparation and reintegration policies in practice. What was their actual effect on the lives of those meant to benefit from them? To what extent did they transform the structural inequalities that gave rise to the conflict, and the gender inequality so persistent in many areas of Colombia? Furthermore, by looking at reparations and reintegration, and focusing both on survivors and perpetrators, I hoped to determine whether these policies would actually balance each other out in terms of paying attention to perpetrators and survivors. Both these policies have an ambitious and transformative focus, but as Purdeková (2015) rightly wonders, what happens if the desired transformation is implemented by a regime that embodies continuity? To some extent, this was already the case with the Santos administration, but doubts about the possibility for social and political transformation became even clearer with President and Uribe supporter Duque. The following pages describe how I studied these questions and these policies, with a particular focus on the decisions I made to avoid over-researching specific themes, individuals and geographical areas (Clark 2008; Boesten and Henry 2018).

In 2015, when I started my research in Colombia, the Victims' Law was in full swing and receiving ample international attention. Through a lawyers' organization accompanying land claims, I established contact with two small communities in the municipality of Chibolo, located in the centre of the Magdalena department on Colombia's Caribbean coast (Figure 1.1). This coast, with a strong tradition of cattle farming for the national market, was not one of Colombia's historically most influential, powerful or affluent regions, a disadvantage that can be felt up to this day (González González 2014). It is known as *La Costa* (The Coast), whose inhabitants are often stereotyped as 'tropical, lazy and wild' (Tate 2018, 422). The region is also characterized as *machista*, including by its inhabitants and my participants, as I will describe in greater detail in the next chapter. It has, however, also been hit hard by conflict, especially in relation to land. After many small-scale peasants had been expelled by more powerful cattle ranchers, a process of land occupations took place in the 1970s. In this period, 2,000 *haciendas* were invaded by landless peasants, often accompanied by the organization *Asociación Nacional de Usuarios Campesinos* (National Association of Tenant Farmers [ANUC]), in an attempt to claim the 'land for those who work on it' (Hylton 2006; Grupo de Memoria Histórica 2010). This made the Caribbean coast one of the regions with the most land conflicts in the 1970s and 1980s (Reyes Posada 1987). The villages where my research took place, called La Pola and La Palizua, were formed through land occupations between 1980 and 1984. They are currently inhabited by

Figure 1.1: Map of Chibolo within the Magdalena department and Colombia

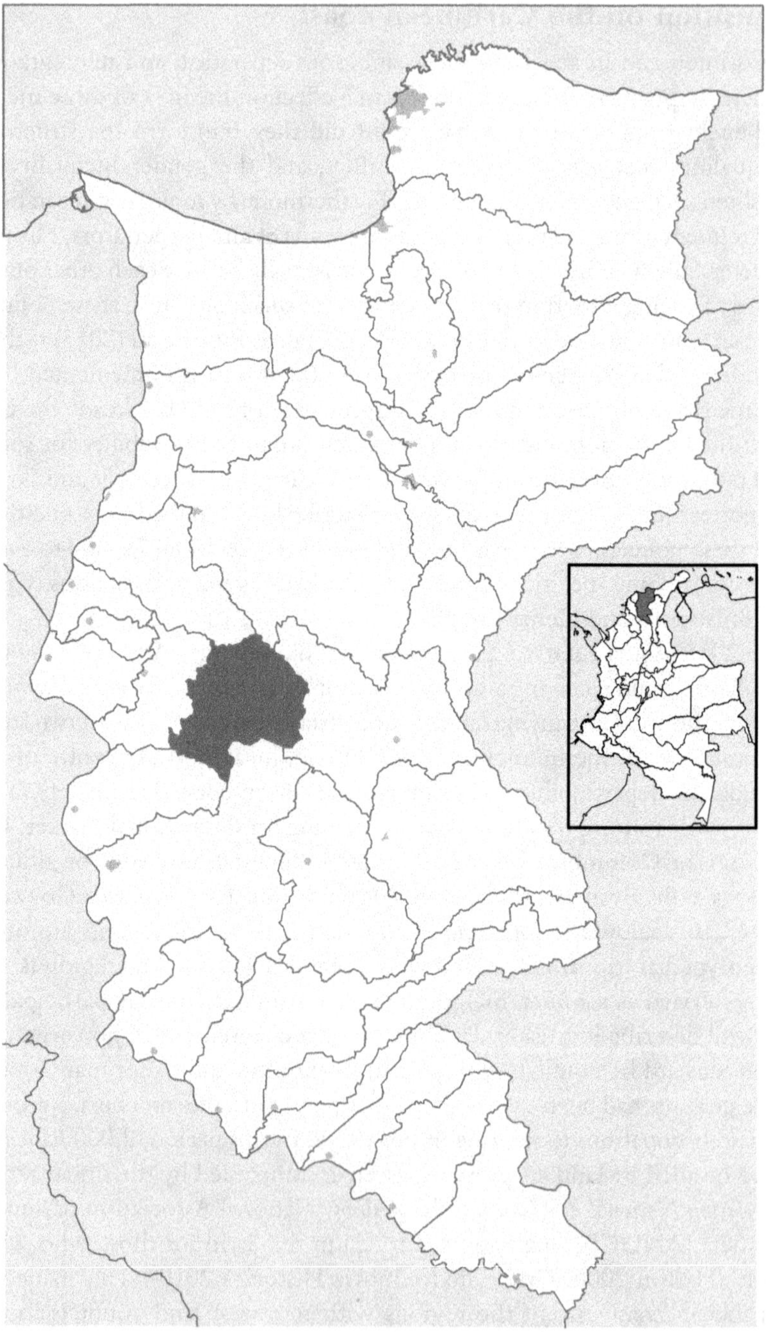

Source: Wikipedia (accessed 28 November 2022), reprinted under CC BY-SA 3.0 licence

campesino[2] families of a *mestizo*[3] ethnic background, most of them involved in the land restitution process.

In the 1990s, this area became a stronghold of the paramilitary group *Bloque Norte*, led by Rodrigo Tovar Pupo, alias Jorge 40, and provides one of the best examples of the collaboration between paramilitaries, narcotraffickers and political bosses (Hylton 2006). Magdalena was of geostrategic importance to the paramilitary, being economically interesting because of large-scale cattle farming, while providing access ways to other departments and the coast for the transport of arms, drugs and other commodities (Richani 2002; Grupo de Memoria Histórica 2010). This led to massive displacement and usurpation of land in Chibolo. La Pola and La Palizua were displaced in 1997, community members scattering throughout the Caribbean coast, some even fleeing to Venezuela. In the meantime, the paramilitary infiltrated justice, security and agrarian institutions throughout the coast. Several pacts were signed between the paramilitary and local politicians, including the September 2000 *Pacto de Chibolo*, leading to the election of senators and members of Congress favourable to the paramilitary (Grupo de Memoria Histórica 2010; Centro de Memoria Histórica 2012). Only in 2007, after paramilitary demobilization, did the people of La Pola and La Palizua start the process of so-called 'voluntary return' without accompaniment by the state. After various violent evictions by the police, their right to be on the land was finally recognized (Planeta Paz 2012), but they found their houses burned down and the divisions of the land undone. Furthermore, the communities lacked basic services such as adequate healthcare, education, electricity and water, and the unpaved access roads became practically inaccessible in the rainy season.

From 2009 onwards, a pilot project was implemented in Chibolo to pave the way for land restitution. Therefore, once the Victims' Law was approved, Chibolo was selected as a pilot case. As several non-community informants explained, the information already available meant that the communities in Chibolo were regarded as the 'low-hanging mangos' of the land restitution process, enabling the government to show quick results (Interviews, 21 December 2015 and 28 January 2016). Moreover, since the villagers had already returned, the process was one of formalization rather than restitution, similar to many other cases (Amnistía Internacional 2014). The communities registered as land claimants in 2011, and the

---

[2] The term *campesino* includes a wide range of small-scale farmers and other rural workers. The term is difficult to translate into English, but in this book I have opted to use peasants.
[3] *Mestizo* refers to a mixed European and Indigenous background. The majority of Colombia's population is of *mestizo* ethnic origin.

land restitution process was soon expanded with the inclusion of both communities as subjects of collective reparation and efforts to reconstruct historical memory about the armed conflict. These communities had not yet been the subject of academic research, making research fatigue unlikely – or at least so I believed.

In 2018, a new research project enabled me to study the reincorporation process of the FARC, which had just started. I decided to keep focusing on the Caribbean coast, as it would allow me to compare dynamics in another location in *La Costa*. Although gaining access to the FARC was not easy, since they had quickly become 'over-researched' (Clark 2008), I eventually managed to contact the reincorporation zone (territorial space for training and reincorporation [ETCR]) in the village of Pondores in Fonseca, La Guajira (Figure 1.2). This reincorporation zone was interesting to me not only for its geographical location, but also because it was one of the few ETCRs that actually continued growing with ex-combatants and their family members, while many such zones were emptying out instead. Pondores consisted by then of approximately 200 ex-combatants and their families, belonging to three different fronts (Sánchez Salcedo and Schnettler 2022). Several interviewees believed that Pondores's success

Figure 1.2: Map of Fonseca within the department of La Guajira and Colombia

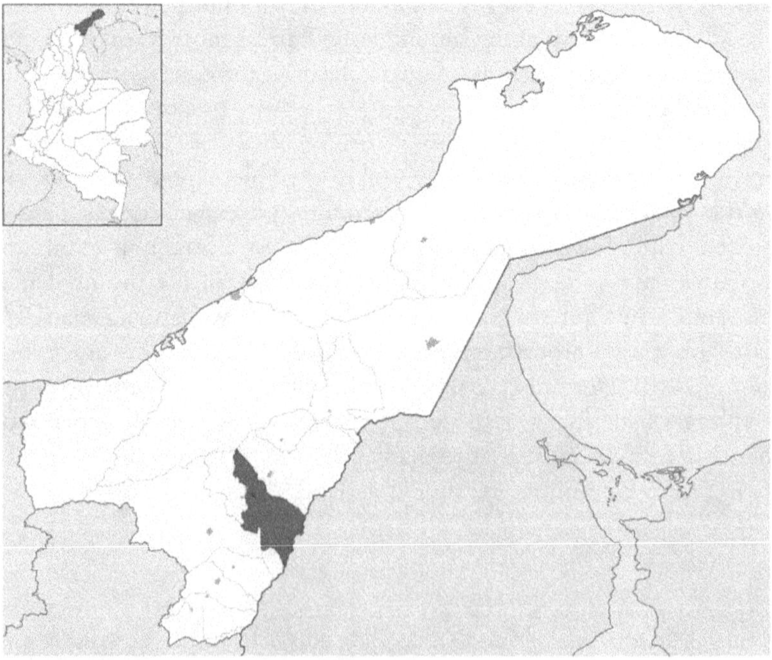

Source: Wikipedia (accessed 28 November 2022), reprinted under CC BY-SA 3.0 licence

stemmed from the leadership of the ETCR, who were actually present and savvy at negotiating with the international community to obtain support. Furthermore, they successfully communicated their hard work, and were lucky that their security situation was better than in ETCRs in other areas. By 2019, only 23 per cent of registered demobilized ex-combatants remained in the ETCRs, the rest having moved to the cities, to join their family members or in search of economic opportunities, while a number joined the dissident groups which have not laid down arms (McFee and Rettberg 2019; Dixon and Firchow 2022). This is important to note, since it means that the reincorporation experience in the ETCR, including in Pondores, is not necessarily representative of the average reincorporation process, as many ex-combatants have taken on an individual reintegration journey. It should also be recognized that the FARC were not a homogeneous group. They were particularly strong in the south of the country, but never managed to gain the same strength on the Caribbean Coast, as paramilitary force was strong here. The FARC only gained a foothold presence here in 1983 (Centro Nacional De Memoria Histórica 2014; González González 2014). Most of the ex-combatants in Pondores belonged to the FARC's former *Bloque Caribe* (Caribbean Bloc), which included a high number of FARC ideologues and top commanders, but, militarily, was among the weaker of the seven FARC blocs. Most of the bloc retreated into Venezuela when military offensives intensified in the early 2000s, and became mainly involved in the drugs and arms trade (Fattal 2018).

At the moment of my research, the ex-combatants in Pondores – most of them *campesinos* of *mestizo* ethnic background, but also including a considerable group self-identifying as Indigenous and one Afro-Colombian – were still receiving a monthly stipend, and some food rations, although these were diminishing. They were living in temporal housing, made of asbestos and meant to last only for six months during the initial reincorporation phase, although it was eventually decided that some ETCRs would become permanent spaces for reincorporation. The ex-combatants were still waiting for their individual productive projects, which they had decided to pool into a collective project that would enable them to build their own houses and establish a village with European Union (EU) support. In the meantime, with the help of funding mostly from the UN, they formed a cooperative with several productive projects, including a farm, tailoring workshop, tourism project and wood-making workshop. The delays in government compliance with its promises, especially in terms of productive projects and safety guarantees, with over 250 ex-combatants killed since demobilization, has generated a sense of despair among most ex-combatants. This was similar to the frustration felt by many community members in Chibolo who had to wait years for the land titles and reparations they were promised. This resembles

Figure 1.3: House in La Pola. "These houses are not suitable for a family, because the material of which they are made does not offer the appropriate security, and they moreover do not have an adequate bathroom."

Source: Caption in Photovoice booklet, April 2016; photograph by Celia, January 2016

research in other contexts in Colombia, where both ex-combatants and civilians are dissatisfied with the state (Dixon and Firchow 2022). In both fieldwork locations, the lack of decent housing, photographed by many women in Chibolo (Figures 1.3, 1.4 and 1.5), was a key element for their desperation. By 2022, a considerable number of FARC ex-combatants, including several of my participants, had moved out of the ETCR to different cities, in search of work. In addition, after former commander Bertulfo died of cancer and the other leader left for security reasons – or because of a new relationship, as participant Maricela told me in March 2022 – unity among the group diminished and people decided to live closer to their families, and, in the cases of some of the women, look after their aging family members.

The tendency to make people wait might result from a combination of poor state capacity and overambitious policies, as a lack of feasibility is a broader problem in Colombia's TJ framework (Sandoval, Martínez-Carrillo and Cruz-Rodríguez 2022). Of course, it is unrealistic to expect that such complex policies as the Victims' Law are implemented within a few years. What is, however, persistently lacking in Colombia is realistic expectation management by the involved state institutions. Instead, ambitious promises create high expectations. Waiting in vain and negative interactions with the state can have strong impacts on people's well-being and their trust in

Figure 1.4: House in La Palizua. "Well, I would like to have a better house. Because you see, it is deteriorated and I would like to have a place where we can be more comfortable. Because this one is very small. We have five children who sometimes have to sleep in the living room."

Source: Interview, 25 February 2016; photograph by Luisa, January 2016

the state. The provision of public goods – or lack thereof – is another key element defining citizens' trust in and support for the state (Mueller-Hirth 2017; Albarracín and Zukerman Daly 2019). All these factors define people's experience of citizenship, as I explain in Chapter 5.

Research methods

There are many ways of researching how conflicts have impacted women and men and the relations between them, and how post-conflict peacebuilding mechanisms have addressed this. Because of donors' and policy makers' interest to show the broader dynamics of conflict and the impact of peacebuilding and TJ, this research has often been quantitatively focused. Quantitative peace research has been critiqued by many, since it isolates

Figure 1.5: Houses in Pondores

Source: Photograph by author, May 2019

violence from its social, cultural and political context, and it only measures those things defined as measurable by outside actors who lack knowledge of everyday, grassroots realities (Boesten and Henry 2018; Firchow 2018; Jones 2020). My interest lies not so much in generalizability but in understanding the lived experience of conflict and post-conflict transitions, and in exploring in what ways such processes can be more gender-transformative. I used a feminist approach to research this, which aims to uncover knowledge that is often taken for granted, especially in relation to women's experiences, while seeking social change and the transformation of different forms of oppression (Letherby 2003; Hawkesworth 2012; Pillow and Mayo 2012). Since oppression and equality are often apparent in everyday experiences, the 'personal is political', making personal experiences and emotions a site for the construction of knowledge (Fonow and Cook 1991; Stanley and Wise 1993; Ramazanoglu and Holland 2002). Critical analysis of lived experiences can, moreover, be a tool to foster social change for oppressed groups (Collins 2019). To uncover the personal, everyday experiences

I wanted to analyse, I used an ethnographic approach, which was better suited than a more quantitative, survey-based approach or elite or policy-maker interviews.

Ethnography is concerned with creating and representing knowledge about other cultures through detailed and complex descriptions of the meaningful social and cultural structures in which people and their actions are embedded in a specific place. This 'thick description' can give insights into the larger issues at stake in society (Geertz 1975). Ethnographers use a range of different methods, including interviews, participant observation, censusing, writing field notes and field diaries and taking or collecting photographs (Geertz 1975; Van Maanen 1988; Pink 2007). Ethnography can help to establish a more 'humanist' and ethical research account, which does justice to people's multiple experiences and perspectives (Robben and Nordstrom 1995; MacKenzie, McDowell and Pittaway 2007). It has, however, also been criticized for being extractive and sometimes exploitative, objectifying people and describing their culture and experiences in the ethnographer's 'outsider' voice, appropriating 'local knowledge' as a new form of imperialism (Mies 1991; Pink 2007; Tuhiwai Smith 2012). This has led to many Indigenous people and 'marginalized' communities feeling simultaneously over-researched and invisible, as they are offered little opportunity to respond to the ways in which they are represented, while their testimonies are 'robbed' and used as academic capital (Castillejo Cuéllar 2005). Ethnography, including ethnographic TJ research, has increased its focus on the 'suffering subject', aiming to generate empathy and lessons for change. This 'damage-centred research' can, however, reinforce negative stereotypes, and distract from understanding the 'better worlds' that people imagine (Tuck 2009; Robbins 2013).

In spite of these critiques of ethnographic research, I found that it can be a positive experience for participants for a number of reasons. As others have also identified, ethnography enables research to take place in participants' own time and space, while ethnographic 'hanging out' requires less investment of time from the participants than formal interviews or focus groups (Krause 2021). This was even more appropriate in a patriarchal context like the communities of Chibolo, where women spent most of their time doing household tasks, which I could observe and help them with. Although in fact they rarely allowed me to do so, as traditional interpretations of gender roles seemed to make them believe that an unmarried White woman in her 30s could not possibly be any good at household chores. That ethnography forces the researcher to fully immerse in the research context is not lost on the research participants. It was clearly appreciated both in Chibolo and in Pondores that, unlike most state and civil society actors, other researchers and journalists, I made the effort of spending a long period of time with them, in their own homes instead of a more luxury hotel, demonstrating a real interest in their lives. The warm goodbyes and continued communication with research participants suggest that this commitment and genuine interest in people's lives can be important. Sharing participants' living conditions and food and trying to understand their lived experiences can be a way of creating bonds of cross-cultural solidarity, making the participants feel less invisible (Pieke 1995). This was literally what one of the female community leaders told me early on in my research, as I described in my field notes in September 2015:

> Josefa said that before she felt like they were invisible, and the fact that people are now coming from so far away to see their experience means a lot to her. To me, it also meant a lot that she told me this, because I feel uncomfortable with her going out of her way to help me while I feel I am not doing that much.

It is important to stress that this long-term 'hanging out' (MacKenzie, McDowell and Pittaway 2007; Robins and Wilson 2015) indeed enabled me to obtain an in-depth, complex and localized understanding of conflict and peace on the Caribbean coast, and to build relationships of trust and also friendship that last until this day. It is, however, also fair to say that fieldwork at times was a very challenging experience. Even though I had previously lived in Latin America for almost six years, I was not entirely prepared for the extremely basic living conditions in Colombia's rural areas. Especially, living in Chibolo was often a struggle, with extreme temperatures that were unfriendly for my white skin, and very limited variation in (not very nutritious) food. Research here also involved endless motorcycle trips on dirt roads, carrying not only my computer and personal belongings but also as many water bottles as I could bring, as there was no running water. The constant male attention and the near complete lack of privacy when staying in very basic houses with no bathrooms further made me wonder whether my research would come at the expense of my physical and mental health.

In addition, I felt uncomfortable with limiting myself to an ethnographic approach, for several reasons. First of all, TJ research is more often than not produced by researchers who do not actually live in or come from post-conflict areas. Such research risks at best to merely reflect outsiders' understandings of conflict and how to deal with it (Jones 2015; Robins and Wilson 2015). I did not feel that as an outsider I had the moral authority to interpret other people's experiences and present them as 'true'. Furthermore, doing research with survivors of conflict and violence involves the risk of re-traumatization, when the researcher's questions invite participants to remember painful experiences. Even feminist research like my own, with social justice goals, is not free of such risks (Sharp 2014; Robins and Wilson

2015). As social justice will likely take a long time to come about, and when its connection to research is unclear, participants may end up feeling frustrated and exploited by the research endeavour, thus leading to research fatigue (Clark 2008; Boesten and Henry 2018). Among the participants in the two research sites, the FARC ex-combatants were especially vocal in their reluctance to complete yet another interview about their conflict experiences. I respected that wish and did not actively probe for these experiences and other topics that were off limits (Hennings 2018). Since it is not always necessary to collect primary data on topics that have already been amply documented, I consulted other sources on conflict experiences and the sensitive topic of sexual violence against the FARC instead (Boesten 2014; Boesten and Henry 2018).

In a desire to prevent re-traumatization, I, furthermore, decided to not focus on the suffering of individual women – unless they explicitly wished to share their experiences – and avoid the global and Colombian 'sexual violence hype'. My objective became understanding the functioning of larger structures of gender inequality, through the exploration of everyday experiences, particularly focusing on women's present-day experiences and hopes for a more gender-equal future. I thus attempted to respond to calls for activist ethnography, which centres the needs of research participants in order to engage in social activism or speak out about the injustices encountered (Manz 1995; Scheper-Hughes, cited in Robben and Nordstrom 1995), specifically with regard to the ways in which communities experience and evaluate the policies that are meant to benefit them (Tate 2020). Nevertheless, I still felt that ethnography on its own would be limited and unsatisfactory, as I could not directly experience or interpret the participants' everyday life. I decided to complement it with a participatory approach, to make my research less extractive and more beneficial for the participants, and give them better tools to speak for themselves and show their own reality.

Participatory visual research

Participatory research refers to both a process and a set of methods for research. It actively involves participants in the process of setting the research agenda and telling their experiences in their own words or images, so that research may become a tool for social change (Cornwall and Jewkes 1995; Lykes and Crosby 2015). Research thus becomes a collaborative experience, in which power is shared more equally between researcher and participants. Participatory research has a long history in Latin America. It was developed there by researchers and practitioners who worked together with grassroots communities in contexts of strong social inequalities, aiming to combine empirical research with activism, valuing grassroots knowledge as equal to academic 'expert' knowledge, and facilitating processes of consciousness raising to enable the design of transformative actions (Fals-Borda 1987; Freire 1996; Lomeli and Rappaport 2018).

Despite its long history and virtuous aims, many community members in Chibolo were not particularly interested in participatory research, although they did show interest in participating in my research. This was a result of the use of participatory methods by the state institutions implementing the Victims' Law through an endless number of workshops and trainings, often involving drawing or map making (De Waardt and Weber 2019). These meetings were often of little utility to the community members, while requiring a considerable time investment. Furthermore, since these communities were pilot cases for the Victims' Law, they had received considerable public and media interest, having welcomed President Santos twice and various groups of journalists from state and non-official media. They had repeated their story of displacement and return so often that it had almost become a script (Krystalli 2021). This meant that, even though these communities had never been the subject of academic research, they nevertheless suffered research fatigue. Since the community women did not experience this fatigue to the same extent as men, because the rigid gender roles in the communities excluded most women from meetings and trainings, I limited my participatory work to the women.

I conducted a photovoice process with two groups of women. They photographically represented their daily lives, the things they were proud of and the obstacles to a better life. I then interviewed them about their images, giving them the control over what they preferred to show and talk about, and privileging their voice in interpreting the images. Their images gave rise to collective discussions, meant to generate knowledge, create connections and raise consciousness (Ponic and Jategaonkar 2012). These discussions helped the women to formulate captions, which together with the images were collated into booklets which I printed for all participants. This process allowed the women to document their own realities, which made it easier for them to speak about their experiences as they themselves had created these images. In the context of more formal semi-structured interviews, women often felt unsure how to answer my questions, sometimes making remarks like 'you should ask my husband'. This shows the limitations of interviews, which can be experienced as somewhat intimidating by women in a patriarchal setting where men do most of the talking in the public sphere. Community leader Alejandro's remarks about his wife were telling in this regard:

> 'With Elena, what happens is that I know what she is going to say. We are the leaders, and I go and fight for her. I say what she would say.

I would say it triple, because I know she knows little about that, and I understand it more than her, and therefore I can better stand up for myself and I talk more.' (Focus group, 19 March 2016)

The photovoice process, instead, showed women they had valuable knowledge too. They were very proud of the pictures they took, showing them to family members and neighbours, whereas in their daily lives, women's roles are often taken for granted. Furthermore, the research meetings allowed them a legitimate reason or a 'respectable social outlet' (Helms 2013) to leave their houses and meet other women. In several of my return trips, women told me how much they had enjoyed the process, even though they did not use the co-produced photo booklets as the lobbying tool that I had hoped they would be, inspired by other photovoice projects (Wang and Burris 1997; Wang, Cash and Powers 2000). This, however, seemed to be more to my own disappointment than theirs. Some of the images taken by the women were subsequently included in collective historical memory reports produced by the National Centre of Historical Memory, as part of the collective reparation process. Many of the images included in this book are produced by the participants, as discussed and consented to by them. Nevertheless, only some of their images were fit for publication because of ethical reasons, as they showed the participants, their family members or other identifiable persons, despite prior discussions about the risks inherent in this. I believe that blurring the identifiable faces may objectify people and damage the pictures the women proudly took (Wiles et al 2008). I have therefore decided not to include them.

These images, and the visual in general, are important in various respects. They offer a means of enabling participants to present their worldview and living conditions through their own eyes. The camera gave women a tool for looking at and showing seemingly trivial activities that are normally taken for granted (Pink 2007; Sontag 2008; Rose 2013), enabling them to show their roles and the aspects of their lives they found most difficult or valued most. These everyday experiences, which might not be included in an interview guide elaborated by an outside researcher, were in many cases illustrative of gendered and other structural inequalities. For example, the women spoke about the difficulty of performing household chores without electricity or running water, and about the absence of bathrooms which complicates women's lives, especially when menstruating. Many pictures were also taken of the severe drought in the villages, prompting me to focus my research more on that aspect of people's everyday experiences. The photovoice booklets produced as a result were received with great interest in the communities, both by men and women. This shows the importance of tangible objects with a visual component as a source of knowledge and communication, which is not sufficiently valued within academia due to its continued focus on and preference for the written (Butler-Kisber 2010; Tuhiwai Smith 2012).

On several occasions, people told me that they felt the photos and booklets represented their story and living conditions, the 'real reality' according to community leader Josefa. Participants considered that their 'truth' contrasted with the reports, photos and videos taken by the institutions involved in the Victims' Law to show successful implementation. Similar complaints were later made by female ex-combatants, who argued that the state institutions only came to take photographs of successful reincorporation projects. They pointed out that these successes were not necessarily due to the state's support. This made them feel that the state, through its depictions, took advantage of ex-combatants' hard work without complying with its responsibility (Asociación Freytter Elkartea 2021). These anecdotes evidence the power of the visual, not only because of the meaning of images but also because of the feelings they – aim to – generate (Callahan 2020). Photos can be interpreted and used in many ways (Sontag 2008): by the state as 'evidence' of their work, but also by women through the opportunity to 'shoot back' (Lykes 2010) to counter outside romanticized perceptions, popular assumptions, negative stereotypes and official representations (Oliveira 2019). This makes the visual political, as it determines who and what are included in or excluded from the social, cultural and political frame. The visual can even shape political events by moving people into action (Callahan 2020). The images also evidence how photographs, particularly effective in showing the materiality and space of people's conditions (Pink 2007), can be an important tool for bridging different worlds (Harper 2010). This enables participants to visually show their living conditions to people in completely different contexts, who might find it difficult to imagine Chibolo. In this way, images can create 'affective communities of sense' (Callahan 2020, 16). Finally, several participants recounted how through these images they had created memories of aspects of their present lives. This was significant for them, because they knew how abruptly life can change for displaced persons. As many participants had lost most of their photographs of the time before displacement, taking photos was also a way of creating new, visual memories.

Because of this positive experience, I initially set out to use photovoice with the FARC ex-combatants too. When I finally managed to gain access to conduct research with the ex-combatants in Pondores, I quickly gave up on this plan. Having been Latin America's oldest and strongest guerrilla group, and being savvy users of social and other forms of media themselves, the FARC's demobilization had quickly become a hype, with their collective reincorporation zones receiving a constant flow of journalists and researchers, as well as a plethora of different state institutions and non-governmental organizations (NGOs) offering different trainings and workshops. This meant that, like the IDPs in Chibolo, the ex-combatants had a very busy schedule of trainings and meetings, on top of their own activities, which was further compounded by the local elections during my stay in autumn 2019. Not all participants are interested in the investment of time and energy that 'deep participation' requires (Cornwall 2000). This was certainly the case for the ex-combatants who constantly expressed a saturation of meetings, trainings and workshops. Furthermore, although in contrast to the FARC's public discourse it is hard to speak of gender equality within the group, as will become apparent throughout this book, female ex-combatants in Pondores did participate to a much higher degree in public life than the women in Chibolo. Research fatigue was therefore shared among men and women here.

Finally, in contrast to Chibolo where I could count the times that gender was mentioned in the workshops and trainings on one hand, gender had become more mainstreamed a few years later, and ex-combatants were bored with all this gender talk. Their gender committee was already working on and preparing for two specific gender projects by international organizations, and while I was in the ETCR, another project came through. Apart from general research fatigue, there was thus an additional gender fatigue that I had to navigate. It took me weeks to have a conversation longer than a few minutes with the coordinator of the gender committee, who repeatedly postponed because of her busy schedule. Hierarchy within the FARC and the ETCR was still strong, making it virtually impossible to start a participatory visual research process without having at least the approval of some of the leaders. While I gathered my thoughts and adapted my methods, ethnographic hanging out came in useful, giving me time to explore other options to make the research more meaningful for the participants, while establishing rapport. As others have experienced too (Hennings 2018), by staying in the ETCR for a longer period of time, having informal chats and watching *telenovelas* together, I was able to build trust, which eventually enabled me to hold interviews with people who initially seemed reluctant, including the gender committee coordinator. This ethnographic approach was crucial for making it clear to participants that, despite their fears due to past experiences, I had a genuine interest in them and was not just there to acquire information quickly to make money or advance my career.

Eventually, when I attended a series of workshops in the ETCR run by an international organization as part of a gender project, I offered to help out, lending equipment and collaboratively shooting a short video on masculinities. This provided an opportunity to discuss the benefits of visual research with some people, which led me to co-produce, mostly together with participant Rebeca, two other videos: a short promotional video for the tourism team and a video about the gendered dynamics of the reincorporation process,[4] based on questions

---

[4] This video was eventually not finalized, as the long COVID-19 lockdown prevented Rebeca from travelling to upload the video, as internet connection was too poor in the ETCR. She turned it into a podcast instead, which can be accessed via https://soundcloud.com/guasimas_radio/mujeres-en-la-paz/s-toE7ZdU9iL9.

we discussed with the gender committee leaders. Although the videos were not as participatory as I would have liked, they were something practical I could do to make the research more beneficial to the participants. Furthermore, the videos had a positive focus, emphasizing the emancipatory experiences of female ex-combatants during the conflict and their hopes and plans for the future. This stood in stark contrast to some of the images produced by the women in Chibolo, who overwhelmingly focused on the challenges they faced as survivors of forced displacement, including some representations of extreme poverty. The experience in Chibolo exemplifies the risks inherent in visual research, which can show people in a powerless position, sometimes to the extent of reducing them to this powerlessness, causing embarrassment, and reinforcing feelings of vulnerability and marginalization (Sontag 2003; Butler-Kisber 2010; Mitchell 2011). Fortunately, the captions in the photovoice booklets countered this to a large extent, expressing agency and hopes for the future. These experiences show how it is often hard to meticulously plan fieldwork in advance. Being open about how research changes and for what reasons is not only part of ethical research practice but can also provide helpful lessons for other researchers and students (Cheng 2018; Krause 2021). This is why throughout the book and in Appendix I include personal reflections about the research; this is not done in an attempt to foreground and focus attention on my experience as a researcher, but to acknowledge my own role in and influence on the research process, the data I collected and its analysis.

A final hurdle in the research process was the global COVID-19 pandemic, which showed how unexpected changes to the field after the research can affect research plans in unexpected ways (Schmidt 2021). The resulting travel restrictions and months-long lockdowns prevented me from returning to Colombia in the summer of 2020 to present and discuss my analysis with the participants, and, more generally, follow the progress of the reincorporation and reparation processes. Although I believe that a return visit to present and discuss research findings is part of ethical research practice, I had to be flexible and adapt (Knott 2019). Instead, I wrote up a summary of my analysis and shared it with participants electronically and produced a short animated video[5] to transmit the main research results, sharing and validating the script with the participants in Pondores. Some participants' comments via voice messages enriched and validated my research data. I also followed the progress of the different FARC activities and committees on Facebook and Twitter, as the FARC have active communication teams both nationally

---

[5] This animated video can be accessed in English via www.youtube.com/watch?v=S9O8N_hmlbc and in Spanish via www.youtube.com/watch?v=lGxaNBhd6Vc.

and locally. This was more complicated with the communities in Chibolo, since internet connection there is less constant, and social media posts tend to be more focused on personal and family situations than the reparation process. Nevertheless, complementing my original data with digital data in a sort of 'multimodal ethnography' has allowed me to obtain a more comprehensive picture of the participants' experiences (Murthy 2008). When I was finally able to travel back to Colombia in March 2022, I caught COVID in Bogotá, and was unable to travel to *La Costa*. I only managed to meet a few participants who happened to be in Bogotá.

All in all, I undertook several periods of ethnographic fieldwork in both locations between August 2015 and November 2019 – excluding the failed fieldwork visit in 2022, in which I did have communication with several participants. Fieldwork periods ranged from a few weeks to three and up to nine months at a time. I spent much time in participants' houses, chatting over shared food, and observed numerous meetings in relation to the reparation and reincorporation process, as well as various community activities. I held semi-structured interviews and focus groups, as well as photovoice interviews with community members in Chibolo, and I interviewed ex-combatants and community members in Pondores. All fieldwork was undertaken in Spanish, without an interpreter. For this book, I draw on 50 formal interviews and countless informal conversations with community participants in both fieldwork locations. I also made short visits to two more ETCRs, in Cesar and Tolima, to gain a more comparative understanding of the reincorporation process. Furthermore, I held over 30 semi-structured interviews and many more informal conversations with stakeholders from the state, civil society and international community involved in the TJ, DDR and wider peacebuilding process in Colombia.

Conclusion

This chapter has provided the contextual background for the research described in this book. I explained the origins and dynamics of Colombia's armed conflict, characterized by historically strong geographical, social and economic inequalities, compounded by gender inequalities, as the next chapter will illustrate in more detail. I have also described Colombia's tendency to develop ambitious and innovative TJ and DDR programmes, and continuing attempts to connect TJ and DDR. Unfortunately, implementing such ambitious policies has proven difficult, causing frustration and even distrust among many participants in my research. To uncover their perceptions and everyday experiences with these policies, their gendered dynamics and track records in transforming gender inequality, I have used a combination of feminist ethnographic, participatory and visual methods. Flexibility and long-term engagement with research sites and participants have proved crucial in responding to unanticipated challenges, especially in relation to research fatigue among participants, and in attempting to make research meaningful for them. The inclusion of the images taken by the participants, and of their living conditions, is intended to give readers an insight into their experiences, needs and dreams, and shorten the distance between them and the women and men whose lives and experiences are central in this book.

2

Tales of Machismo and Motherhood: Gendered Changes across War and Peace

Having set out the theoretical and contextual framework of the book, I now explore the gendered experiences of the women and men in Chibolo and Pondores during and after the conflict. As described in the Introduction, 'gender' is often understood as attention on sexual violence in conflict and transitional justice (TJ) research and policy. This, however, frequently leads to a failure to analyse the underlying structural gendered inequalities which produce sexual and other gender-based violence in the first place. In this chapter, I describe the everyday gendered dynamics of conflict and post-conflict lives, and how these are defined by structures of gender inequality. An understanding of these gendered changes across peace and conflict is important, as recognizing that gender relations are not rigid, and identifying and building upon instances of agency and change, provide entry points for reparation and reintegration processes to transform gender inequality in a more sustainable way.

I start this chapter by explaining traditional gender roles on Colombia's Caribbean coast, including how *machismo* – the hegemonic form of masculinity in Latin America – defines family relations. The private sphere of the family in turn is crucial for understanding the lack of success of gender-sensitive TJ and disarmament, demobilization and reintegration (DDR) described in the following chapters. In this chapter, I set out how conflict disrupted traditional gender relations, both for IDPs and combatants, producing emancipatory experiences for women in both groups as well as changes in dominant models of masculinities. I contrast these fluid gender roles with the post-conflict situation, where maintaining those more equal gender roles has proven hard. I specifically look at women's participation in community structures, as well as their own organizational spaces. I explain the gendered relapse in the continuation of structural inequalities and gender roles for men and women, and connect it to agency and citizenship, concepts which are crucial to make gender justice more transformative.

Conflict-related gendered changes

Colombia's society is defined by a patriarchal social structure with clearly prescribed roles for men and women. This patriarchal regime is particularly strong on Colombia's Caribbean coast (Grupo de Memoria Histórica 2010). Patriarchy in Latin America and beyond refers to a social system of male domination over women, in which authority is exercised by men in many spheres of life, including social relations, norms, institutions and language (Anthias and Yuval-Davis 1992; Lagarde y de los Ríos 2014). Patriarchy is centred around the 'nuclear family', which is led by the male head of household who provides for his children and wife (Gutmann 2003; Olavarría 2006). The female role lies in being the support base of the family through caring and household tasks, expressed in traditional values as motherhood, sacrifice and submission. Pateman (1988) described this arrangement as a sexual contract, in which the wife receives subsistence in return for her labour, as an unpaid assistant to her husband who, moreover, gains sexual access to her as his 'patriarchal right'. The symbolic force of the nuclear family as an organizing unit has been strong in Colombia, leading, for example, to agricultural policies which target the male heads of household, assuming that supporting men will automatically lead to support for women too. This model ignores women's exploitation through unpaid domestic and agricultural labour, and maintains their unequal position and vulnerability when families fall apart, as often happens in conflicts (Meertens 2019).

Patriarchy tends to be articulated with other axes of oppression, such as class and ethnicity (Crenshaw 1989; Lagarde y de los Ríos 2014). In the communities where I worked, patriarchy is mostly compounded by class, as community members in Chibolo and most former combatants belonged to the peasant population, which composes the underclass of rural society. Whereas in Chibolo, like most of the peasant population, participants were of mestizo descent; in Pondores, there is also a considerable number of Indigenous men and women, thus making ethnicity an identity marker too. Geographical location is another aspect of inequality, as rural communities have particular disadvantages, described in the previous chapter, in terms of the lack of public services and gendered dynamics in relation to the division of labour in rural communities (Meertens 2019). Nevertheless, it should also be recognized that women's insertion in the labour market, which is greater in urban areas, does not necessarily lead to a change in increased bargaining power for women, since they are often employed in informal and badly paid jobs which provide little security. Paid employment, moreover, does not necessarily diminish women's responsibility for household and caring tasks, especially since employment in the informal sector allows to combine both activities more easily (Ellerby 2017). In rural settings, land is the basis of income generation. Although the whole family works on the land, power within the household and the communities tends to lie with men, whose work is valued most since they tend to cultivate agricultural produce which is sold at the market and generates income (Zuluaga-Sánchez and Arango-Vargas 2013). Women's agricultural work, focused on family consumption, is not remunerated and therefore not equally valued (Jiménez Ocampo et al 2009; Federici 2012). In addition, patrilineal kinship values mean that land is inherited from father to son to guarantee that land remains family property. Women tend to live with their husbands' family upon marriage (Brydon 1989; Grupo de Memoria Histórica 2010; León 2011).

Following the logic of patriarchy, especially strong in Chibolo, women's principal role and sphere is the household, to which they dedicate most of their time. In the afternoon, they may have some recreational time to watch *telenovelas* (soap operas), but, in general, women are expected to continuously be at the disposal of others. The culture in *La Costa* is collective and welcoming. People – that is to say men – visit each other frequently, and they must be attended to. Some women, both in Chibolo and Pondores, would be reprimanded by their husbands when they spent too much time *'en la calle'* (on the street), chatting with neighbours, and, as a result, left their houses unattended. The household is defined by caring tasks, including for family members. Being a mother is therefore an important aspect of women's role in patriarchal societies (Jelin 1994). Although motherhood is often embraced by women themselves for giving them a sense of identity and a means of survival, it also tends to result in their dependence on their husbands, and their domination by men in various spheres of life (Chant 2003). Although most families in *La Costa* no longer have as many children as a few generations back, there are still examples of large families. Most women have children very young; the age of 16 or younger is not an exception. Social pressure to conform to traditional gender norms is strong, as single women lack a defined and accepted social place (Pateman 1988). This reflects how women are valued in patriarchal societies for the roles they represent, rather than as individuals. Not all women were happy with this role division. In Chibolo, María José complained that she had become a "slave of the household". Nevertheless, disrupting interiorized gender roles is not an easy process. Clara, for instance, explained that in spite of her difficult 38-year marriage to an extremely jealous and controlling man, she never considered separating, because she would never be able to leave her 13 children. Claudia described how her deceased husband never let her participate in any activities outside of the household:

'No, my husband wouldn't let me! Imagine, I had all those children! If I remember correctly, *doña* Reyna asked my husband if he would let me participate, but "No, she has enough work with the children she has to look after, and the house. And I have to be working on the land. And otherwise, who will cook for me? Who will look after those children?" Never, nothing, I didn't participate.' (Interview, 19 December 2015)

Having children is not just connected to women's roles but also to male roles and behaviours, which are prescribed by rigid notions of hegemonic masculinity, which identify what it means to be seen as a successful man in *La Costa*. *Machismo* is the most dominant form of hegemonic masculinity in Latin America, and it is particularly strong in certain regions of Colombia, such as the Caribbean coast. *Machismo* is demonstrated through wealth, (hetero)sexual conquest – and the fathering of many children, often with different women, as an indicator of virility – and the exertion of power over others. *Machismo* is thus defined by gender inequality between men and women, but also by competition among men (Baird 2015). It is displayed by an exalted virility, competitiveness, strength and toughness, not showing vulnerability or expressing emotions (Kaufman 1987; Lagarde y de los Ríos 2014). Descriptions, however, easily result in stereotypes about male abusive behaviour, while reality is often more nuanced (Viveros Vigoya 2003). Stereotyping, moreover, risks blaming men while ignoring the underlying social gendered structures which create these masculinities (Barker 2005).

Men's main gender role is to provide their wives and families with protection, food, clothing and other basic needs. In return for fulfilling these obligations, men enjoy privileges, or what Connell (2001, 43) calls the 'patriarchal dividend'. Their main privilege is to be cared for by their wives, receiving the best food and other attention they need. In addition, they enjoy the freedom and power to do as they like (Kaufman 1987). They are also those mainly responsible for the public functions in agricultural communities. For example, in Chibolo, all but a few members of the communities' peasant associations are male. Although women have played an important role in the peasant movement, including in the land occupations in the 1960s and 1970s, they were not recognized for this in terms of decision-making positions in peasant organizations like ANUC. They were seen as supporters of the main activists and leaders: the men. Although many peasant women were organized in women's committees and arranged small fundraising activities, this did not generally result in leadership roles either (Meertens 2019). It should, however, be recognized that although these gender norms benefit men more than women, the continued need to prove their masculinity, being a successful breadwinner and competing with other men over manliness, can also produce anxiety for men (Connell 2005). This is especially true for men who experience disadvantages in terms of class, ethnicity or other factors of social inequality, or in times of crisis when it becomes harder to live up to gendered role expectations. This was evident when conflict intensified, and gender roles became more fluid.

Gender roles during conflict

These rigid gender norms changed as a result of conflict, both for survivors and combatants. In Chibolo, although displacement and the move to the cities changed the lives of both men and women, it is likely to have produced a more radical shift for women. For many women, their daily routine changed from taking care of the household to working outside the house to provide income for their families, which was crucial because most families' incomes plummeted as a result of displacement, since men's agricultural skills were of little use in the cities. This is a common pattern in situations of conflict and displacement (Bop 2001; Calderón, Gafaro and Ibáñez 2011; Zuluaga-Sánchez and Arango-Vargas 2013). Initially, working outside of the household produced shame for women, as Marta described:

> 'When I was displaced, I went to La Estrella. I did laundry there. ... I had never washed "on the street" before, but I had to wash in La Estrella, on the street. The first days I felt ashamed, but when you get used to it, you no longer feel ashamed to walk with that bag of clothes.' (Interview, 26 February 2016)

Following patterns of women's entrance to the labour market in urban areas (Federici 2012), most women worked in line with their gendered roles in domestic and household tasks, doing laundry, cleaning or selling food or handicrafts. Yet reflecting a common pattern in Latin America (Jelin 1994), women's new roles did not alleviate their household tasks, while men's contribution to household or caring tasks did not increase either. This produced a double burden for women. Moreover, women often had unstable and low-paid employment with long hours, making it difficult to maintain a normal family life (Olavarría 2006). Some participants expressed sadness for not having been able to provide their children with the food, care and attention they needed. Patricia told me how she worked as a maid and was only able to come home every other week. Even though she and her husband worked very hard, they earned barely enough to survive. Her children were looked after by her eldest daughter, herself a teenager. Working so hard and still being unable to provide a good childhood for their children produced stress and anxiety. Ligia told me how she and her children worked in the market, and still were almost always hungry. Claudia also described the hunger and tiredness she experienced during displacement, and the difficulty in providing her children with schooling, food and healthcare. This feeling of failing in motherhood's central roles of caring and providing food and education for their children was strong for some participants and provoked a sense of powerlessness, 'maternal failure' and being incompetent as women, for whom motherhood and caring for others are defining tasks (Lemaitre 2016).

Displacement, however, was not entirely negative. Some women spoke positively about their changed gender roles. Ana explained how she attended training in the city where she sought refuge, giving her a sense of pride: "When I went to Valledupar, I went to declare, I was given some training and they even gave me a travel allowance for the taxi. My husband didn't continue but I did go – I attended. They even gave me a diploma – I have it there in the folder" (Focus group 18 March 2016). Palizua's leader Josefa explained how she ended up working in a small factory, earning a good salary. She enjoyed this new role, unconnected to traditional gender roles, since she explained that she was not made for working in other people's houses anyway. Other women also expressed pride for having been able to raise their children in difficult circumstances. Luisa showed this visually in the photovoice process, through a picture of herself milking a cow (Figure 2.1).

Figure 2.1: Woman milking a cow

Source: Photograph by Luisa, January 2016

She explained that milking, a male activity, was how she used to maintain her family in times of great difficulty, when her husband worked outside of the village. She cried while presenting the photo to the other women, since the image represented a painful memory of hard times. But it also gave her a feeling of pride: "I don't milk anymore, my children do it, or my husband. ... But this is, like I said, the way I raised my children, and therefore it is like a reason for pride" (Interview, 25 February 2016). These examples show that caring for others, even if based on stereotypical gender roles, can also create a sense of pride, for having demonstrated agency in maintaining the family in difficult times (Lemaitre 2016). The image also demonstrates that conflict often shakes up existing power relations, and can therefore provide unexpected opportunities for producing change and increasing women's agency (Björkdahl and Mannergren Selimovic 2015; Berry 2018).

Conflict also had gendered impacts for men, as during times of crisis, it often proves hard to fulfil the ideal of hegemonic masculinity. As in other cases (Kabachnik et al 2012; Myrttinen, Khattab and Naujoks 2017), being displaced produced a sense of emasculation for men in Chibolo, who felt useless as peasants in the city and unable to comply with their gendered role as breadwinner. Unemployment produced a lack of self-respect for men, and whereas women generally take on any job to maintain their families, men tend to have or consider fewer options, as they regard more feminine roles such as selling food on the street to be off limits (El-Bushra and Gardner 2016). These dynamics of emasculation applied even more to men whose families broke up as a result of displacement, as Mauro described: "All the time I remembered the seven years of work with my children that I left behind. That was really ... The first days after we left were very hard for me. I was left without my wife, without my land" (Interview, 19 January 2016). Mauro's experience resembles 'masculinity nostalgia', a longing for the (idealized) masculinities of the past, which are connected to key elements of male power such as fatherhood and authority, land ownership and being a successful breadwinner (MacKenzie and Foster 2017). For many men in and beyond Chibolo (Jiménez Ocampo et al 2009), returning to the land therefore meant the restoration of a sense of successful masculinity. Nevertheless, some relationships did not survive displacement, as many women preferred not to return because of the painful memories attached to the land, or because the stress and anxiety deteriorated the relationships. Some of these single men were admired for managing to get by well by themselves, but, in general, people frowned upon them, wondering why they did not look for a new wife. One of these men even told me that I could come and visit him, but that I should know that he was a *macho solo* (single man) and therefore not able to attend me well. A man without a woman was seen to be incomplete, lacking a wife to take care of him, and considered unsuccessful as a head of household, an essential male role (Brandes 2003).

Gender roles also changed for combatants. In fact, gender roles and norms are connected to the reasons why many women joined the FARC, and why the guerrillas accepted women in their ranks. Initially, the FARC was a predominantly male group. Women accompanied their husbands, but they only had support roles such as cooking for the troops. Their role diminished even further in the 1960s when the FARC turned into a mobile guerrilla force, and the men had to leave their families behind. It was not until the end of the 1970s that the FARC started to admit women, both to guarantee the supply of troops for their now more formalized guerrilla army but also because they believed including women would show a softer image that would enable them to engage better with the peasant population and particularly women, for example, through messages on Mothers' Day. Women were formally accepted as equals in the FARC statutes in 1985. Seeing women and relative gender equality in the movement inspired more and more women to join. From the 1990s onwards, they even became commanders (Welsh 2015; Gutiérrez Sanín and Carranza-Franco 2017; Gutiérrez and Murphy 2022). For some women and girls, joining the FARC was a way of gaining greater equality and showing their worth in a context where options for girls and young women were limited (Herrera and Porch 2008).

This might have been even more the case for Indigenous women. For example, in the Arhuaco cultural tradition, the youngest daughter receives no education since her role is to care for her parents (Santamaría and Hernández 2020). María, an Indigenous woman, indeed told me that her poor parents could only afford education for her brother. This is why María joined the FARC aged 11, because she wanted to continue studying. Although she did not receive a formal education, during over 20 years in the FARC, she worked as a nurse. Luz, a mestiza woman, explained that she was raised by an aunt after her mother died when she was only 3. This aunt treated her very badly, so Luz started threatening she would join the guerrillas when she was 10. This improved the treatment somewhat, but, being moved around different places and family members to prevent her from getting involved with boyfriends, at 17 she decided to join the FARC anyway. Most women, and in fact men in Pondores, joined at a young age, often between the ages of 14 and 17. While some women explained that they joined the FARC to save themselves from violence, either generalized or selective violence by other armed groups, testimonies from other ex-combatants list a diversity of reasons to join the ranks, including the desire for adventure, the desire to make a change to the country and looking for possibilities to study (Nodo de Saberes Populares Orinoco-Magdalena 2018; Millán Cruz 2019). In different countries around the world, escaping domestic violence is one of the main reasons for girls and young women to join armed groups (Specht and Attree 2006).

Even for those women who did not join for reasons related to gender inequality, their conceptions of gender roles and relations changed during their time as guerrilla members. Both women and men do not tire to stress the practice of gender equality in the guerrilla movement, demonstrated in the sharing of everyday tasks like cooking and laundry between men and women, and in all guerrilla members carrying guns and participating in combat. Natalia explains: "In that time, men and women were the same. For example, if I carried a certain weight, so did the men. The weight we [as women] carried was sometimes even heavier, because we carried more stuff than the men" (Interview, 9 October 2019). A former commander who participated in the peace negotiations in La Habana explained how he saw gender equality in theory and practice: "The right of women is present and considered in all our documents, and as a guerrilla, I always found that an armed woman was a real act of gender equality: the right of the woman to go to combat" (Interview, 20 May 2019). Many people remember with fondness the solidarity and respect between men and women that they experienced. Values such as solidarity and mutual care, traditionally considered feminine values, were adopted by both men and women, making femininities and masculinities fluid and creating what are sometimes called 'insurgent masculinities' (Dietrich Ortega 2012), which differ from normal masculinities depending upon the specific context.

Guerrilla membership offered women the possibility to study and gain opportunities that young women did not otherwise have. For example, Andrea, Tania and Gloria, like María, were nurses. María explains her satisfaction at her achievements:

> 'In the mountains, I was a nurse, and so I have a lot of knowledge of health. I worked with sick people, with viruses, epidemics, paludism, dengue, I know how to differentiate all of them. I took courses on first aid and then I started to practise, to attend the ill. This didn't scare me, because it's about the lives of the comrades. I know about medicines, about IVs. I feel satisfied that I learned all of that.' (Interview, 8 October 2019)

At times, María also served as an 'economist', which means that she was in charge of dividing and managing the food and other resources in the guerrilla camps, a complicated logistical effort which she clearly felt proud about. Other women were radio operators. Female leader Anita, although reluctant to talk much about her time in the guerrilla movement, told me she used to be a commander. Women stressed that tasks such as radio operator or nurse, although considered support roles or more 'feminine', were actually crucial to guerrilla operation. Moreover, women who held those functions were still also combatants, clearly not a stereotypical women's role. Guerrilla membership therefore offered an emancipatory experience which many women, like female ex-combatants from other guerrilla groups, remember in terms of the joy of personal development and the learning of new skills (Nieto-Valdivieso 2017; Weber 2021b). Civilian women inside the territorial space for training and reincorporation (ETCR) recognize this. Ana, whose sister and partner are ex-combatants, admired these women:

> 'They don't find it hard to use the machete, dig holes, things that a civilian perhaps would find hard because we are used to household activities, like the food, watching the children. But not them, they are used to anything. I always say that they are all-terrain – they will survive anywhere.' (Interview, 17 October 2019)

Nevertheless, women only made it to leadership positions in the lower and middle ranks, while the top FARC leadership was exclusively male (Barrios Sabogal and Richter 2019). The commander who I cited before said:

> 'In the FARC, there were no feminine tasks – we all performed all the tasks equally. The activities of men and women, even the right to go to combat and die in it, were organized according to the military organization of the day. But, of course, we all carry traces of *machismo* – we cannot overcome 5,000-year-old hegemonies in a few years.' (Interview, 20 May 2019)

As was the case in other revolutionary movements, gender-equal practices in the everyday activities of the guerrilla movement were part of the strategy to achieve the revolutionary goal, but not a goal in itself (Gonzales Vaillant et al 2012). Rather than promoting true gender equality, gender relations were temporally suppressed and inequalities rendered invisible in the pursuit of the goal of liberation shared among 'comrades', an identity that transcended gender identities and 'defeminized' women (Bernal 2001; Dietrich Ortega 2012).

A complicated aspect of guerrilla membership for women was motherhood. Although men and women within the FARC could have relationships, and there was a relatively liberal attitude towards sexual relations, they were not permitted to have children and generally received forced anticonception, which was established as a policy in 1993 (Giraldo-Gartner 2020). Nevertheless, some of the women in Pondores did get pregnant, perhaps because the contraception was not always available or effective. Although, as described in more detail in Chapter 3, some women were forced to undergo abortions, like many other women in the FARC, others were able to have their babies. They could not keep their babies with them, however, and had to hand them over to family members, if they were lucky, or otherwise to guerrilla sympathizers. Some women in Pondores remember how hard it was to separate from their children. Tania was able to see her son regularly, as her mother-in-law would visit the guerrilla camp with him during holidays. María, however, never saw her daughter, who was raised by her sister, until after demobilization, as she considered it too dangerous for her family to visit. Others, like Luz, completely lost contact with their children. This pattern is common in armed groups, and often generates feelings of guilt among women and problematic family relations which outlast the conflict (Ibáñez 2001; Weber 2021b). This means that the equality of everyday practice in the guerrilla movement came at an emotional cost for many women, as the revolutionary goal trumped personal aspirations (Rayas Velasco 2009). Yet, as I will show in Chapter 6, this revolutionary goal did not mean that women put aside the personal and gendered desire to become mothers.

The post-conflict situation: back to normal?

As other research in and beyond Colombia has confirmed (Bop 2001; El-Bushra and Gardner 2016; Berry 2018), changes in gender roles during conflict are often temporal, failing to lead to structural changes in gender relations or increased bargaining power for women within their households. This is apparent in both Chibolo and Pondores. After returning to the land, women in Chibolo took up their traditional gender roles again. Being able to take care of their families properly reduced their feelings of stress and 'maternal failure'. This contrasted with the stressful period of displacement, in which they had the double burden of working within and outside of their own households. Edilia, for example, explained that despite the pride in having raised her daughters alone after separating from her partner, she stopped working as soon as she married again. After all, now she had a man who would help her with everything once more. This illustrates how women's role as breadwinner is frequently seen as a 'disturbed order of things' by both men and women (Kabachnik et al 2012, 775).

Returning to pre-conflict gender roles is thus often seen as a symbol that the conflict and the corresponding shifts in power structures are over, and normal life can be resumed again (Björkdahl and Mannergren Selimovic 2015; Sjoberg 2016). Ana explained why she came back to the land to join her husband who had already returned: "The girls [her daughters] told me: 'Mommy, you have to go to Daddy because Daddy is skinny!' Haha! 'And he has a bad colour.' And I said OK, I will go" (Focus group 18 March 2016). In spite of her pride and joy for the trainings followed and new experiences during displacement, she returned to her traditional role of caring for the family within the household. This enabled the men to return to their traditional role as cattle farmers and heads of household. A notable exception was Josefa, one of the female community leaders. People in both communities talked about Josefa admiringly, commenting that she was such a hard worker, that she was like 'a *macho*' – and thus, in a way, somewhat less of a woman. People also talked negatively about her husband being a drunk. Indeed, he would sometimes disappear for days, leaving Josefa to fend for herself at the farm. Elderly widow Marta would sometimes also undertake activities not seen fit for women. In the photovoice process, a neighbour took a video of her fixing the roof of her house. With a mentally disabled son living with her, another son killed by the paramilitaries and a third one living outside of the village, Marta had no men to help her out. Like Josefa, she had to undertake 'male' tasks by herself, thus presenting examples of when women can disrupt gender roles without being criticized for it.

In Pondores too, the more equitable everyday practices in the guerrilla movement did not persist in the post-conflict scenario. Although somewhat less rigid than in Chibolo, overall, it can be observed that women here are also in charge of most household tasks such as cooking, washing and cleaning. Initially, the FARC aimed to maintain their collective practices, including the preparation of collective meals by a cook, based on the pooling of the government food supplies. This required a monthly contribution from all, but would enable everyone, both men and women, to participate in other activities as they did not have to spend time on preparing food. It would, moreover, enable them to maintain a collective spirit. Nevertheless, several participants explained that, gradually, this practice was lost, as people preferred to consume their meals in their own family. Tania, for example, explained to me that she did not want to continue paying for food that was not prepared with love. As a result, women are doing most of the cooking, while the men, who learned how to cook in the guerrillas, tend to cook only when their partners are not able to do so.

Even female leader Anita, who had struggled to teach her much younger civilian partner some of the conflict-era gendered role divisions, would get up at five in the morning to prepare breakfast and lunch when her partner would leave for work at six. She herself was not less busy than him, spending most of her days in meetings, yet even for her, the most natural thing was for her to cook. According to her partner, this was because he worked and she did not. When she challenged him about that, arguing that her leadership in the ETCR was also work, he reluctantly agreed, but this did not change the role division between them. It shows the persistent understanding, also among ex-combatants, of work as that which is remunerated. Ana, the sister and partner of two ex-combatants, half jokingly used to describe her work in the household as '*economía solidaria*', the term used for the cooperative model in Colombia, which the FARC aspire to. She called it that way since nobody paid her for her work, so it was based on solidarity. Luz explained that her husband always washes his own work clothes, and when she is busy, he also cooks. Yet when she is not busy, she cooks. This exemplifies the general role division among demobilized families and couples: the women are in charge of household chores, and men help them by washing *their own* dirty work clothes, or cooking when the women are unavailable. But the equitable division of tasks that was common among comrades during the conflict is seen by most as an 'exceptional transgression' (Dietrich Ortega 2012, 504). Other research suggests that for ex-combatant men, it is hard to maintain such caring masculinities, as they are frowned upon by their civilian family members, who expect these tasks to be performed by women (Gutiérrez and Murphy 2022). Roberto lamented this:

> 'Over there, women felt more free, independent, how shall I put it? They had more liberties in relation to the men, but here they have adopted that old attitude again. They have the same attitude of total servitude towards the man [*el macho*]. And wherever you look, you will not find any men doing laundry, but only women washing the men's clothes, cooking for them.' (Interview, 24 September 2019)

This shows that, in spite of temporary changes in gender roles, changing gender relations and norms more structurally takes a long time (Žarkov 2006; Aguirre and Pietropaoli 2008). Women's gains often mask continued oppression, which can even result in a 'patriarchal backlash' of increased violence against women (Berry 2018, 201).

The transformation of those gender roles is also hampered by persisting structural inequalities. In Pondores, those gendered inequalities are mainly economic, since men tend to have more access to paid work, whereas women's work is not or hardly remunerated and tends to reconfirm traditional gender roles which limit women to work in the household. They either work in the household or sell self-cooked food or items ordered through magazines, collected from town and dispatched by the women from their houses, like Anita and others do, through an initiative called 'entrepreneurial mum'. Another source of work for women is in the productive projects run by the ex-combatant cooperative. These projects, including the tourism and tailoring projects that involve most women, have so far failed to be profitable enough to enable regular and well-paid salaries. In contrast, many men in the ETCR are employed as private security guards of their former commanders, through an arrangement with the National Protection Unit (NPU) as part of the reincorporation process. This work involves irregular working hours and a considerable amount of travelling, thus making it harder for men to play a stable role in family and household tasks. Women mostly prefer not to become security guards because the travelling would not allow them to look after their children. Although a childcare facility does exist in the ETCR, it only receives children older than one year, and, furthermore, only functions in the mornings, thus making it hard for women to have a formal, full-time job outside of the ETCR when they have a child. Due to the COVID-19 pandemic, even this limited childcare support ceased to exist – it was reinitiated after the lockdowns. Via WhatsApp, young mother Rebeca explained to me that, as a result, the women ended up taking on most caring tasks, thus producing a double burden for them and reinforcing traditional gender roles even further (Personal communication, 13 April 2021). Natalia, not a mother herself, regretted this:

> 'Many girls have had babies, and they have to look after them. They can't leave because the child is in the house, because they have to make food for their husband, etcetera. So it's more like you see with the civilian population. Basically, the girls have become housewives. Well, they do work, but what I am saying is that it's the work in the house. They need to do all the work in the house, and the babies and all that, because the men have taken on a different way of life than we had back then.' (Personal communication, 28 March 2021)

Also other research confirmed that traditional gender roles have been largely reinstated in reincorporation camps, where many female ex-combatants have become housewives (Gutiérrez and Murphy 2022).

In Chibolo, structural inequalities are even more striking. The lack of electricity and running water makes women's household tasks very time-consuming and physically straining. During the first years of my research, most women cooked on woodfire, using very basic stoves made by placing iron bars on bricks. In later years, many women had been able to buy a gas stove, but they often continued using the woodfire stove too, claiming that the food tasted better like that, even though this required them to cut firewood, on top of their already demanding household activities like the daily sweeping of the patio, the washing – often by hand – of clothes that were extremely dirty because of men's work on the land and, in some cases, also fetching water from the community or their own wells, when they had run out of rain water to drink. Women sometimes complained about the health effects of these chores. Irene said: "I like doing laundry, but standing and scrubbing gives me back pain, and at night I can't sleep because of the pain. One has to be strong. But not with a washing machine" (Interview, 1 December 2015). María José explained one of the photographs she took: "There I am cooking. ... On woodfire, I wish there would be natural gas, so that one would not have to use that fireplace with smoke. ... Sometimes I am coughing, and I think it's because of the smoke I have in my lungs, living in that smoke" (Interview, 5 March 2016) (Figure 2.2). In addition to the adverse health effects, the performance of such time-consuming and straining household activities represented an obstacle for a more active role for women in their communities, simply because they

Figure 2.2: Cooking on wood fire. "This is where I cook, here on the wood stove. That is something complicated, with the smoke, a real inconvenience too. A real stove would be more comfortable, but the resources we have more or less allow us to eat, but not to buy that sort of things."

Source: Interview, 23 January 2016; photograph by Cecilia, January 2016 (image cropped to protect anonymity)

lacked the time for that, and had interiorized gender roles which limited women to the household.

Although women in Chibolo generally took their household responsibilities very seriously, as they enabled them to fulfil their socially expected gender role, they also complained about them. Juana, for example, whom it took months to allow me to help her with simple household tasks such as doing the dishes, once asked me: "Why has God decided that we have to eat three times a day? It is so much work all this cooking, and it never stops, not even on Sunday!" (Informal conversation, 5 September 2015). Many women in Pondores also resented their household responsibilities. Anita, who used to be a commander in the FARC, complained that she found peace much more work than war, since during the conflict, for 11 years she did not touch a pan, and now she had to cook every day. The combination of unequal access to paid jobs, lack of childcare facilities, the persistence of traditional gender roles, in Chibolo compounded by the lack of basic services such as electricity, gas and running water, led most survivors and female ex-combatants to lose the gendered gains they made during the war.

I could somehow experience the gendered role divisions and the extent of their interiorization in my own experience of doing research. For example, it was easiest for me to participate in most of the everyday activities in the ETCR. In Chibolo, I often felt frustrated at not being able to do much more than my research, as working in the field was not seen to be appropriate for women, whereas the community women, especially initially, did not accept any of my help with their chores. Household tasks thus became a way in which

I could measure the level of trust I had gained. Initially, most women would not let me help them with their household chores. Perhaps they saw me, a single woman over 30, as rather useless according to their gender standards, and therefore not to be trusted with these tasks, or as a guest and therefore an outsider who should not be burdened with household tasks. But at the end of my stay in the villages, my help in simple chores was accepted, and in an exceptional case, I was even trusted with frying yucca. From being a complete outsider, I had become a little bit more of an insider. In Pondores, in contrast, female leader Anita, in whose house I stayed, immediately accepted my help with daily chores like sweeping the house, doing the dishes or cooking. This reflects how household tasks for many female ex-combatants were additional tasks, which were mounted on top of their activities in the cooperative or their participation in education, trainings and workshops. They were keen to be relieved of these chores, whereas in Chibolo, these tasks defined a woman's role and identity. Apart from household tasks, I also joined various agricultural activities in Pondores, which was unimaginable in Chibolo.

Organization and decision making

One of the conflict-era gains, or in the case of Chibolo pre-displacement assets, that were lost was organization. In Chibolo, common to rural peasant communities, as described earlier, before displacement, women had organized in women's committees. Some of the older women remember these committees, which were organized locally, held regular meetings and managed to obtain several funded projects that benefited the communities, for example, enabling the school and health centre in La Pola, and projects to breed goats in both communities. These committees were in close contact with peasant union ANUC, which provided them with trainings on healthcare, alimentation, maintaining vegetable gardens and the like. Nevertheless, upon return from displacement, these committees no longer existed. Many of the 'old' women did not return from displacement, and the younger women had no experience in organizing. ANUC was no longer able to support, since, as its leader explained, they had been hit hard by repression during the conflict, and no longer had the resources to provide sufficient physical and political accompaniment to facilitate women's organization and participation (Interview, 30 October 2015). In the remaining forms of community organization, the peasant associations, most members were male, with the exception of a few female leaders and widows, who could not be represented by their husbands.

Some of the female community leaders saw my research as a way to revitalize women's organization. Surprisingly, some male leaders also insisted on my support to organize the women. I gradually understood that these leaders believed that women had good chances to obtain funded projects to improve the well-being of the communities, especially because of the attention for gender in the post-conflict context. Most women considered a women's committee as a way of obtaining livelihood projects to improve their economic situation, to develop skills through trainings, start a small women-led business or lobby local politicians for the improvement of basic services in their communities. Others mentioned that the women's meetings provided a distraction from their everyday tasks and an opportunity to leave the house and talk to other women. Nevertheless, attendance of the meetings was irregular and organizing the women proved difficult. This was partly explained by women's interiorization of traditional gender roles, making them prioritize their household tasks, their part of the 'contractual basis of family life' (Kabeer 2012, 224), over activities outside of the house. Others saw outside activities like women's meetings only as a 'respectable social outlet for women' (Helms 2013, 110) if they had a clear benefit, for example, in the form of a productive project that would generate income. Obtaining such a project took more time and perseverance that many women had expected and possessed, making the meetings seem useless to many of them.

A final factor related to a lack of confidence, not being used to voicing their opinions in a deeply patriarchal culture in which men represented their families. Ana often mentioned that she was afraid to participate in meetings because she could not read or write, whereas 21-year-old Jenifer told me that she was too nervous to speak in front of the other women – although she eventually did, presenting the images she took as part of the photovoice process. Leaders like Josefa or Lucía, and some other women who participated more actively in the meetings, expressed their frustration at the apathy of most women. These women, in turn, often complained about the authoritarian nature of the leaders, and were not keen to take on leadership roles. In spite of some productive projects that were eventually obtained, which will be described in Chapter 4, the women in these communities were not able to re-establish effective women's committees, thus leaving most of the public roles in the communities to the men, and largely confining the women to the household. This means that for most women their role remained, according to Josefa, "to be born, have children and die" (Informal conversation, 21 August 2015).

Although the FARC's organizational dynamics and history in many ways were very different from the communities in Chibolo, in other ways, women's organizational practices were strikingly similar. The FARC was known for its strong internal cohesion and discipline (Ugarriza and Quishpe 2019), which gave it a strength that allowed it to negotiate its own conditions for reincorporation. The rural and collective reincorporation process was meant to maintain this organizational force, which led to the creation of cooperatives in many ETCRs, including in Pondores. In contrast to Chibolo, both men and women were members of this cooperative. Although its president was a man, women were included as board members in functions such as vice-president and secretary. The vice-president was in fact the wife of the former commander, reflecting the views of several UN and non-governmental organization (NGO) interviewees that the current female ex-combatant leaders are often family members of former commanders, and also showing how commanders' partners tended to have certain power and benefits as active guerrillas (Barrios Sabogal and Richter 2019). Although as a non-member I was not allowed to attend the cooperative's assembly, I did attend other meetings in the ETCR. It always struck me that, aside from female leaders like Anita and Mónica, it was always the men doing the talking. This might not be surprising, since although women were admitted as equals in the guerrilla ranks, in practice, they hardly made it to the level of commanders, and they were not expected to voice opinions that were different from their partners (Herrera and Porch 2008). Furthermore, in a strongly hierarchical context like an armed group, voicing critical opinions in itself was not valued positively or encouraged for men or women (Ocampo et al 2014). Funnily enough, in some of the meetings with both ex-combatants and community women that I attended, the civilian women from the neighbouring community were much more vocal than the ex-combatants. This might be explained by the fact that they had not spent years or even decades in a strongly hierarchical environment. They ran a successful coffee association, according to them mostly led by single mothers, who as such had probably been forced to become more active publicly and economically in order to maintain their families.

Similar to what happened in Chibolo, gender committee leader Mónica frequently expressed her frustration at the lack of active participation of the other women, even in the meetings of the ETCR's gender committee, which were practically women-only spaces, since the few male members hardly ever attended. Mónica complained that the other women never wanted to help, for example, when they needed to work in the restaurant run by the committee, but that when there was a trip somewhere, they all wanted to go. Like in Chibolo, female leaders like Mónica and Andrea, who led the tourism project, in turn often received criticism from others for being authoritarian. Similarly, an employee from a women's organization criticized many female leaders for being very masculine, focused on giving orders (Interview, 12 November 2019). Such criticism is gendered, since an authoritarian leadership style is often accepted without complaints from male leaders, who are expected to be less communicative and are admired for being strong-willed. Female leaders often have little other option than being somewhat authoritarian and undemocratic, for lack of active participation and discussion by other women who are not used to speaking up, and in order to be taken seriously by men. For example, when the building of an imitation guerrilla camp for the tourism project was not done according to Andrea's instructions, Pedro suggested that this might be because the workers were only used to listening to their former commanders, men like now deceased Bertulfo, but that they had to learn that Andrea was their boss now. Female leaders thus need 'masculine authority' to be taken seriously by the men they have leadership over. At the same time, the lack of more democratic leadership can result in the fragmentation of women's organizational spaces. This was very clear in Chibolo, described in more detail in Chapter 4, but also in Pondores, where Roberto left the committee because of the "dominance of that little group, of two persons [Anita and Mónica]" (Interview, 24 September 2019) and women like Tania participated very irregularly, complaining that the leaders only invited people to help them out with hard work on the projects, but not for a trip somewhere nice. Women thus did not have strong collective structures which would enable them to lobby for more equality in public and private spheres, and, as a result, most decision-making spaces were occupied by men.

Ongoing machismo and violence

Unfortunately, the persistence of gendered stereotypes and role divisions does not only lead to a double burden, a lack of economic independence and decision-making power for women, but also risks producing other harms. In Chibolo, *machismo* continued to be strong. This was evident in various ways. First of all, men were often promiscuous, producing tensions in marriages and sometimes even among wider families. Juana, the lady of the house where I often stayed, struggled for a long time with her promiscuous husband, until she finally decided to accept his sexual escapades as he would never change, and at least he provided her and the children with everything they needed. Nevertheless, since her husband had been unfaithful with her friends and one of her nieces, she considered that things get really bad "when even your own family doesn't respect you anymore. One has to put up with a lot here" (Informal conversation, 30 March 2016). Juana often told me that she hardly had friends, since no other women could be trusted around her promiscuous husband. Men's promiscuity therefore reduces women's support network. At the same time, women's promiscuity is not to be tolerated, making many men extremely jealous, sometimes even causing violence.

Machismo can also have economic effects for women. Sara, who was not originally from Chibolo, came to live in La Pola after she met Jorge in a workshop that was part of the reparation process. They had children quickly, making young Sara decide not to continue her studies to become a teacher. Once they had two small children, Jorge left her, according to Jorge because she was not a good wife and made him do the dishes and cook food. Sara moved back to her parents' house as a single mother. Jorge moved in with his new girlfriend, economically providing for her and her children instead, to the indignation of his own family members. Another economic impact was men's tendency to consume alcohol, an inherent part of male identity in Latin America (Brandes 2003). On Friday, Saturday and Sunday afternoons, the *cantinas* of the villages were full of men, the regionally popular *vallenato* music blasting through the communities and copious amounts of beer, rum and *aguardiente* being consumed. National holidays and celebrations were notorious for the large quantities of alcohol consumed – by the men, as the women stayed at home looking after the house. Being drunk was not seen as a motive of shame for men, although the few instances when women were drunk unsurprisingly led to community gossip. Although holiday periods were looked forward to because of family visits and parties, for some women, they were overshadowed by tensions with their husbands, who would spend days in a row in the bar, spending the little money that the family had on alcohol, as Marta explained: "It is the woman who is suffering. Because the men go drinking and when there is no money left to drink, they sell what they can sell, but they won't look for food" (Interview, 26 February 2016).

Beyond emotional and economic harms, some women suffered physical harm, sometimes connected to alcohol. During my stay in the villages, I heard several anecdotes of men coming home drunk and forcing their wives to make food for them, sometimes pulling them out of bed by their hair, or trying to beat them. In a group discussion, it was jokingly commented that sexual violence within marriage occurred "when he comes home drunk" (Meeting notes, 8 October 2015). Alcohol hence intensifies *machista* behaviour, reinforcing its negative effects on women (Greenberg and Zuckerman 2009; Theidon 2013). But it should also be recognized that alcohol in itself is not the problem, but only reinforces an already existing problem of gendered inequality (Hume 2009). Although it thus became clear to me that different sorts of violence took place, this was not talked about much in public. Incidents were often mentioned in the third person, or the frequency of women's rights violations was described without speaking about any violence that the narrator herself might be experiencing. Nevertheless, over the course of my fieldwork, I heard of cases of physical violence against women, often for seemingly trivial things like preparing rice without salt or not buying a husband his cigarettes. Juana told me in the beginning of my fieldwork that she found it difficult to be married, since as a woman, she always had to attend her husband well, even if he arrived drunk in the middle of the night, or was in a bad mood and hit her. Several women mentioned that they hit their husbands back after having been on the receiving end of violence. One of them said she decided to leave her ex-husband because of violence. Another woman saw no alternative than to tolerate violence and threats thereof, feeling she had nowhere to go with her children.

The public silence about violence against women is common in Latin America, suggesting that women consider violence as a naturalized aspect of dominant masculinities that they have to endure without making a fuss (Jelin 1994; Hume 2009). Marriage is regarded as a social contract, which entails taking care of their husbands and obeying them in return for the provision of food and shelter. Failing to fulfil part of this contract – for example, by not attending to their husbands' well-being or being unfaithful – justifies violence as a form of correction (Chant 2003; Barker 2006). The family is seen as a private space outside the scope of state intervention, and problems are solved 'from the door inwards' (Molyneux 2010; Gutiérrez Bonilla et al 2015). Lack of economic independence, reinforced by early marriage, makes it harder for women to end oppressive or violent relationships, since they believe that they depend on the male breadwinner for their livelihood (Mies 1998; Calderón, Gafaro and Ibáñez 2011; Federici 2012). These examples of violence against women in Chibolo were not discussed in any of the meetings I attended between community members and the institutions and organizations linked to the reparations process. This reflects TJ's gendered hierarchy of abuses which privileges political violence in the public sphere over the intimate violence that women experience, which often takes place in the private sphere (Ní Aoláin 2006; Tabak 2011; Kent 2014). Transformative gender justice should recognize all those gendered harms, and the connection that exists between gender inequality before, during and after conflict, as a first step to transforming it (Swaine 2018).

Gendered violence was also a sensitive topic in Pondores, as I will describe in more detail in the next chapter. This was not only because of its naturalization as part of hegemonic masculinities but also because it undermined women's self-image of emancipated women who took up arms against state injustice. In fact, in an online public discussion forum, while some of the women accompanying the reincorporation process from Bogotá-based institutions mentioned the increase in violence against women, the female ex-combatants participating in the forum, including Anita and Mónica, did not mention gender-based violence at all, and focused their attention on the poor state compliance with the peace accords, including the lack of childcare facilities which specifically affected women (Asociación Freytter Elkartea 2021). This, however, does not mean that violence or other expressions of *machismo* did not exist. A male ex-combatant once pointed out a girl who had beat her partner in the eye, after he had hit her out of extreme jealousy. Maritza had experienced both gendered violence and irresponsible paternity by her ex-partner, a former ex-combatant. He left her for another woman when she got pregnant, refused to recognize their baby and then once a DNA test proved his paternity, he tried to prevent her from taking care of the baby, furthermore, failing to provide her with alimony for the baby. Neither the management of the ETCR nor the Agency for Reincorporation and Normalization (ARN) seemed to prioritize resolving her case. According to Natalia:

'We see that there are men here that abuse the girls. Well, maybe they are not many, but there is abuse in any case, from not letting anyone visit the house, to not being able to have a phone because you are writing with so-and-so, all of that is abuse. And other, bigger abuse as well.' (Personal communication, 28 March 2021)

Much of this abuse is related to jealousy, and the *machista* conception of women almost as men's property. That is why Natalia insists that "we need training, so that we become conscious that life and for one to live does not depend on a man" (Personal communication, 28 March 2021). Other reflections of *machismo* were the consumption of alcohol – albeit on a lesser scale than in Chibolo – and promiscuity, with many men, including some of the leaders, having children with different women, and failing to provide adequately for them. Roberto agreed on the existence of *machismo*: "Here, the domination of the *macho* is very present, precisely because the woman herself has let herself be subjected" (Interview, 24 September 2019). This attitude is common in Latin America, where men often blame women for reproducing *machismo*, rather than analysing or recognizing their own role in it (Hume 2009). Although it is important to work with women to raise their self-esteem and independence, as Natalia suggests, engaging men to transform *machismo* and other harmful practices of hegemonic masculinities is equally important.

I also experienced *machismo* myself during my research. Throughout my fieldwork, especially in Chibolo, I was continuously asked why I was not married and did not have children – especially given my age. My negative response was often followed by pitying looks, questions about my cooking skills or comments about the need to find myself a Colombian husband so that I could dedicate myself to the household. This made the research quite personal as I myself became the subject of questions and judgments (Coffey 1999). I frequently felt objectified, being talked about in my own presence because I was considered a status symbol for being White, Western and tall. This obvious interest was not limited to my research participants. I was once halted by the police on my way out of the communities, first to be asked what I had been doing there, and then asked for my number. It also did not end when fieldwork was over, as several years afterwards, I still received Facebook messages with questions about my love life, compliments and invitations. At times, this extreme interest made me feel unsafe, for example, when travelling on the back of motorbikes on the quite desolate dirt roads towards the villages, with bad phone signal. I do not share these experiences with the intention of focusing attention on myself, but in the interest of being open about the unexpected and gendered experiences of field research in patriarchal settings, often not taken into consideration by research training and ethics review processes (Gifford and Hall-Clifford 2008). I come back to this in the Appendix.

Apart from annoying me on a personal level, the patriarchal culture and strong *machismo* at times also presented ethical challenges and produced discomfort towards some of the male participants. This was particularly true when hearing them talk about women and seeing how they treated their wives, which contradicted my feminist research principles and personal beliefs about gender equality. Like other authors (Fruehling Springwood and King 2001; Hume 2007), I sometimes wondered how open I should be about my own goals and convictions in undertaking research. Yet I did not want to lecture participants about gender either, and as I was interested in better understanding gender relations, I tried to adhere to the observer role, which involves not disturbing the research setting (Hsiung 1996). At the same time, the (temporary) shared experience of patriarchy in this *machista* setting allowed for the discovery of shared affinities (Sultana 2007) with women with whom I shared little apart from our gender. This relation of intersubjectivity generated data about life in such rigidly gendered societies and sparked interesting and insightful conversations. Women often agreed that Western culture offered women more opportunities to decide over their own lives. My alternative, Western understanding of gender roles thus made me become a participant in the everyday gender politics in the villages (Hsiung 1996). Nevertheless, it is needless to say that my Western and middle-class background and ability to leave the research site meant that my positionality was very different from the women in Chibolo.

Compared to the often challenging experience in Chibolo, my research in the FARC reincorporation zone was easier in many respects. Since men and women had experienced living together in more equal relationships during the war, I felt much less objectified and received less catcalling and unwanted attention. This did not mean that I did not receive male interest; if anything, invitations for relationships were much more direct, and several men even suggested that we could arrange something just for the duration of my fieldwork. This was perhaps evidence of the greater sexual liberty that the FARC had historically experienced. Fortunately, men seemed to take my rejections in good spirit.

Positive changes

In spite of the ongoing and sometimes strong *machismo*, not all is negative. There are also positive examples of women – and men – who have managed to disrupt gendered expectations and these cases deserve attention. Women in Palizua, for example, selected photos for their photovoice booklet that visualized their connection to the land and cattle, and their desire to receive training to increase their participation in this work (see Figure 2.3). They thus showed that the relationship to the land or the animals was not limited to the men.

Figure 2.3: Women as veterinarians. "This photo represents that we could be doctors of our animals, in our *fincas*, with a veterinary course. ... That could promote productivity because we could keep our animals healthy and well. Our income could increase and our quality of life would change to a better future as personas in society and as families."

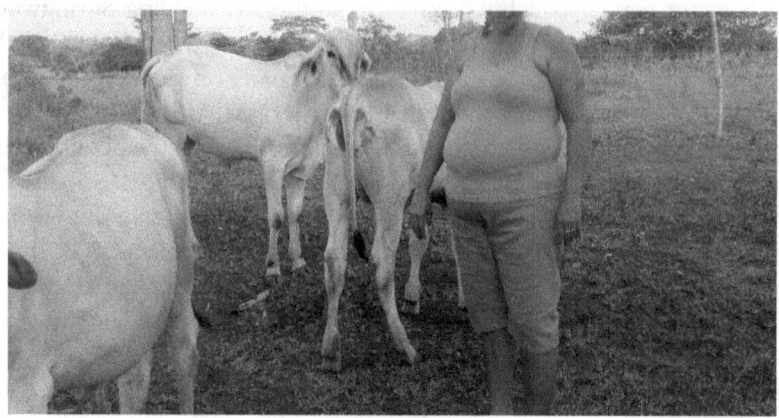

Source: Caption in Photovoice booklet, April 2016; photograph by Irene, November 2015 (image cropped to protect anonymity)

On several occasions, they, moreover, expressed that they believed they were better prepared for life than men, since they combined household tasks with agricultural work, whereas men only knew how to do one thing. This shows that women's consciousness about their roles and the value of their work was in fact changing. Other examples include some of the female community leaders, such as Josefa, the leader in La Palizua. In the first years of my connection to the communities, she not only invested much energy in organizing the women in her community but was also a leader in the wider land restitution and reparation process. Gradually, however, her role diminished, as she repeatedly complained that the male community leaders did not invite her for meetings and activities, while she also became increasingly absorbed with the shop she opened in the village centre. An example of a female leader whose leadership did not diminish was Carola. Apart from being an active member of the women's committee in La Pola and one of the very few women joining the peasants' association here, she also became active in the cooperative that was formed between different communities, including La Pola and La Palizua, to collectively sell milk. She became a member of the credit committee which checked the cooperative's finances. Part of what made Carola's participation easier was her husband, who is a good example of what 'new masculinities' could look like in the countryside. Alfonso was a very friendly man who never complained about Carola's outdoor activities, and who did not hesitate to cook and serve me lunch when Carola was not at home. His behaviour was quite a contrast to most men in the communities, who could not even offer a coffee, and expected their wives to prepare lunch before they left for any activities. Other positive examples were several young women from both communities who continued studying to fulfil their own life projects of becoming psychologists and nurses, instead of marrying young and having children. It should, however, be noted that their cases reflect the socio-economic disparities in these villages, as these girls' families, in contrast to most households, had the resources to pay for their daughters' education, and, moreover, had family members or close friends in the cities where the girls were boarded. This was inaccessible to most others.

In Pondores, there were also examples of women refusing to conform to the civilian gender norms which they considered oppressive. Andrea was one of them. She used to be together with one of their former commanders, but after demobilization, when she started to travel because of trainings for the tourism project she led, he started cheating on her. Andrea decided it was better to be single than to be with someone who cheated on her. Although she experiences social pressure to hurry and find a partner and form a family, since people tell her she is still '*buena*' (good) but is getting old, Andrea prefers to study and work. She told me she might not even have children since she does not want the '*desgracia*' (misfortune) of a life that most women have, who end up suffering to maintain their children with irresponsible partners (Informal conversation, 20 September 2019). Maricela is another example. She worked very hard as a communications officer for the ETCR's housing project, while finishing professional education at the same time. Although she was dating, she preferred not to move in together, so she could focus on her own plans. A year or so after my fieldwork ended, she moved to Bogotá for a job and studied for a degree at the National University. She is one of the only women in the ETCR who is economically independent.

There are a few female leaders in Pondores, of whom Anita and Mónica are the most influential and active. In Mónica's case, her husband's attitude is crucial. Whenever she goes to a meeting, he takes care of their young son, makes dinner and attends to the shop they own. When an employee from the National Ombudsman's Office asked him to join a Bogotá-based group on masculinities, he told me he first asked Mónica for permission. This shows that sharing household and productive tasks more equally is an important factor in enabling women's active public or economic roles. Pablo too is an example of new masculinities, which the FARC prefer to call 'insurgent masculinities' (FARC 2020). Besides being the FARC focal point for the reincorporation process, paid by the government to manage all relationships and meetings with the reincorporation institutions, he worked as an informal doctor, having been an experienced nurse in the guerrilla. Furthermore, he was a very committed father for his 3-year-old son, being involved in childcare at least as much as his wife. He once told me that men and women used to perform the same tasks in the guerrilla, so why should there be a difference now? Unfortunately, he saw that most men had returned to their old ways, making women responsible for most household work. He therefore wanted to sensitize other men and transform the strong *machismo* in the *costa*, which mocks men who help out in the household as gay. Andrea considered that "many women have wanted to have children, and that is understandable, but sometimes I don't understand that after so many years of training, struggle, work and experience, they are staying there. Everyone would need to make their contribution, participate a bit more" (Interview, 5 November 2019).

What is apparent from the examples in this chapter is that women experience varying degrees of agency, over time, across spaces and between women. This is apparent from the different degrees of public participation of women in Chibolo and Pondores. Yet even in Pondores, where women seem to enjoy more equality, many women's capacity to act independently in the public, political and economic spheres is limited by underlying structures of gender inequality, which maintain imaginaries about women's proper role and place. This complexity is evident in the person of Anita, who on the one hand is a strong female leader in Pondores, and on the other experiences inequality in the relationship with her partner, who expects her to be responsible for household tasks, as he has a paid job. The persistence of traditional gender roles, in spite of gendered changes during conflict, prevents women from having an equal degree and quality of political and public participation to men. The rigid and persistent distinction between the public and private spheres, with women expected to take on the main burden of childcare and housework, is an important element in maintaining women's inferior economic position and thus their low self-esteem and lack of independence (Lister 2003). Yet the fact that gender roles did change during conflict, and led to important emancipatory experiences, should be recognized more broadly and publicly. Pablo and Andrea, like female FARC leaders such as Olga Marín (Millán Cruz 2019), point to the importance of emphasizing and building upon the gendered role changes experienced during the conflict. Also, the FARC's gender strategy for reincorporation and its own feminist strand, called 'insurgent feminism', recognize and aim to build on the greater equality in gender roles when men and women were still in arms (Comisión Nacional de Mujer Género y Diversidad – FARC and Sandino Simanca Herrera 2018; FARC 2020). But at the local level, these policies do not seem to resonate much. Gender roles for rural *campesino* women, especially when they have families, are quite different from those of the probably mostly urban women with higher educational attainment who designed these policies.

TJ mechanisms, like historical memory, should play a greater role in overcoming this relapse in gendered gains. For this, they first need to *recognize* positive gendered changes more prominently, as Fraser's trivalent justice suggests. Failing to recognize such gendered changes in women's roles creates a gap in social memory (Theidon 2003), which maintains the status quo in which men are protagonists in most spheres of life. It is also important to recognize that conflict-era gendered gains were not only beneficial for women, who enjoyed emancipatory experiences, but also for men, especially ex-combatant men. Former commander José, during an event about masculinities organized as part of an internationally funded project, regretted that many men seem to want to behave in their families like their former guerrilla commanders, expecting their wives to be submissive and follow their orders. He called on men to be self-critical and change themselves first in order to change the world. This requires further unpacking conflict-era masculinities, since, for most men, these did not consist of *giving* orders, but of *following* them together with their female comrades. In return, they received clothing and food. This is why many men and women stress that they were better off as active guerrillas, as they did not have to worry about their daily needs. The current stress of providing for their families is a burden that men did not have prior to demobilization, and which could be relieved when they would return to more equal role divisions. More equal role divisions in turn would allow women a more prominent role beyond the private sphere. Similarly, in Chibolo, recognizing more explicitly women's conflict-era gains can prove important to motivate them to move beyond their household tasks. For this, TJ should broaden its focus beyond the 'victimizing experiences' included in the Victims' Law, and instead start unpacking and analysing a wider range of conflict-era experiences of women and men which can prove more fruitful for changing gendered role expectations and relations. Recognizing women's agency is therefore a crucial aspect of building the conditions for their equal and active citizenship. As I will show in the following chapters, TJ and DDR in Colombia are currently failing in this effort.

Conclusion

In this chapter, I have described how gender roles changed during conflict, including changes for men and masculinities, and gains for women in terms of increased agency, albeit often at a personal cost because of the double burden that these new roles implied. After conflict, gendered changes mostly reverted back to the pre-conflict situation, diminishing women's agency in many cases. I have described how structural gendered and socio-economic inequalities present barriers to women's agency, and prevent an active practice of citizenship in which they exercise agency to demand their rights and fulfil their own life projects, instead of complying with socially expected gender roles. These gender roles make women struggle to organize themselves, even though collectively they could more successfully demand their rights. In the next chapter, I further unpack how, unfortunately, the reparation and reintegration processes in Colombia currently fail to promote such citizenship-building processes, and through their persistent victim–perpetrator binary in fact often achieve the opposite.

3

Between Victimization and Agency: Gendered Victim–Perpetrator Dichotomies

As I described in the Introduction, victimhood is a central term and category in transitional justice (TJ), and it is a crucial one when researching the gendered dynamics of current reparation and reintegration laws and policies on the ground and their effectiveness in enabling communities to move forward by transforming structural gender inequality. Victimhood is essential for understanding the potential, or rather the obstacles, for gendered transformation, because it suggests passivity, vulnerability and a lack of agency, and it may result in ignoring the resistance and agency that people displayed (Kapur 2002; De Waardt 2016). In this way, it is unhelpful for retrieving the instances of agency described in the previous chapter, which could help to promote processes of citizenship building. In this chapter, I describe the problematic victim–perpetrator binary inherent in TJ and disarmament, demobilization and reintegration (DDR) in and beyond Colombia, and why it is an obstacle for *salir adelante*. I also describe how the categories of victims and perpetrators produce moral questions and sometimes discomfort for researchers working with both groups. I suggest the overarching category and identity of citizenship to overcome these rigid binaries which ultimately maintain divisions, inequality and polarization in society.

Victim–perpetrator hierarchies in transitional justice

One of the defining elements of a 'true victim' is innocence, implying that victims cannot have been actively involved in conflict (Bouris 2007; Madlingozi 2007). Innocence and moral purity make victims deserving of justice and reparations. Those seen as somehow responsible for their own victimization, or worse even, as perpetrators of violence, tend to be excluded from the support reserved for innocent victims. This creates a binary between the good, innocent victim and the bad perpetrator (Moffett 2016), ignoring a 'grey zone' of people whose experiences are not so easily classified (Levi 2013). This grey zone includes those who joined armed groups after having experienced injustice, who suffered harms after joining armed groups and people who were forced to commit crimes as part of self-defence groups or as child soldiers (Viaene 2011; Theidon 2013). These individuals could be seen as victims and perpetrators at the same time, and it is often difficult to establish which of those roles, victim or perpetrator, is dominant in individual experiences (Borer 2003; Orozco 2003). Others might not have been direct perpetrators, yet were complicit bystanders who did not intervene (Madlingozi 2007; McEvoy and McConnachie 2013).

Dichotomies are also created because the victim label is mainly reserved for those who suffered direct violence, or civil and political rights violations such as torture or killing, whereas socio-economic crimes generally receive lower priority (Miller 2008). Furthermore, TJ tends to prioritize violence that took place in public spaces, while violence that can be connected to conflict but does not take place during it is also generally excluded. This, for example, means that domestic and gender-based violence used to reassert pre-conflict gender norms, or resulting from traumatization during conflict, is unaddressed (Ní Aoláin 2006; Tabak 2011; Swaine 2018). This categorization can lead to competition between people who have experienced conflict in different ways, creating hierarchies between those considered more and less deserving of the victim label. This in turn can create distrust which undermines social repair and reconciliation (Bar-Tal et al 2009; Shnabel, Halabi and Noor 2013). Especially in protracted and complex conflicts, with horizontal victimization characterized by cycles of victimization and revenge, it can be difficult to distinguish victims and perpetrators, and 'genuine' or 'deserving' from 'undeserving' victims (Orozco 2003; Saeed 2016).

To add some nuance to this narrow understanding of victimhood, several authors (Bouris 2007; Moffett 2016; Baines 2017) have argued for the recognition of 'complex political victims', referring to victims who do not comply with the 'ideal victim' characteristics of innocence, purity and moral superiority. Complex political victims include victims who supported discourses that led to their own victimization, those who participated in forms of resistance and are therefore not seen as entirely innocent or those who suffered the same harms in which they were also complicit. Although complex political victims are normally regarded as 'bad victims' (Madlingozi 2007), it is argued that they should not be excluded from certain forms of support because of the complexity in their experiences. Because of this, the Extraordinary Chambers in the Courts of Cambodia included former Khmer Rouge cadres as complex political victims, since they also suffered harms. Nevertheless, the inclusion of perpetrators as victims, thus ignoring the specificities of their situation and the choices they made, has been experienced as offensive by some of the 'real victims' in Cambodia (Bernath 2016).

To overcome this risk, the category 'complex political perpetrators' has been coined, although it has not received much take-up. Baines (2009) suggested the term specifically to address the situation of child soldiers. They are perpetrators of violence, although, at the same time, their responsibility for their actions is mitigated by the fact that they were victims of child recruitment, moulded by their superiors into committing human rights violations. This nuance allows for the acknowledgement of the crucial impact that political frameworks, social identities and the 'persuasive power' of specific situations can have on people, which makes it unfair to scapegoat only certain people (Govier and Verwoerd 2004, 375). The nuance included in the categories of complex political perpetrators and victims enables a more complex analysis of how situations of chronic crisis, political violence and mass atrocity lead to gradations of innocence and responsibility in the same persons, with some people becoming victimized perpetrators and others somewhat responsible victims. Unfortunately, such nuance is not often recognized by TJ mechanisms.

Victim hierarchies have gendered dynamics. The disproportional attention to sexual violence by TJ tends to result in a gendered victim hierarchy, in which only women who have suffered sexual violence are considered 'real victims', confining other women to the role of witnesses about human rights violations committed against their male family members. Other wartime experiences, such as socio-economic crimes, the impacts of displacement which may affect women disproportionally or gendered harms such as forced marriage or labour, frequently remain unaddressed (Franke 2006; Ní Aoláin 2006). If TJ only considers women who suffered sexual violence as 'real' victims of gendered crimes, it risks exacerbating the differences between survivors, and creating or reinforcing divisions in communities (Berry 2018). This hierarchy can, moreover, create a situation in which women may feel forced to talk about having suffered sexual violence in order to receive reparations or health and welfare services (Olujic 1995; Theidon 2007a; Boesten 2010). Yet breaking the silence about sexual violence can result in re-victimization and stigmatization. Women's silence may be a form of protection for themselves and their families, and can also be a way of dealing with pain (Eastmond and Mannergren Selimovic 2012; Kent 2014). TJ has failed to respect and listen to these gendered silences, while simultaneously silencing other experiences, such as women's agency, resilience and resistance, which do not fit the vulnerable 'women and children' category (Otto 2010). In the remainder of this chapter, I illustrate how these gendered victim hierarchies are interpreted and performed in different ways and for different reasons at the community level, by both IDPs and former combatants in Colombia.

Gendered victim categories in Colombia

Colombia's Victims' Law creates a clear victim category, defining victims as those who have suffered harm (called 'victimizing events') as a result of human rights violations that took place after 1 January 1985. Land restitution is only accessible to those who were displaced after 1991. While members of the armed forces can be victims and will be compensated out of a specific fund outside of the Victims' Law, members of illegal armed groups are generally not considered victims, with the exception of children who were illegally recruited by armed groups. For these children, a specific programme was created after the 2016 peace accord, called *Camino Diferencial de Vida* (different life course). Despite these exceptions, this categorization results in a binary between guilty perpetrators and innocent victims, neglecting the 'grey zone' of people who were members of guerrilla or paramilitary groups and who also suffered harms (Theidon 2009).

In terms of gendered victimhood, both Colombia's TJ mechanisms and women's organizations focus strongly on sexual violence against women. For example, the then coordinator of the Victims' Unit's (VU's) Women's and Gender Group proudly explained that their flagship strategy provided reparations for victims of sexual violence, attending only to women. Although she recognized that there are also cases of sexual violence against men or LGBTQ persons, these are not addressed by this programme. The strategy provides victims of sexual violence with symbolic reparation measures designed and implemented by the women themselves, such as ceremonies, rituals or artistic activities (Interview, 25 January 2016). Women's organizations in Colombia also predominantly focus on women's roles as victims, especially of sexual violence. This is unsurprising given the international 'sexual violence hype' described in the Introduction, which leads to greater funding and attention for this crime (Hilhorst and Douma 2018). The women's movement, especially organizations like Humanas and Sisma Mujer, supported by the Constitutional Court, have strategically used the idea of the paradigmatic woman victim of sexual violence to lobby for specific rights for women. The centrality of sexual violence was also apparent in the women's movement's efforts to incorporate gender in the peace negotiations with the FARC, for instance, through the '*cinco claves*' campaign, which called for the specific treatment of sexual violence, as distinct from that of other crimes (Céspedes-Báez 2018). The same can be said for the Subcommission on Gender in the peace negotiations with the FARC, which positioned sexual violence as a priority area (Flisi 2016).

A representative of Humanas, one of the women's organizations involved in the *cinco claves* campaign, explained why sexual violence was important for her organization:

'Because we believe it's a type of violence that has a very important gendered weight. It reflects the gender order of society. ... So we are essentially interested in sexual violence for the meaning it has, because it organizes and maintains unequal power relations, because it sends a message of masculine supremacy, because it's a social organizer, because it is directed principally against women. But that doesn't mean we do not recognize that other crimes were committed against women, right?' (Interview, 12 November 2019)

Although she recognizes that sexual violence was not the only crime women suffered, most of women's organizations' public framing of the gendered consequences of conflict centre on sexual violence. The portraying of sexual violence as emblematic of gendered conflict impacts has contributed to a 'hyper-attention' to sexual violence, which risks neglecting other gendered harms that women have suffered or their needs beyond the attention for this crime (Rubio-Marín 2012). This limits support possibilities for women who experienced other forms of gendered harm, such as the gendered impacts of displacement – for example, poverty, sexual or labour exploitation, the struggle to feed their children – or forms of physical violence that take place in the public and private sphere, by armed actors but also by family members. Such intra-family violence is often not seen as conflict violence and thus not addressed by TJ or other post-conflict programmes, but it is caused by the same gender inequality that gender-sensitive TJ aims to address.

The recognition of sexual violence as a key gendered victimizing experience even extends to the situation of female ex-combatants. Although they are normally considered perpetrators, Colombia's Constitutional Court recently recognized that a female ex-combatant who was forcibly recruited and forced to undergo an abortion should be recognized as a victim and included in the Victims' Registry (Zulver and Weber 2020). Also, the Colombian Commission for the Clarification of Truth, Coexistence and Reconciliation (CEV) addressed abortions against female ex-combatants. Although the recognition of the often dual experience of female combatants is laudable, it is striking that sexual and reproductive rights violations are at the basis of this recognition, whereas other crimes and injustices that ex-combatants – including male ex-combatants – have suffered are not regarded as sufficient grounds for recognizing their victim status. This position confirms the treatment by the Constitutional Court and by many women's organizations of women's vulnerability based on their sexuality. The 'vulnerability frame' is not new to Colombia. The 1991 Constitution created the 'subject of special protection' category for groups who 'due to their economic, physical or mental condition are in a clear state of weakness' (Peláez Grisales 2015). Women are included as subjects of special protection, together with groups such as Indigenous peoples, the elderly and young people. Besides – literally – stressing weakness, this strategy means that attention is placed on the need for the protection of vulnerable groups, rather than the need to address the underlying inequalities that produce these vulnerabilities.

Some argue that such positions at the margins of power, including specifically the category of victimhood, can be used as a political tool and a strategy to claim rights, or fight for justice and non-repetition (Rudling 2019; Krystalli 2020b). Yet, as I will show in the next sections, victimhood is not the way in which the participants in my research preferred to frame their stories. Internally displaced persons (IDPs) in Chibolo – the 'actual victims' – do not seem to feel that this category adequately represents their situation, nor that it covers all gendered experiences. The FARC, although denying gendered victimhood, at other times strategically adopt a victimhood narrative to circumvent their responsibility for violence. This suggests the need for a better way of representing conflict experiences, that does more justice to the complexity of lived realities and the post-conflict needs of survivors and ex-combatants.

Gendered victimhood in Chibolo

In Chibolo, the language of victimhood made its entrance with the communities' claims to land restitution and reparations through the Victims' Law – unsurprisingly, given the name of the law and the institutions and processes involved, such as the VU and the Victims' Registry. Nevertheless, the victim label was not natural for most community members. Although they emphasized that their experiences before and during displacement had been really difficult, I hardly ever heard them describe themselves as victims. They rather talked about their life as *campesinos* (peasants). People also described themselves as IDPs or *desplazado/a(s)*, a term used less by the stakeholders. This is because the Victims' Law turned the humanitarian category of IDPs into victims, who could claim rights to truth and reparations in contrast to the ineffective humanitarian assistance of before (Sandvik and Lemaitre 2015). Yet although TJ stakeholders as the Victims' Law institutions and accompanying non-governmental organizations (NGOs) used the victim category to refer to IDPs, community members like Carola considered that the victims were those who were killed: "those really were victims, because we no longer see them" (Focus group 19 March 2016). Community participants spoke mostly about the link between their past and ongoing *lucha* (struggle) for the land and a better future, therefore not only focusing on their experience of victimization but also stressing their agency. The stories most shared were somewhat heroic ones about the men's return to the land, with no state accompaniment to resist those who the paramilitary had brought in to occupy it. Women's experiences during displacement emerged in my own conversations with women, but were less part of the community narrative. Yet, as in other contexts, the diminishing of the recognition of women's role in conflict also reduces the space for women's political participation in the post-conflict situation (Theidon 2003).

In addition to these memories of *lucha*, community members emphasized their everyday social and economic needs. Marta complained: "They are only interested in the past, but they should see the needs we have today" (Interview, 26 February 2016). This illustrates how for the participants in Chibolo, their experience is broader than the specific 'victimizing event' of displacement. It also includes their present-day experience of structural violence, as well as the agency they showed during and after the conflict. TJ institutions and NGOs, on the other hand, have a backward-looking focus on victimization, framed in terms of civil and political rights. The two narratives seem like parallel discourses that emphasize different sides of survivors' experiences, reflecting how TJ, in spite of its acclaimed victim-centredness, often remains far removed from the reality, views and needs of the people it pretends to benefit (Robins 2012). In Chibolo, TJ stakeholders made clear efforts to teach the community members this new victim-centred language. In one meeting I attended, the VU employee even explained to the communities that they were victims and that those who called themselves survivors were wrong, since even though they had survived, they would always be victims.

These stakeholders' understanding of gendered victimhood was less evident. As described before, the VU's gender strategy addressed sexual violence, whereas its gendered approach to collective reparations at the time mainly boiled down to approximately ten processes of reparations for women's groups, thus evidencing the persisting understanding of gender as women. Since there were not many female-headed households in Chibolo – another traditional focus of gender-sensitive public policy in Colombia (Meertens 2019) – nor clear evidence of sexual violence, the VU did not seem to consider that a specific gender perspective was needed here. The use of sexual violence was widespread in Colombia's conflict. Records from the prosecutor's office show that the *Bloque Norte*, which was active in Chibolo, was the paramilitary group responsible for most cases of sexual violence (Gutiérrez Bonilla et al 2015). There are records that show that this crime was committed in the municipality of Chibolo (Meertens 2019), potentially also in the two communities where I worked. Community leader Guillermo repeatedly mentioned that several women in a part of his community to which not all people had returned – since opponents of land restitution were still occupying this land – had suffered sexual violence, but did not want to speak about this publicly. This frustrated Guillermo, who was aware of the sexual violence 'hype' among state and civil society, making him believe that the reporting of this crime could galvanize support for the communities.

These women's silence shows how refusing to speak can be a protection strategy for women in patriarchal societies, while they might also prioritize other aspects of their stories, or present-day insecurity, over talking publicly about sexual violence (Enloe 2000; Crosby and Lykes 2011). Silence can thus be a form of agency, or a form of grassroots resistance against domination by international legal and humanitarian norms and agencies (Eastmond and Mannergren Selimovic 2012; Helms 2013; Kent 2014).

Nevertheless, this silence does not mean that women did not experience the conflict in different ways from men, even though the TJ institutions and civil society organizations active here did not seem to perceive the need to dig deeper into this. Although beyond sexual violence other forms of gender-based violence occurred, including forced labour such as cooking for different armed groups, people did not seem to consider this as particularly gendered, or even as a significant aspect of the conflict period. Instead, most community members used to remember the direct violence, the people who were killed, most of whom were men, or the fear that both men and women experienced. The present-day gender inequality and *machismo* described in Chapter 2, which included domestic violence such as physical and psychological abuse, were also not discussed in any of the meetings I attended between community members and the institutions and organizations linked to the reparations process. This reflects TJ's 'gendered hierarchy of abuses' which privileges political violence in public spaces over the intimate violence that women experience, which often takes place in the private sphere and frequently persists after the conflict is over (Ní Aoláin 2006; Tabak 2011; Kent 2014; Swaine 2018).

Although, in some ways, the participants in Chibolo did not identify with the way in which TJ gives substance to the victim label, in other ways, their narratives did comply with the requirements of the 'ideal victim' label. The emphasis on innocence, which is key to this category, led to the erasure of the role of the guerrilla movements in these communities. Although several informants close to the communities recognized that the guerrillas did have a presence here, and some community participants whispered that certain people were indeed involved with guerrilla groups, their role was downplayed or even neglected in order to maintain an image of innocence and thus of deservingness of reparations and restitution. For instance, when I visited Chibolo in the autumn of 2019, I spoke to the brother of Juana, who I by then had known well for over four years. She and her husband used to call me their daughter, since they only had sons. Her brother told me that he was the first of the family to arrive to the land in Chibolo in the 1980s, when the land was still 'fought for'. He explained that he came as a member of an armed group, which promised him a piece of land. Eventually, he had to leave because of family problems, came back later to then be persecuted by the paramilitary – presumably because of his prior involvement with the guerrillas – after which his family claimed the land on his behalf. Nevertheless, when Juana, who was not present during this conversation, later explained her brother's situation to me, she only mentioned that he had been forced to leave Chibolo because of personal problems. In spite of the relationship of trust that we had established over the years, in which we had shared many personal experiences, she clearly did not want to share her brother's involvement in an armed group with me.

In this way, innocent victimhood becomes 'narrative capital' (Theidon 2013, 113) in the 'economics of memory' (Theidon 2013, 109). This creates 'untruths' in the narrative (Baines 2015, 318) and obstructs the possibility of a more complex account of the past that does justice to survivors' various experiences and the different choices they made. An innocence-based understanding of victimhood encourages people to present a 'whitewashed' version of theirselves, transforming a multi-layered experience with the scales of grey produced by complex protracted conflicts into a neat history of innocence, in order to maintain an image of 'good citizens' who are worthy recipients of government assistance (Moffett 2016). In this image of good citizens or good victims, stories of agency only fit when they do not compromise survivors' moral superiority. Therefore, although there is space for recognizing the struggle for the just cause of claiming one's land – although less so for the everyday gendered agency described in Chapter 2, which is taken for granted – there is no space for recognizing involvement in armed groups, as this could suggest that people were in some way responsible for their victimization. Ex-combatants have a different interpretation of these shades of innocence, responsibility and agency, showing how those involved adapt categories of victims and perpetrators to best fit their own situation and needs.

Perpetrators as victims?

According to the victim–perpetrator dichotomy, the FARC ex-combatants who participated in this research are logically seen as perpetrators, with the potential exception of female ex-combatants, who are considered to have had higher risks of suffering sexual violence or forced recruitment (MacKenzie 2009; Henshaw 2016). In Colombia, sexual violence against ex-combatants has become a touchy subject. Even though the FARC is historically known for having strictly regulated the sexual life of its members through forced contraception and abortion, and although sexual violence against women and girls, even by FARC commanders, has been documented, its degree and nature was long debated, especially when committed against its own members (Centro Nacional de Memoria Histórica 2017; Gutiérrez Sanín and Carranza-Franco 2017). A heavily militarized and hierarchical context in any case makes it hard to distinguish consented from non-consented sexual relations, especially if refusing implies punishments like performing heavy tasks or standing guard (Herrera and Porch 2008; Baines 2017). In recent years, this issue has received media attention thanks to corporation 'Rosa Blanca', a controversial organization formed by women who claim to have been forcibly recruited as minors and suffered sexual violence and forced abortions within the FARC. Several interviewees suggested, however, that the organization is either financed or at the very least used by right-wing politicians to delegitimize the FARC and the TJ process (Interviews, 9 May and 23 August 2019). Nevertheless, the CEV report firmly establishes that the FARC was the group second most responsible for different forms of sexual violence, committed both inside its ranks and against the population, including the LGBTQ population. Reproductive violence such as forced abortions was common, although the practice varied between different fronts (Comisión de la Verdad 2022a). There is not much information about whether male ex-combatants might also have suffered gendered or sexual violence, as the possibility of male combatants being victims is generally ignored altogether (Hauge 2020). This maintains gendered victim–perpetrator dichotomies even within the category of ex-combatants, while it also upholds notions of hegemonic masculinity (Berry 2018).

In the FARC reincorporation zone where I worked, many women had had children while they were *guerrilleras*, and some even saw their children regularly while being active combatants, as described in the previous chapter. This means that not all women were forced to undergo abortions, although they were not able to raise their children themselves. Some women, including an ex-combatant I spoke to in another territorial space for training and reincorporation (ETCR) south of Bogotá, claim that they themselves decided to have an abortion, as there were no conditions to have children (Barrios Sabogal and Richter 2019). I avoided the topic, as this was not the subject of my research, and I did not want to ruin the rapport I was building, knowing how sensitive the issue was. But I later saw media reports in which women in Pondores admitted having undergone abortions (Janetsky 2021). Ana, who had joined her ex-combatant sister in the ETCR, told me her sister had undergone forced abortions repeatedly, leading to later complications with her desired pregnancies, and that other women experienced the same problem. Perhaps this was a result of the precarious conditions in which abortions were often performed, leading not only to emotional but also physical damage (Centro Nacional de Memoria Histórica 2017). Ana argued that these women did not talk about this publicly, for fear that media attention would reinforce already negative public perceptions of the FARC (Informal conversation, 25 September 2019). With the different practices across FARC fronts and over time, it is hard to make claims as to how frequent forced abortions were practised, although it has been evidenced as a pattern by the CEV. What is clear is that some women in Pondores may have been forced to undergo abortions, whereas others had more freedom in their reproductive decisions.

Participants, both men and women, were, however, unanimous in their dismissal of claims that sexual violence took place in the FARC. This was, for example, stressed by a member of the ETCR's tourism team when showing me around the 'memory house', where they had included photographs of women with babies to counter the stereotype of the FARC raping women. He said that, on the contrary, those who committed rape were sanctioned and sometimes even executed. One of his – also male – colleagues, when showing me the FARC imitation guerrilla camp on another occasion, made a point of stressing this prohibition and punishment too, which indeed corresponds to the FARC's statutes (Herrera and Porch 2008). Nevertheless, they could not testify to having actually seen such punishments being meted out. Women too insisted that there were no sexual violence cases within their ranks. Andrea, for example, said: "They have told us that we were raped and what not, but who can believe that? I spent 20 years in the FARC and nobody ever touched me without my consent, without me wanting to. Everyone was respectful and I feel offended by that, because it really didn't happen" (Interview, 5 November 2019). In a video made by the ETCR's communication team about the 'ethnic perspective' of reincorporation, which a participant sent me in December 2020, two Indigenous ex-combatants gave a short testimony about their experience. Both of them stated, in almost identical terms, that their rights as women or Indigenous persons had never been violated, and that, instead, their experience in the FARC had been like a 'university of life' for them (Gutierrez et al 2020). This suggests that both men and women attempt to protect the FARC's image of a united and disciplined organization (Céspedes-Báez 2019), explicitly pointing out the equality and respect between men and women within the ranks, emphasizing women's agency, demonstrated by the fact that women carried guns and would not have let themselves become victims (Millán Cruz 2019). Interestingly, this same argument is also used in the FARC's gender reincorporation strategy to explain why female ex-combatants are often stigmatized when denouncing violence in the reincorporation phase, as it is allegedly believed that they would not let themselves be injured since they used to carry arms. In this way, although during the time of the conflict the practices of equality within the guerrilla movement prevented them from suffering violence, at the same time, the FARC recognizes that women can be victims of gender-based violence in the reincorporation phase, as they are now 'inserted in a patriarchal matrix that exists in Colombian society' (FARC 2020, 38).

Civil society organizations and researchers working with ex-combatants confirm the salience of such equality and agency narratives, indicating that women often claim they preferred to have abortions rather than becoming mothers in a guerrilla camp (Giraldo-Gartner 2020; Interview, 7 May 2019). Various women's organizations, furthermore, point out that no armed group from whatever ideological position is eager to admit to having committed sexual violence in a systematic way (Interviews, 21 May and 12 November 2019). Fear of international prosecutions prevents them, as does the fear of moral sanctions. Admitting sexual violence is embarrassing, as it reveals war to be an erotic experience (Nguyen 2016; Meertens 2019). In addition, female ex-combatants themselves refuse to be regarded as victims of sexual violence or other forms of oppression. In the words of one of the FARC's female political leaders, they prefer to show women's 'real stories', which prioritize women's desire to resist state policies instead of their victimization (Informal conversation, 16 May 2019). Echoing similar patterns in countries like the Democratic Republic of the Congo (Baaz and Stern 2012), women's main interest is to uphold the stories of agency and equality that were described in Chapter 2. Silence, or at least silencing certain aspects of wartime experiences, thus becomes an agentic tool that can be deployed strategically to uphold a preferred account of the past (Touquet and Schulz 2020). This approach, however, presents agency and victimization as a zero-sum game, ignoring that dual experiences of agency and victimhood are possible, and that one does not diminish the other.

This attempt to portray female ex-combatants as emancipated women who did not experience violence and oppression can have damaging effects for women. Apart from making it hard for them to access psychosocial or physical support to overcome past experiences of sexual and reproductive rights violations, it also complicates their attempts to denounce or seek support for present-day violence. In many contexts, including Colombia, domestic violence tends to increase among ex-combatant families once conflict is over, as a result of male inability to deal with changed gender relations, because of trauma and resulting alcoholism, or simply because ex-combatants have learned to use violence as a way to resolve conflicts (Theidon 2009; Tabak 2011; Weber 2021b). Interviewees from the UN and an international lawyer's organization recognized that, in many ETCRs, there was a rise in intra-family violence (Interviews, 23 August and 7 November 2019). Nevertheless, although FARC senator Victoria Sandino has recognized that such violence should be addressed, both UN and civil society stakeholders accompanying the reincorporation process recounted instances in which women who decided to denounce gendered or intra-family violence were bullied by their former comrades, and excluded from leadership and decision-making spaces (Interviews, 7 and 12 November 2019). A women's organization mentioned that the few cases that female ex-combatants were willing to take forward involved instances of stigmatization and inadequate health treatments by the state, but not those of abuse by their former comrades (Interview, 12 November 2019).

Although during my stay in Pondores I did not get the impression that there were high levels of gendered or domestic violence, I did hear about isolated incidents, and instances of verbal abuse of women and the fear this generated. The women who told me about it did so reluctantly, and when asked whether they had denounced it, they claimed this was no use, since the leadership would not do anything anyway. In conversations I had with Rebeca and Maricela in 2022, they both admitted that there were many cases of intra-family violence. Rebeca herself had separated from her partner as he became controlling and violent. Both agreed that the leadership and the gender committee did little about this. Rebeca, not an ex-combatant herself but a former militant, considered that the ex-combatants had each other's backs, leaving civilian partners unprotected (Informal conversations, 28 and 31 March 2022). They were clearly demotivated about the reincorporation process's gender perspective, arguing that there was a lot of gender talk but no real changes. The careful protection of a public image of unity, discipline and agency, and the continuation of practices of hierarchical leadership, render female ex-combatants and civilian women in the ETCRs unprotected in cases of gendered violence. That this violence continues to exist is unsurprising, since little is being done to transform gender inequality, as will be discussed in greater detail in the next chapter.

Although there is no space for the recognition of gendered victimhood, when this is convenient to their narrative, ex-combatants do represent themselves, implicitly or explicitly, as victims, especially of the state. In the first place, they believe they have been fooled by a government that never took the implementation of the peace accords seriously. Jorge, for example, said: "I thought that since these are lofty accords, on the state level, that therefore the government would start to implement them, a 100 per cent. So it has been quite a … hard experience, because the expectations that I had aren't the ones that we have now" (Interview, 16 October 2019). In reality, the lack of progress with the accords' implementation also stems from the fact that the section on reincorporation was not very well developed. The difficulties this presents serve the FARC's discourse about the government's lack of political will (Cárdenas and Pérez 2019). In addition, and perhaps more importantly, ex-combatants argue that they have been victims of structural violence and state terror that left them no other option than to take up arms and fight against an unjust state. They thus portray themselves as victims at various points in time, both during and after the conflict. On many occasions, both men and women insist that the state was responsible for initiating and committing violence in the countryside. María, for example, argued that "the government will need to pay the victims for what they suffered, because in the end, all of that came from the government" (Interview, 8 October 2019). On several occasions, I heard female leader Mónica make similar statements, moreover, explaining that their new mission now that they are demobilized, is to "give a new life to the countryside through its development" and improve the situation of all Colombians.

Ex-combatants' attempt to present themselves as victims is unsurprising, as perpetrators usually try to maintain a positive self-image while coming to terms with their past actions (Williams 2018a). Pointing to past abuses of the enemy, in Northern Ireland referred to as 'whataboutery', is also a way of claiming that the enemy's violence was more serious and thus to avoid recognizing responsibility for violence (Orozco 2003; Lawther 2020, 12). Although it is unfair and can be damaging to survivors to treat FARC ex-combatants equally to 'real victims' who did not take up arms in spite of suffering the same structural injustices (Bernath 2016), there is nevertheless truth in ex-combatants' stories which victim–perpetrator binaries fail to recognize. As described in Chapter 2, many ex-combatants joined the FARC because of experiences of poverty, lack of possibilities to study or broken families as a result of illness or violence. Other research has confirmed such reasons, moreover, listing escaping intra-family violence and patriarchal societal structures, and a desire to combat social inequality, as motivations to join (Florez-Morris 2007; Denov and Ricard-Guay 2013; Gutiérrez Sanín and Carranza-Franco 2017). Furthermore, several ex-combatants' families were displaced, and others lost family members due to conflict violence.

This shows how victimhood and perpetrator-hood are often closely connected and can coexist in a single person. This is even more so for women, who have experienced different forms of gendered inequality or violence. María, for example, was not able to study, as her parents could only afford her brother's education, showing how gendered inequality compounds poverty for girls and women. Yet these experiences, including the structural violence that pushed many people to join the FARC, either because of a conscious decision to fight for a fairer society or since they saw no other option, tend to go unrecognized. Instead, perpetrators are simply that, an exception only being made for forcibly recruited children or female victims of sexual violence. This view is, for example, reflected in the position of women's organizations, who are only willing to work with *farianas* if they will recognize that they suffered sexual violence (Céspedes-Báez 2019). In Pondores, projects and support in relation to gender were all provided by either the state or international organizations, not by women's organizations. The before-mentioned lawsuit which led to the recognition of an ex-FARC member as a victim of forced recruitment and abortion was brought by the international organization Women's Link Worldwide. A representative of an international lawyer's organization recognized that it is mostly international organizations working on gender with the FARC, because of the insistence of women's organizations to address sexual violence committed by the FARC and the FARC's reluctance to address this. Although this organization eventually managed to collaborate with a Colombian feminist lawyer's organization to pursue legal cases of present-day gender-based violence against *farianas*, the Colombian organization decided not to continue the project because of the impossibility to work on any form of violence with the *farianas* (Interviews, 23 August and 12 November 2019). Another women's organization described the dilemma they struggled with:

> 'Politically, we have always positioned ourselves with the victims, right? ... At some point, we will have to build bridges with the reincorporated women, because they have had an interesting experience in terms of the [peace] negotiation. We will have to build bridges in the future, but for now, let's say that what we work on is very much in relation to the visibility and political agency of the women who have been victims.' (Interview, 21 May 2019)

That a woman could be both perpetrator and victim at the same time is still not something natural for these organizations (Krystalli 2021). This illustrates how victimization and agency continue to be seen as mutually exclusive by many actors in TJ and peacebuilding, in and beyond Colombia (Touquet and Schulz 2020).

Social identity – victim, perpetrator or citizen?

These examples from Pondores and Chibolo show that survivors – victims in TJ terminology – may not be entirely innocent, while perpetrators may not be only responsible. Reality is more complex and ambiguous, illustrated by the example of Juana, whose brother was a member of an armed group while she and her family were displaced. Mariana, who lives in the neighbouring community to the ETCR, was not an ex-combatant herself, but spent years displaced in Venezuela. She explained to me that her uncle was killed by the paramilitary, while one of her cousins had joined the FARC. Ex-combatants living in the ETCR had family members who were soldiers in the Colombian army. An ex-soldier and a female ex-combatant are now a couple and have a baby together. Many people here thus seem to understand that it is often just a matter of coincidence or (bad) luck whether one was displaced, joined one armed group or another, or even the army. This awareness is less present at the national level, as is evidenced by the defeat of the peace plebiscite in 2016. In this question of coincidence, structural violence plays a key role, since situations of poverty or violence and lack of opportunities for a life project mean that for many people joining an armed group is simply a way to survive and have some chance of gaining a livelihood and opportunities to develop themselves. This shows, as Nwogu (2010) has explained, that identities of victims and perpetrators should be seen as a temporary state, which any person could enter and exit, based on the presence or absence of a certain mix of circumstances. Greater awareness of this, and of the shared experience of structural violence, which emphasizes commonalities rather than differences, might help to promote understanding between groups.

In spite of victim and perpetrator categories thus being quite blurry, TJ tends to force people into one of these categories. Social identity theory, which analyses inter-group behaviour based on individuals' emotional attachment to a particular group, and the way in which this affects their well-being and behaviour (Haji, McKeown and Ferguson 2016; Hogg 2016), offers a useful tool for exploring the benefits and risks of such categories. Membership to a particular group can give people stability and well-being by prescribing who they are, what they should believe and how they should behave based on group prototypes. For instance, victims are innocent and morally pure, and therefore deserving of support. In an uncertain situation, people will choose to identify with groups that are clearly defined, as this helps them have a clearer understanding of their place in the world. Different groups or categories will become salient for people at different times (Tajfel 1974; Hogg and Terry 2000). As a result of the Victims' Law, some people in the communities in Chibolo started to categorize themselves as victims, as this presents a clearly defined identity, which, moreover, is supposed to lead to support. One of the community leaders, for example, described how he saw his community: "I say as victim community. Because we are one single community and we are all victims. ... Yes, I believe it is something like victim community, it sounds right. Victim community of Palizua" (Focus group 18 March 2016). The risk of clearly differentiating groups or categories is that it may create deep divisions between groups, sparking inter-group competitiveness. Members of a group with lower social status often attempt to move to one with higher status. This is, for example, what happens when ex-combatants attempt to 'pass' as victims of social injustice and state terror, since victimhood is a morally superior category to perpetrator-hood (Orozco 2003). Such passing, however, frequently leaves people in a limbo, being excluded from both groups, which eventually undermines their sense of identity and well-being (Hogg 2016). Survivors also attempt to downplay their potential responsibility for activities that might have led to their victimization in order to comply with the victim prototype. Yet recognizing such responsibility could in fact help to overcome the rigid divisions between categories and social groups and thus reduce polarization. Increased social cohesion can in turn aid collective action among different groups of people to demand rights, or organize themselves to improve their living conditions.

Overcoming tensions through shared experiences

According to social identity theory, a way of overcoming inter-group tension is what Hogg (2016) calls cross-categorization, which means that people acquire a less threatening understanding of the other group, based on the recognition that, although the groups are distinct, they share certain identity dimensions. Understanding how structural violence is central to the experiences of both survivors and perpetrators could provide a basis for recognition. The experience of gendered inequality, in some cases leading to gendered violence – before, during or after conflict, by armed groups and private actors – presents an element shared between female survivors and female ex-combatants, as does the agency and emancipation that many women from both groups have exercised during and as a result of conflict. Such shared identity elements could help create connections rather than divisions between survivors and combatants.

A more nuanced understanding of the duality of, and connection between, victim and perpetrator experiences also shows the need for more equal support for survivors and perpetrators. As described in the Introduction, one of the tensions between DDR and TJ is that most resources are frequently spent on DDR, which can generate discontent among survivors (Theidon 2007b; Sriram and Herman 2009). I could not help but notice that FARC ex-combatants received more support than the neighbouring community Conejo, whose inhabitants had mostly been displaced by the conflict, or survivors in Chibolo. Although FARC ex-combatants constantly complained that the government was not providing them with the promised support, since food rations diminished, the collective productive project had not yet materialized and people were still living in supposedly temporary asbestos-made housing, at least ex-combatants had received an individual lump sum, and over two years after the start of reincorporation, they were still receiving a monthly stipend, as well as gas, energy and water. This is in stark contrast to participants in Chibolo, many of whom are still waiting for their compensation cheque, while they have no access to running water and only some people, since relatively recently, have access to electricity. Conejo too suffers from unreliable electricity, many people there live in great poverty and according to some of the community members I interviewed, the promised support for the community has been slow to materialize. They had not yet received reparations either. This suggests a prioritization of support for ex-combatants over survivors. Ana's story is a case in point. Her sister was lured into the FARC by a family friend, after which her father was killed by the paramilitary and the family was displaced, losing their land. Ana never received reparations for the violence endured and ended up in extreme poverty, eventually moving into her sister's house in the reincorporation zone, since there, at least she and her three children had a roof over their heads. Similarly, Mariana and her sister, whose situation was described earlier, have not yet received compensation for displacement by a paramilitary group. A representative of the Agency for Reincorporation and Normalization (ARN) recognizes the tensions that this creates in the communities: "They comment, privately let's say, but there are actors in the communities that say 'well, we expected that this would bring us some benefits that had been postponed for being in a conflict zone'" (Interview, 11 October 2019). The relationships between ex-combatants and receiving communities, and the effect of unmet expectations of increased public services in these communities, was not addressed in the peace agreement (Carrillo González 2017). Recognizing structural violence as a key element in the situations of both survivors and ex-combatants makes clear that prioritizing ex-combatants over survivors, apart from being unjust, is not a viable strategy in the long run. Since structural violence can push people to join armed groups or find other illegal ways to make money, the choice to support survivors or perpetrators is in fact a false dilemma, because people can be or become both. Although the Colombian government has the tools to provide non-combatant communities with similar support, through the development and infrastructural measures included in the land restitution sentences, and the rural development and reform aspects of the peace agreement, these rural support policies have not yet been a priority, according to an interviewed UN representative. The ARN official agreed:

'This is the sensation that exists in the countryside, for example, in relation to the development plans with territorial perspective, the PDET [territorial rural development plans], in the prioritized municipalities. ... Fonseca is one of them. But that sort of things, I feel it is not advancing. That influences the perception of reincorporation, because that [the PDET] is for the territory, not for the specific population group but for the territory, and that would help us a lot in terms of diminishing the tensions, to have a more organized process and one that is more oriented towards resolving structural problems of that territory.' (Interview, 11 October 2019)

Of course, it is not desirable or feasible in the short term to treat survivors and ex-combatants as complete equals and include them in one overarching category (Hogg 2016). It is important to acknowledge the harm done to people and allow them to identify with other victims. This can create solidarity and help the healing process (Bar-Tal et al 2009). It should, furthermore, be recognized that conflict experiences can have a lifelong effect on people, since traumatic experiences create a split between the sense of self before and after the event (Nordstrom 1997). As Marta's quote earlier illustrates, survivors might continue to feel victimized by structural violence, thus making victimhood a continuous experience (Mueller-Hirth 2017). At the same time, it must be recognized that victimhood is a temporal identity, since people have not always been victims. Therefore, the category of victimhood may be necessary for legal or policy purposes, but it should not become permanently attached to people's subjectivity or sense of identity (Moreno Camacho and Díaz Rico 2016). Furthermore, whereas survivors might not have been completely innocent victims, it is also important to recognize victimization among perpetrators, albeit without ignoring the responsibility they hold for their actions (Orozco 2003; Bernath 2016). This use of the complex political victim and perpetrator categories would allow recognizing the nuance and complexity in people's experiences, which can consist of victimhood but also agency and responsibility (Bouris 2007). They also allow more space for the stories of gendered agency described in Chapter 2, which are not of interest to most TJ institutions.

Adding a complex political perpetrator lens, less commonly advocated for by TJ scholars, is crucial to acknowledge the role that structural and other violence played in turning people into perpetrators. It allows for their recognition as simultaneously victims of gendered and other violence and agents of violence bearing responsibility for the harms they have done, even though they might have been motivated to join armed groups for social justice goals (Baines 2009; Weber 2021a). Truth commissions, for example, can play a role here, by recognizing more complex narratives of the past, and adding a stronger focus on perpetrators' stories, thus enabling a better understanding of the motivations for violence (Nwogu 2010). The CEV has given an interesting example in this regard, recognizing FARC ex-combatants were victims of reproductive violence. Adding this complexity blurs the victim–perpetrator binary and makes cross-categorization and mutual recognition possible, thus helping to overcome some of the inter-group tensions and eventually bringing reconciliation a bit closer (Orozco 2003). Julia, the leader of a women's coffee association in a neighbouring community, believed that seeing the humanity in the other was essential for reconciliation:

'Well, we live in a community where they [the ex-combatants] are too, they are already a part of our community and we need to learn to live with them one way or another. In the end, they are human beings, and although they might have made a mistake, like all human beings, we all make mistakes and we all have the right to a second opportunity.' (Interview, 1 November 2019)

Recognizing that people may respond differently in similar circumstances of structural violence is part of this reconciliation process, which can be aided by a societal understanding of the categories of complex victims and perpetrators. Ana argues that "it is important to raise people's awareness that they were indeed guerrillas, but they were also victims, and perhaps the soldiers, the police, they were victims too" (Interview, 17 October 2019).

Eventually, however, even complex political victim or perpetrator categories will not provide people with a stable identity in the long run, since victim and perpetrator prototypes will only be meaningful as long as TJ and DDR processes convert such categories into support. And, as Chapter 5 will show, assumptions of receiving support simply for being victims or ex-combatants risks instilling a passivity in people which is not helpful for moving forward, especially when such support is inefficient and little effective. Furthermore, eventually, people depend on the state to decide who to classify as a victim, rendering people powerless and leading to what Buchely (2018) calls 'precarious citizenship'. Instead, a future-oriented post-conflict identity can help to prevent people from becoming trapped in the past and to unite rather than divide them (Shnabel, Halabi and Noor 2013; Meertens 2015). People have multiple social identities, with different identities becoming salient in different contexts over time (Hogg and Terry 2000; Wessels 2016). The idea that victimhood is a temporal identity corresponds to how one of Chibolo's leaders understands his community's identity: "We have always identified ourselves as a peasant community. That we have been victims is true, we have been victims, but …" (Focus group 19 March 2016).

TJ must aid with the adoption of a self-identity that will help people in the post-conflict process of rebuilding their lives. Like IDPs in Chibolo, FARC ex-combatants like to stress that they are peasants – even though many of them have not actually spent much of their life as peasants. Being peasants could thus be an identity that survivors and ex-combatants share. The conflict-era agency that the women in Chibolo and Pondores have exercised, described in Chapter 2, can be another element that connects the experiences of both groups of women. Historical memory processes and other forms of storytelling, for example, through films, books or other forms of art, could help uncover such instances of agency, to use them as an instrument for building a political community (Baines 2017). To create a collective identity for women as socio-economic and political actors in their families and communities, such processes should stop focusing only on 'victimizing experiences' and instead also recognize more diverse representations of women's roles, which can help to transform gendered stereotypes that mostly stress their vulnerability (Williams and Palmer 2016; O'Reilly 2017). A collective sense of identity and agency is an important element of citizenship (Lazar 2013a). Citizenship, and the sense of being citizens who all share the same entitlements, can therefore be an overarching social identity to connect people (Wessels 2016), even though some suffered political violence while others experienced other forms of injustice. Thus, based on temporal and instrumental categories of complex political victims and perpetrators which stress similarity instead of differences in experiences, TJ should prepare and support people for a future-oriented identity as citizens, which recognizes different pasts but unites them based on a shared future. Identifying as citizens first and foremost, with corresponding duties and rights of citizenship, could in turn enable people to overcome the sometimes passive attitude described in this book, and help them to organize and demand their rights to transform their lives.

The ethics of researching 'victims' and perpetrators

Although I have always been critical of the victim–perpetrator dichotomy in TJ, and have tried to create a more complex and nuanced understanding of gendered conflict experiences through my research, putting this more nuanced understanding into practice was challenging at times. Although convinced of the appropriateness of the complex political perpetrator lens, I sometimes struggled with the FARC ex-combatants' self-representation as victims. Especially, their constant complaints about the government's failure to implement their promises, which a UN representative agreed had become like a mantra (Interview, 7 November 2019), was hard to accept, as was their dismissive talk about 'small' projects of 35 million pesos (approximately £7,300), which they saw as virtually nothing. Of course, I could also see that many parts of the peace agreement were not being implemented and I obviously understood their anxiety at the ongoing attacks against ex-combatants, but I could not help but think of the people in Chibolo, who had received much less government support and were still struggling to keep their heads above water, whereas the FARC had all their basic needs covered. I noticed that my aversion against their often self-pitying stories was growing.

Several researchers have discussed the ethical complexities of doing research with perpetrators, such as the need to avoid abetting their crimes, identifying perpetrators through research, risking potential stigmatization and building rapport with individuals whose actions the researchers do not approve of (Williams 2018b; Broache 2019). In addition, I was not sure how to write up the stories I heard. On the one hand, my goal was to represent the views of the participants as accurately as possible, and I was convinced that knowledge about ex-combatants' experiences of (structural) violence could help to promote understanding and reconciliation. On the other hand, I did not want to uncritically share unreflexive accounts of victimization that I found unrepresentative of reality. But I was concerned participants would not want me to publish more critical accounts. On top of this, the COVID-19 pandemic meant that I was unable to travel back to share and discuss my results with the participants, making it even harder to follow all the steps of what I considered to be ethical research (Knott 2019). Eventually, I shared a short, written report with my main results with all the participants I was still in touch with, and asked them to comment and share it widely. I did include my criticism in the report, albeit worded diplomatically, and also introduced some rebuttals to the FARC's complaints mantra. The few reactions that I received were positive, and edits mostly consisted of spelling corrections and minor additions.

I also struggled with another dilemma. Initially, I had intended to focus my research on reincorporation not mainly on the ex-combatants' side of the story but to also actively involve the community members in Conejo. Nevertheless, I soon realized that the ETCR was in fact quite separate from the community, and I simply did not have enough time to spend equal periods in the ETCR and in Conejo. Gradually, I did get to know some people from Conejo in activities and workshops in which ex-combatants and community members both participated, and, eventually, I was able to interview some of them, in addition to some non-combatant inhabitants of the ETCR. Nevertheless, I did not manage to divide my attention equally, thus reproducing the tendency to prioritize ex-combatants which I critiqued. In the meantime, I kept in touch with the communities in Chibolo, whom I visited during a break in my stay at the ETCR. I felt a bit uncomfortable telling them I was doing research with the FARC, thinking they might feel offended that I was now siding with 'the enemy'. Nevertheless, although some people in Chibolo believed the FARC were just drug traffickers, others seemed to agree with the reincorporation process and were aware of the support the FARC were receiving, as well as the killings of ex-combatants and the partial lack of government implementation. They did not show signs of jealousy of the process or of my research with the ex-combatants. Most people did not even seem too interested in what I was doing now that I was no longer mainly researching the Victims' Law; their main interest was to know whether I had finally married.

When I returned to the ETCR after this visit, I found it even harder to listen to the FARC complaints mantra. When Anita, the female leader I lived with, asked me how my trip to Chibolo had been, I could not help but tell her, aware that this might offend her, that, in a way, people there were worse off because they had received even less state support and did not receive any food or other services. Rather than feeling offended, Anita said that life is hard for the Colombian people, and that therefore it is hard to understand why people vote the way they vote. Apart from making me feel a little better for at least having voiced my discomfort, albeit perhaps indirectly, her comment and the responses of the participants in Chibolo showed that many people in fact are able to empathize with the other group's situation, and realize that, to a certain degree, they share the same experience of ongoing structural violence and a government that does not comply with its obligations and, essentially, does not care for its citizens' well-being.

Conclusion

This chapter has showed how the prescribed scripts of gendered victimhood do not fit the stories of participants in Chibolo and Pondores, or the ways in which they want to represent their experiences. At the same time, the moral dynamics inherent in victimhood and its emphasis on innocence do feature in the representations of both survivors and ex-combatants. This leads to one-dimensional stories which obscure complexities that shine light on the role that structural violence, and structural gendered violence, play in the process of becoming a victim or a perpetrator. I have showed that paying greater attention to this gendered structural violence can not only help to create a more complex and realistic account of the past but also to increase understanding and empathy between groups. Initially, the categories of complex political victims and perpetrators are instrumental for this. Eventually, however, TJ should enable and support people to become citizens in a post-conflict country. Rather than innocence-based victimhood, it should promote a citizenship identity, based on a prototype connected to practices of active citizenship. In the final chapters, I will explain in more detail how gendered practices of active citizenship can enable people to claim the redistribution of economic resources and (gendered) power relations, thus not only overcoming a sense of victimhood but also a crucial obstacle for a better and more gender-just post-conflict future. In the next chapter, I first show that such an approach is so far largely absent from TJ and DDR mechanisms in Colombia, which in fact currently often lead to weakened practices of gendered citizenship.

4

Gendering Reconciliation? The 'Differential Perspective' of Reparation and Reintegration

The previous chapter discussed some of the more structural problems with how transitional justice (TJ) and disarmament, demobilization and reintegration (DDR) view and categorize the people that benefit from and participate in these mechanisms, and how that approach does not help to promote reconciliation and gendered transformation. This chapter looks at how Colombia's reparation and reincorporation processes incorporate a gender perspective. It thus answers the first part of the question guiding this book: what are the gendered dynamics of current reparation and reintegration laws and policies on the ground, and do they effectively transform structural gender inequality? Early DDR and TJ processes in Colombia, such as the demobilization processes of the 1990s, or the Justice and Peace Law (JPL) of the mid-2000s, did not have a clear gendered perspective. In the last decade, Colombia has started to address the gendered impacts of its decades-long conflict. Its 2016 peace process was widely commended for its inclusion of a gendered perspective, and the Victims' Law too has a 'differential perspective'. What change does this make to the way in which peacebuilding and reincorporation are approached on the ground? This chapter will contrast the way in which gender is formally integrated in reparation and reincorporation policies with the ways in which conceptions of gender and gendered changes are – or are not – translated into concrete actions. It will analyse what impact these actions have on women's positions and gender relations, describing how, in some cases, well-intended strategies and projects can end up having counterproductive effects.

The 'differential perspective' of reparation and reintegration

The 2011 Victims' Law adopted a so-called differential perspective, which aims to counter the situation of vulnerability of certain groups of victims due to their age, gender, sexual orientation and disability, to protect their rights and enable their participation. Rather than a gender perspective per se, it offers a more intersectional view of how people have been affected differently by conflict depending on the intersection of different axes of inequality, including, but not limited to, gender (Crenshaw 1989). Furthermore, the Law adopts a 'transformative perspective', understood in Article 5 as the intention to 'eliminate patterns of discrimination and marginalisation ... to prevent repetition' and 'restore or reconstruct a stable and dignified life project for the victims'.

Although the Law's differential focus enables a wider analysis of structural inequalities, this risks overlooking gender as a specific cause for discrimination. This is especially true for the way in which gender was incorporated into land restitution. The Land Restitution Unit (LRU) at the time of my research had a 'Social Unit', which dealt with issues related to gender but also with the participation of survivors more broadly. As a result, there was no clearly gendered expertise or personnel in the LRU. This made its well-intended gender policies largely unsuccessful. Attention to gender is largely translated into the prioritization of female heads of household, women who suffered sexual violence and women's access to issues such as credits, training and other social security benefits. Furthermore, a key aspect of the gendered dimensions of land restitution is the fact that land titles are allocated to both men and women. This could constitute a clear transformative measure for women, since it is estimated that women in Latin America currently represent, at most, 25 per cent of land owners (León 2011). Owning land and property makes women less vulnerable in cases of divorce or their husbands' death. A problem with the way in which this potentially gender-transformative measure is implemented is that a land restitution case can only have one claimant. This tends to be a man, in his traditional role as head of household representing his family, while women are included as the claimants' wives or permanent partners. The view of men as *real* owners of the land therefore continues to dominate (Meertens 2019). It was not until 2013 that the LRU, in coordination with the Ministry of Agriculture, started a 'Women and Land Programme' to promote the participation of women as land claimants within the judicial phase of the land restitution process. The programme included measures to support and protect women and gender training for the involved personnel and judges. This shows that the translation of a gender or differential focus into practical actions often only occurs along the way, when it becomes clear that policies without a gender perspective actually reinforce gender inequalities. Unfortunately, the Women and Land Programme was soon suspended because it failed to turn women into 'viable' economic subjects (Meertens 2019, 148).

In spite of a nationally led women's programme – at least for some time – the need for a gender perspective did not necessarily trickle down to the local level. The LRU official working in Chibolo, for example, never even mentioned the joint land titles as a gendered element of the restitution process. She admitted that "I don't handle this issue of the [differential] perspective very well. That's why I'm telling you, we're always talking about this perspective but sometimes we don't know …" (Interview, 19 October 2015). As a result, the land restitution process in Chibolo mainly engaged the men as landowners, and meetings were largely attended by men, with the exception of just a handful of women. A former LRU official admitted the consequence of this:

> 'I believe that she can appear in the title and she will not even notice that she is included. She isn't aware of anything that happened in the process. She knows that her husband went to many meetings and that the land title is there, but she is not aware what this means, and what it means that the land is hers. And you cannot achieve that in one meeting. That requires a conception of a process.' (Interview, 21 December 2015)

It is unrealistic to expect a transformation of gender relations if a gender perspective is not included from the design of a programme onwards, but is only 'added on' along the way. It is even harder to expect transformation when the staff involved in these programmes are not able to undertake a gender analysis or recognize gendered forms of structural violence (Bueno-Hansen 2015). From 2013 onwards, there is no gender disaggregated data available on land restitution under the Victims' Law (Meertens 2019). The lack of clear gender-sensitive measures on the ground instead leads to the persistence of traditional ways of viewing men's and women's roles in rural communities.

The gender perspective of reparations is directed by the Victims' Unit's (VU's) 'Women's and Gender Group', and guided by Conpes 3784, a national-level policy for the protection of the rights of female conflict victims, which was adopted in 2013 – again, two years after the adoption of the Victims' Law. As described in the previous chapter, the main gendered policy resulting from Conpes 3784 was the reparation strategy for female sexual violence survivors. Furthermore, at the time of my research, the VU implemented collective reparation processes with a number of women's groups and organizations. The director of the VU's Reparations Area admitted that it was only several years after the launch of the Victims' Law that the VU started piloting a methodology to apply a "differential perspective" to mixed collective reparation processes (Interview, 25 January 2016). The realization that gender had to do with relationships, rather than simply women, again came rather late. An understanding prevails of 'gender' as 'women', who merit special protection on the basis of their vulnerability. Women are therefore included in the group of 'subjects of special protection', as described in the previous chapter. Such vulnerability-based understandings and approaches tend to ignore what the experience of displacement has meant for women's roles and agency, and how this can help to see women in a new light, as social and economic actors. Instead, the state's discourse resonates with historical relations of power and inequality, maintaining certain groups as rescuers of others, without transforming these inequalities (Boesten 2014; Crosby, Lykes and Caxaj 2016). This is reflected in how the coordinator of the VU's 'Women's and Gender Group' saw their reparation strategy for female sexual violence survivors: "Well, this is like our most loved strategy within the Unit, because of the moments of satisfaction it has generated for us, but also because, for the women, it is most important, well, has been very important" (Interview, 25 January 2016).

Comments like these raise doubts about whether the Victims' Law is actually victim-centred, or whether it is rather a way for the state to be *seen* to be providing justice and 'doing gender'. The gender approach of the Victims' Law is limited to specific teams, advisors or programmes, rather than being an integral part of all its processes. 'Adding women' is common to TJ and human rights processes (Theidon 2009; Bueno-Hansen 2015), but it risks creating a 'women's ghetto' of women-focused projects or programmes that have less resources, lower priority and fail to address or transform the underlying gendered inequalities (Charlesworth and Chinkin 2000). The VU's specific reparation strategy for female sexual violence survivors is a case in point. According to an interviewee from a Colombian women's organization, this strategy, though well intended and integral, has attended to very few women (Interview, 23 May 2017). It was only in September 2021 that the VU published guidelines for the understanding and implementation of a differential gender approach, as well as indicators to measure its implementation (Echavarría Álvarez et al 2021). The publication of this document, ten years after the adoption of the Law, came too late for me to study its implementation. Up to that point, the VU's work on the ground seemed to have little gender perspective, much less aim towards the transformation of structural gendered inequality. This chapter will provide examples of that lack of awareness of structural gendered inequalities and how to transform these.

Gender and reincorporation

Prior DDR processes in Colombia did not have a proper gender perspective, but in 2014, in response to the challenges encountered in the paramilitary demobilization process, the then responsible institution, the High Council for Reintegration (ACR), developed a gender strategy. This strategy is quite progressive and complete, dealing with the need to transform gender roles, prevent gender-based violence, promote women's leadership and address violent masculinities. Although the actual impact of this strategy on the ACR's work is unclear (Flisi 2016), the document provided a good starting point for integrating gender in the reincorporation process of the former FARC guerrillas. The 2016 peace accords signed between the FARC and the Colombian government were praised for their gender perspective. In contrast, the gender perspective of the reincorporation process is rather disappointing. Perhaps this can be explained by the fact the Subcommission on the End of the Conflict only had one female member (Corredor 2022). Moreover, reincorporation was among the last topics to be discussed in the peace negotiations, and there was a sense of haste to finalize the process as the population's patience was running out (Cárdenas and Pérez 2019; Arias Ortíz and Prieto Herrera 2020). Even the FARC itself admitted that this was the part of the peace accords with the most generalized dispositions (FARC 2020). The accords' section on reincorporation does not refer to gender in any meaningful way, except making a general call for the process to have a gender and differential perspective. The lack of a concrete gender perspective might also have to do with the fact that, in spite of its public attempts to demonstrate the opposite, gender was never a priority for the FARC. This is, for example, reflected by the fact that, initially, only about 20 per cent of the FARC's delegation were women, most of whom without full negotiating power (Corredor 2022). The Gender Subcommission was only created in 2014, two years into the peace negotiations, whereas the agreement's differential perspective was only formally presented in July 2016 (Flisi 2016; Koopman 2020).

The national policy document which guides reincorporation, Conpes 3931, does include a gender perspective, but this is simply copied from the gender perspective defined in the peace accords. It emphasizes women and the need for specific measures in the design and implementation of the peace programmes, in recognition of women's position as autonomous citizens. The Conpes outlines specific actions towards this goal, such as the creation of institutional reflection spaces about gender and masculinities among the Agency for Reincorporation and Normalization (ARN) – the ACR's successor – and the Presidential Office for Women, and the design of specific strategies to increase women's economic independence. Nevertheless, the step from turning these policy guidelines into actual programmes is taking a long time. Reports from the international monitoring commission of the peace accords repeatedly identified the lack of progress made in this respect, pointing out that the advances made were mainly thanks to the efforts of the FARC ex-combatants and political party, whereas the state was slow to provide services and benefits for women (Secretaría Técnica del Componente Internacional de Verificación CINEP/PPP-CERAC 2020).

The coordinator of the reincorporation process in the regions of Magdalena and La Guajira explained that, at the time of the interview, autumn 2019, the ARN was implementing pilot projects on gender, based on prior experience in the paramilitary reintegration process, which would give them the necessary input for incorporating gender in the longer-term reincorporation process (Interview, 11 October 2019). Although it is, of course, laudable that the institution tries to make its previous gender strategies fit for reincorporation, it is unclear why two years are needed to start this process through pilot projects. In a similar vein, other 'gender institutions', like the 'Gender Table' of the National Reincorporation Commission and the High-Level Agency for Gender, were also created along the way, as researchers from the international monitoring commission of the peace accords pointed out: "I believe that they hadn't thought out nor gauged what gender inclusion would be and that has complicated things, although I believe that it is now advancing, but it has complicated its effective mainstreaming" (Interview, 21 August 2019). A representative of an international lawyers' organization believed that the recently created High-Level Agency for Gender was an ineffective institution. It consists of different government agencies but provides no clarity about its actions, achievements or budget, while there is no way of asking for this information. She believed the institution was created to make it *seem* like something was being done (Interview, 23 August 2019). Again, gender is being added along the way, in spite of prior experience and expertise. A women's organization pointed out that in Colombia, "there is very little capacity on the part of public officials to learn from past experiences. There is always this attitude of a clean slate" (Interview, 12 November 2019). As a result, there is an abundance of laws and policies on reintegration, as well as other TJ and post-conflict mechanisms, which are often implemented by a multitude of different state and civil society institutions, making both its implementation and its understanding by the general public a complex task (Peñaranda Currie 2020). As a result, there is not yet a clear and well-designed gender strategy for reincorporation. Furthermore, unlike the Victims' Law where at least the VU has a gender team, the ARN does not have a team or even an expert to deal with gender and its challenges. Although this could suggest that gender has been mainstreamed in the ARN's work, a representative of a women's organization believed:

> 'This is what happens in Colombia, it's all about the statements. ... To have a policy, a designated person to do the work, but, in practice, it is not really incorporated and the policy is a very empty policy, which remains on paper without any specific elements, specific actions that

allow one to say that there is a gender perspective.' (Interview, 12 November 2019)

In the absence of a state-sponsored gendered reincorporation strategy, the FARC developed its own – although rather than on gender, it specifically focuses on the reincorporation of women. The strategy, which was developed in 2017 and updated in 2020, is in fact very detailed and comprehensive, dealing with aspects as diverse as political reincorporation and the promotion of female leadership, social reincorporation including the reunification of families with children raised by others, but also addressing, albeit rather generally, 'new insurgent masculinities' and the need to start treating caring responsibilities as a collective rather than a women's task (FARC 2020). Nevertheless, few of the admirable and well-designed suggested actions in this strategy are implemented in Pondores, reflecting the all too common gap between policy and practice, and national and local levels within TJ and DDR processes.

Representations of masculinities and femininities

The previous chapter described the persistent victimhood focus in TJ and, to a certain extent, DDR processes. It also showed that this focus, translated into a specific sexual violence approach when a gender lens is added, does not apply in the cases of Chibolo or Pondores, or at least that participants do not feel represented by the prescribed victim label. Furthermore, a victimhood focus is backward-looking, instead of providing a more future-oriented identity. How do the reparation and reincorporation processes regard and address post-conflict femininities and masculinities, and how effective are these to transform gender inequalities?

One striking way in which women are commonly addressed, already hinted at in the Introduction to this book, is in relation to their role as mothers, who are assumed to be peaceful by nature and therefore to have a special task in peacebuilding. This representation is common among Colombia's women's organizations, who often portray women as mothers who 'don't give birth to children for war' (Cockburn 2007; O'Rourke 2013). This discourse was present both among survivors in Chibolo and ex-combatants in Pondores. In Chibolo, for example, women often mentioned an activity organized by the VU's psychosocial reparation programme *Entrelazando*, to celebrate Mothers' Day and pay homage to the *madres luchadoras*. This term can be translated as the 'courageous mothers' but also refers to the women who came to the communities as part of the first group of peasants who occupied the land in the 1980s, who are still referred to as *luchadores*, or fighters. Although it should be applauded that women's role was recognized, at the same time, they were predominantly seen in their motherhood role, reinforcing traditional gender patterns. Furthermore, this Mothers' Day celebration was, to my knowledge, the only instance that a specific gendered activity was organized. The focus on motherhood risks viewing women exclusively in their reproductive role, essentializing them as peaceful, while, at the same time, seemingly suggesting that women are superior or more moral than men, simply for being mothers (Dietz 1987). Furthermore, it excludes women who do not or cannot comply with the gendered role expectation of motherhood (Werbner and Yuval-Davis 1999).

Some of the comments made in stakeholder interviews, for example, with the VU and a leader of peasant organization ANUC, echoed this view of women as peacemakers:

> 'We are convinced that women are precisely those who reconstruct the social ties that were affected by the conflict. Since they are survivors of the conflict, they will be rebuilding those social ties. They are the ones who will rebuild the families, the community contexts. We want to support the women to be leaders.' (Interview, 25 January 2016)

> 'Us women, in our hands are many things.' (Interview, 30 October 2015)

Ideas about women's special role as mothers and peacemakers are also commonly heard among FARC ex-combatants. María, for example, believed that, in a conflict, "the mothers always suffer more, both the mothers of the soldiers and the mothers of the *guerrilleros*" (Interview, 8 October 2019). Leader Mónica also stressed that women often bear the brunt of conflict because they are mothers, and that this also makes them those most supportive of peace:

> 'We have our sons, our daughters, and as women, I believe we are those most interested in peace, not in war. ... As women, we have given birth to those persons that die in war. So we are those most affected in a war. A man that is killed, or a woman that is killed, they were born of a woman.' (Interview, 29 October 2019)

Edilberto believed that motherhood shows the commitment of the *farianas* with peace:

> 'Well, the ex-*guerrilleras* here are different, you know. Look, every *guerrillera* here is looking for future development – she wants to have a baby because we were in a place where they could not have a family. Now they want to have a family and they think: "I want a child and I will work to have a house, raise my child well educated, so my child moves forward, becomes a doctor". ... Look at the thinking of those

guerrilleras about their children, and look how almost all are having babies.' (Interview, 24 September 2019)

In this way, Edilberto points at an aspect of reincorporation that speaks strongly to the public attention: the so-called baby boom among FARC women. In June 2017, there were 164 pregnant women and 98 children in the Territorial Spaces for Training and Reincorporation (ETCRs) across the country, with 258 new pregnancies registered by December 2018 (Giraldo-Gartner 2020). This baby boom was also noticeable in Pondores, with many women being pregnant and several babies being born during my fieldwork period. In the media, this is often portrayed as a symbol of peace, of female ex-combatants having become 'harmless mothers' whose priority is now to look after their babies' future (Giraldo-Gartner 2020).

Yet although such affirmative essentialisms of women as mothers committed to peace and providing a better future for their children can carve out a new space for women, beyond victimhood or perpetrator-hood, their long-term utility for gendered transformation is unclear. Such discourses romanticize and idealize unpaid women's roles, while they pay little attention to women's political projects (Berry 2018; Meertens 2019; Gutiérrez and Murphy 2022). Furthermore, they maintain ideas about women being most responsible for raising children, and make no mention of fathers' role in this. Broadening the recognition of men's roles to include fatherhood, disrupting the idea of raising children as women's domain, is a pending task for TJ and other peacebuilding processes, and a step towards gender justice in Nancy Fraser's model. Building peace and rebuilding communities that are still characterized by patriarchal relationships is not easy, and can place an additional burden on women, especially if they are not supported by actions to transform the structural gender inequalities that limit their agency. Motherhood and the caring tasks it entails often represents an obstacle for women to participate in spaces beyond the private sphere of the household.

As mentioned, a missed opportunity is that men are rarely, if ever, addressed as fathers. In Chibolo, men were engaged in the Victims' Law process as those principally responsible for agricultural activities on the land. Although, as explained, joint land titles were allocated to men and women, men were those most involved in the land restitution process, and the productive projects provided emphasized their role as cattle farmers, an activity in which women's role was not promoted in any way. As I have described elsewhere (Weber 2018), these projects reconfirm the idea that men have the principal relationship with the land, making Patricia exclaim that "What we would like is to also have a project as part of the reparations. So that it is not just for the men, because those projects that they have given are just for men" (Interview, 15 October 2015). This was also reflected by comments from women like Claudia and Elena, who were not even aware that they would now also be included in the land titles, and wondered if they would receive compensation, since all the paperwork was in their husbands' name. One of the latest land restitution sentences initially only addressed male owners and did not even include all female partners (Focus group 19 March 2016), a mistake that needed to be corrected through a demand by the accompanying lawyers' organization.

As a result of this persisting understanding of only men as peasants, I was not able to identify *actual* changes in the way men's and women's relationships to the land were perceived. Juana, for example, when asked about her husband Juan's whereabouts, would say "he went to one of his *fincas*". She accompanied Facebook images of the pavilion they built in front of their house with the caption 'the pavilion of Juan García'. During a visit in 2019, she talked about her sister-in-law, criticizing how she organizes and manages everything in her house, from the food and the medicine for the cattle to all the building work, claiming ownership by saying things like "I built that fence". Juana did not agree with this; she believed her tasks were those in the house, while the rest was done by her husband and she would never claim any recognition for it. The idea that she also owned or contributed to their business had not been interiorized, even though she was the person in charge of managing the finances of the family's milk and cheese business. Even leader Josefa, who played an important role in the post-displacement return process in La Palizua, told me that she did not attach much importance to actually owning the land, despite buying her own cattle to obtain more security and independence from her husband.

These examples show how the Victims' Law's potentially gender-transformative measure of joint land titles seemed to be mostly a formality. Unfortunately, having de facto property rights is often not enough for women to actually enjoy these rights (Greenberg and Zuckerman 2009; Meertens 2019). Specific attention and accompaniment is needed to start reconceptualizing women's relationship to the land, including the recognition and promotion of women's contribution to the farming economy as agricultural workers and administrators of the land in their own right (León 2011). That women are actually keen for this was demonstrated in the number of pictures they took of the farm animals. These included images of chickens, ducks, pigs and goats, considered traditionally as agricultural work for women close to the household (León 2011), but also images that showed the importance they attached to the cattle and of their own role in cattle farming (see Figures 4.1 and 4.2). It is a missed opportunity that the Victims' Law institutions did not take this chance to engage women more fully and equally in agricultural life. This would have promoted a more autonomous and independent post-conflict future for women, rather than being included simply as wives of peasants or mothers of their children.

Figure 4.1: The farm as a family business. "This photo represents that we have a company, in which we work as a family. The man, woman and children all work in cattle farming."

Source: Caption in Photovoice booklet, April 2016; photograph by Ana, January 2016

Figure 4.2: The importance of the animals. "The cows and other animals are suffering with the strong drought."

Source: Caption in Photovoice booklet, April 2016; photograph by Luz, March 2016

FARC ex-combatants also commonly talk about themselves as peasants. Indeed, 66 per cent of demobilized ex-combatants come from rural regions (Consejo Nacional de Política Económica y Social 2018). This, however, does not mean that they have agricultural skills that could make farming a sustainable way of life, since the long time spent in the *monte* means that most of them do not actually have much farming experience. This is also demonstrated by the fact that, although many people in the ETCR have planted some crops in their patios for personal consumption, and although both men and women participate in collective working days on the agricultural projects, the number of ex-combatants working on the collective *Finca Nueva Colombia* is very limited. Of the approximately 20 people working there regularly, many are not even ex-combatants; they are members of neighbouring communities or Venezuelan migrants, often simply working for three meals a day in the absence of a salary. During my fieldwork, the number of women working on the farm could be counted on one hand, and they did not seem to be involved in the same tasks as the men. On the occasion I accompanied Gerardo, who was in charge of the plantain project, I was the only woman, evidently leading to confusion for the coordinator of the *finca*, who was unsure which task to give me – not only a woman but a European one at that. One of the other men took me under his wing, and when he did not return from the breakfast break, hanging out with others drinking the leftover alcohol from the weekend, I joined Gerardo to prune the plantain trees. I only saw other women on the farm during the breakfast and lunch breaks. Although participants like Roberto were quick to stress that, in the beginning of the reincorporation process, men and women worked equally on the farm, even from their comments, one could sense that things no longer were that way:

> 'You know Susana, right? Well, Susana is one of those women who will take on any type of work. But, well, she now dedicates herself to taking care of the chickens, because they have a project producing those, but that is a different matter. But she works and all of them [women] use the machete, all of them here, we used to all go together.' (Interview, 24 September 2019)

The fact that Susana now looks after the chickens is telling, as keeping chickens is regarded as a traditional female agricultural task. Rather than including women more fully in the agricultural projects, the gender committee is setting up its own project, with support from the UN: a nursery with trees and plants of the region, as well as medicinal plants and a herbal tea production line. According to gender committee leader Mónica, the goal of this project is not only to generate work and income:

'We believe that we must focus on nature as well, and stop to consume so many chemicals. ... The gender committee includes the diversity of human beings, and therefore we want this to have a component for children, so that the children can be learning there, getting to know things ... so that from when they are little onwards, they are acquiring knowledge about what one can and cannot do in nature. We also want there to be participation of the elderly, because of the knowledge they have and so that they also have a space where they feel that they can work.' (Interview, 29 October 2019)

Gendered dynamics are obvious here: whereas men are involved in the 'proper' agricultural work of managing the farm, women combine agricultural work – also physically straining, as I experienced myself when weeding the nursery plot – with wider goals of caring for the environment, the children and the elderly.

New masculinities?

A further dimension of the gendered nature of reincorporation is that it is mostly men who are involved in the training process to become security guards for the National Protection Unit (NPU). Although both men and women are eligible for this process, I saw only two or three female guards during my time in the ETCR. An interviewee from CINEP explained that the selection process was indeed gendered, since the NPU was hardly selecting women for the training, even though there was a large demand for female guards (Interview, 7 May 2019). Furthermore, the fact that the guards travelled a lot, accompanying the FARC leaders on their meetings around the country, made it more difficult for women with children to become guards. Several times, the ETCR's leadership asked Anita, a former commander, if she wanted to start the training process. She said that if she had not had her son, she would have signed up immediately, but now she did not want to be away from him too often. A result of the majority of the newly trained security guards being men is the continued connection between violence, aggression and arms with men and masculinity. During the conflict, weapons had a special meaning for both men and women. Many people found it hard to give up their arms because, according to María, "the weapon is a part of you, and when it is no longer there, you miss that part" (Interview, 8 October 2019). Whereas during conflict, the weapon had been a symbol of equality between men and women, in the reincorporation process, men were more likely to maintain their attachment to weapons, contrasting with the image of women as mothers who handed in their arms to raise children (Giraldo-Gartner 2020). This enables men more than women to continue conflict-era models of masculinity, maintaining the stereotypical view of men's special relation with weapons (Myrttinen 2003), whereas women more often tend to return to traditional gender roles and caring tasks, as the FARC themselves also recognize (FARC 2020).

Although the FARC party's gendered reincorporation strategy includes a strategic line on 'insurgent masculinities' – which included the more equal sharing of both combat and caring tasks – and the UN is also starting to address this issue, there is not much evidence of this work in practice. It is remarkable that many female ex-combatants were interested in this topic, as was evident from a meeting I attended of a British Council/ARN project on gender and active citizenship. The participants in the meeting – almost all women – chose masculinities as one of the topics they wanted to work on. In preparation for the resulting event on masculinities in the ETCR, I helped Rebeca to make a short video about masculinities, holding short interviews with some male ex-combatants. These interviews showed that many men thought that masculinities had to do with homosexuality and "men who paint their nails". They also believed that men's role was to be head of the household, even though they agreed women had rights too. Apart from evidencing the lack of awareness of what masculinities means, and therefore the gap between policies and actual practice, this anecdote shows the ongoing sensitivity of the issue of LGBTQ rights among FARC ex-combatants. Homosexuality was always prohibited in the FARC and even though there must have been LGBTQ combatants, they were forced to hide their sexual orientation. Although the 2016 peace accords were the first in the world to explicitly recognize LGBTQ rights (Cairo et al 2018; Thylin 2018), this does not mean that these rights are socially accepted in the ETCR. Horacio, for example, said that LGBTQ people were problematic because they are very promiscuous and "mess things up". When asked whether he believed heterosexual men were not promiscuous, he merely laughed. Several women mentioned that the gender committee's attempt to integrate more men had failed after several of them attended an event on gender and diversity. Being shocked by the presence of LGBTQ people, including some transvestites, they decided that 'gender' was not for them. Again, there is a gap between formal and actual acceptance, the national and local levels and urban and rural peasant culture.

LGBTQ rights are a touchy subject in Chibolo too. Although I once heard a VU official in a meeting with the communities explain that the Victims' Law's differential perspective included the need to protect LGBTQ rights, she did so in a way that caused great amusement among the community members, suggesting that this was not an issue to be discussed in a serious way. Jokes were sometimes made about single men being homosexual, or 'gaytorade' as Cesar once joked, referring to the popular sports drink. During one of my last visits in 2019, Juana explained to me that a problem had arisen in her husband's family, since their niece had decided to marry someone who part of the family considered to be 'fokifoki', in other words, gay. This reflects how heteronormativity defines how hegemonic masculinity is understood and performed in Chibolo. For many men, homophobia is a way to deal with insecurity about their own maleness (Kaufman 1987; Jones 2006). At the same time, although it was a public secret that one of La Palizua's leaders was homosexual, he was accepted and respected as a leader. Gender norms are thus not completely rigid. In the same way, FARC leader Mónica explained to me how she had started to understand and accept LGBTQ rights when she was in prison, together with many bisexual or lesbian women. She initially found this strange, but asked them questions about it and gradually began to accept it as normal. It is a shame that not more efforts are made to help such perception changes among the wider groups of survivors and ex-combatants. There are no visible efforts either, in Pondores or Chibolo, to change power relations between men and women, to engage men in 'feminine' tasks such as caring responsibilities, or to engage women more actively in 'male' activities. Femininities and masculinities continue to be seen as largely separate. A comment by an LRU official about the need to make sure that productive projects benefited women too is telling in this regard:

> 'It's a bit of fighting with a cultural issue again, very difficult. So we said: no, let's design a specific programme line, only for women. ... Of course, the male head of household will be addressed, so let's do something specifically for the women, where they can also say "I would like to work in handicrafts, or I would like to cultivate a specific crop". ... Because we don't want to cause fights between the husband and wife, you know?' (Interview, 29 October 2015)

Her comment shows the recurring tendency to add something for women to otherwise male-centred programmes, rather than actually transforming gender relations. The following sections describe in more detail how 'inclusion' is envisioned and women are 'added on' to reparations and reincorporation.

Gender in practice: inclusion, transformation or ticking boxes?

Victim-centred TJ has generally led to calls for stronger participation of survivors in TJ processes. This has inspired the creation of an elaborated framework for survivors' participation in the Victims' Law at the local, regional and national level, through which survivors were supposedly able to influence their reparation process. This led to the creation of a number of participatory spaces in relation to the collective reparation process in Chibolo. These included a steering committee in each community, a group of 'weavers' (*tejedores*) for the psychosocial support strategy, 'memory managers' (*gestores de memoria*) for the historical memory process and the participation of survivors in the local and departmental 'victims' tables' (*mesas de víctimas*). In addition, the development of the collective reparation plans had involved many meetings in which participatory exercises were undertaken. Nevertheless, as I have described in more detail elsewhere (De Waardt and Weber 2019), these spaces did not necessarily lead to survivors' opinions being taken into account in terms of the measures included in the reparation plans and much less in terms of their implementation.

Furthermore, in these participation spaces, gender seemed not to be a priority. Most of the meetings I observed were attended primarily by men. In addition, when the Victims' Law's differential perspective was explained in these meetings, officials emphasized LGBTQ rights rather than the need to ensure women's participation in meetings and decision-making processes. In fact, women could often not attend these meetings, or missed parts of them, since they were expected to cook the *olla comunitaria* (literally communal pot; usually a large pan of soup cooked and eaten collectively) which was shared after the meetings. This reconfirmed traditional gender roles of women as those responsible for looking after the well-being of those, mostly male, making the decisions. Women were therefore less aware of what was being discussed, making it even harder for them to participate in decision making. When in 2016 a new cooperative was formed to enable several communities, including La Pola and La Palizua, to collectively sell milk, the list of members was overwhelmingly male-dominated. Community leaders Pedro and Tomas told me that, in their understanding, only one person per family should sign up. Unsurprisingly, it was always a man. The UN and state institutions accompanying this process did not raise this as an issue of concern. This reflects traditional 'familistic' attitudes to rural and agrarian policies in Colombia, which assume that support to the male heads of household will benefit the entire family (Meertens 2019). Although a few years later a handful of women were part of the cooperative board and committees, its leadership continued to be male. Furthermore, there were clear tensions between the cooperative and the community's women's group, as I will describe in the last section.

In contrast to the marginalization of gender in the Victims' Law's daily practice, gender was very much at the forefront of the reincorporation process, as a result of the inclusion of gender in the peace agreement and the public and international attention for this. Nevertheless, the effect was not equally impressive. The UN focal point for gender in Pondores told me early on in my research that people in the ETCR were quite bored with gender already, since they had received many gender trainings before coming to the ETCR, while they noticed that the leadership continued to be male and *machismo* persisted. For example, the leader of the ETCR's *junta de acción comunal* (community action board), in spite of formally being a member of the gender committee, was frequently criticized by others for misunderstanding gender and feeling threatened by it, seeing it as something that would divide the ex-combatants. This leader, like other men, firmly believed that once capitalism would be defeated, other inequalities would vanish as well. This shows how some of the FARC ex-combatants' strong Marxist ideology can be an obstacle for prioritizing gender or even taking it seriously. I also heard men and women talking dismissively about this 'gender business', while some men mentioned that women should not confuse *libertad* (freedom) with *libertinaje* (excessive, immoral sexual activity), thus showing yet another misunderstanding of what gender means, and how it was perceived as a threat to the traditional moral order.

This illustrates that a strong formal focus on gender does not necessarily lead to tangible changes. For example, of the productive projects implemented by the cooperative in the ETCR, only one is led by a woman. On the national level, a similar trend exists: the 47 collective projects approved in early 2020 involved 2,454 ex-combatants, of whom only 688 were women. Of the 705 individual projects approved, only 178 were implemented by women (FARC 2020). A member of the Gender Commission of the FARC political party confirmed that the main frustration for many female ex-combatants was that, in spite of all the gendered and other training they completed, they were still not given leadership roles or positions of responsibility in cooperatives and other decision-making spaces: "They know how to do all sorts of things in a cooperative, but they don't have leadership positions … they don't have decision-making positions, so what is the point?" (Interview, 1 October 2019). This confirms Maricela's remark, cited in the previous chapter, that all this gender talk produced few real changes.

Although, of course, transforming gender relations is a long-term process, which cannot be expected to take place in a few years, it at least requires that real efforts are made to change gendered power relations from the start of policy implementation. As the previous section described, in Colombia's reparation and reintegration process, this was rather incorporated along the way, and, even so, in an ineffective way. In both scenarios, the inclusion of a gender perspective often remains a discursive tool, or an effort to formally train people about what gender means, but without measures to actually strengthen women's position as leaders or their decision-making power in communal spaces. According to one of the researchers involved in the international monitoring commission of the peace accords, this reflects a tendency of '*mujerismo*' or 'womanism', meaning that, for most institutions involved in the implementation of the peace accords, 'the implementation of a gender perspective is to mention "and for women too" or "and the LGBT population", or that in a participatory process like with the PDETs [territorial rural development plans], the gender perspective means to have 100 women there, even if those women are not able to influence the decisions that are being taken.' (Interview, 7 May 2019)

This focus on formal gendered activities rather than changing power relations is common to TJ and other peacebuilding processes. It is an important lesson for the national action plan (NAP) on Women, Peace and Security (WPS) that the Colombian Commission for the Clarification of Truth, Coexistence and Reconciliation (CEV) has recommended, and shows the importance of integrating measures that go beyond the discursive level and actually aim to transform gendered power relations – even though this takes a long time. As I will describe in more detail in the next chapter, trainings and workshops are easier to measure than changes in gendered identities and power relations. Whether these workshops and trainings, or the participatory spaces in the Victims' Law, actually manage to transform communities' situations seems of less interest. Community members themselves do not seem to believe that they do. In Chibolo, participants had become disillusioned with all the meetings, which had cost them a great deal in terms of time and effort, while they were still waiting for genuine change to happen. In Pondores, participants frequently mentioned that they were not interested in any more workshops and trainings, and that they wanted actual changes to their situation.

Pablo, the FARC's reincorporation focal point in the ETCR and one of the only people paid for their work in the reincorporation process, explained that all institutions and donor agencies wanted to do things in their own way, which first required a survey to establish a baseline study, and so they all repeated the same activities. A UN representative agreed that reincorporation and gender projects had become very 'sexy' among international donors. Everyone wants to support these projects, and be seen to be supporting them. At the same time, they want them to be implemented in the way *they* think is best, which does not necessarily respond to the beneficiaries' priorities or needs (Interview, 7 November 2019), nor to what is most feasible or likely to be sustainable, as I will show in the next section. As a result, recipients of these projects often lose interest or, even worse, become disillusioned. In other contexts, like Rwanda, questions have been raised about whether activities and workshops are always meant to transfer knowledge, or are rather a form of governmentality, controlling people by consuming their time and energy and thus preventing their participation in collective rights-claims processes that could challenge the status quo (Purdeková 2015). Similar questions have been raised about prior, individual reintegration processes in Colombia, where ex-combatants struggling to make their fragile individual productive projects work were believed to be less likely to engage in political activities which the state saw as undesirable (Fattal 2018). In Chibolo, the intense participation in Victims' Law activities and its disappointing results considerably weakened other communal forms of organization, such as the community peasant association and the cooperative. And even though the communities were interested in receiving support for the reactivation of their women's committees, a measure included in the collective reparation plan, this measure was not a priority for the VU. The VU representative argued that, before creating another group, they should first make sure that the other organizational spaces functioned properly (Weber 2018). That these other spaces were created by the VU for the purpose of the reparation process, in contrast to authentic organizational spaces with higher potential for activism and rights claims, might be telling. In other contexts, survivors actively driving and demanding their own participation in TJ processes was more effective than invited participation spaces (Vegh Weis 2017). Unfortunately, such capacity and interest for collective mobilization to demand victims' rights, key elements of active citizenship, were in fact undermined by the way reparation and reintegration were implemented in Chibolo and Pondores. This was reinforced by the disappointing 'productive projects' provided.

Gender as women's projects

Perhaps to compensate for a more comprehensive gender strategy, in both Chibolo and Pondores, specific gendered projects were implemented, although they are better described as women's projects. In Chibolo, these projects were not provided by the LRU or VU. Instead, it was CODHES, a civil society organization, that provided a project for the women's groups in both communities. After intense discussion, the women in La Pola chose a bakery project, while La Palizua's women preferred a tailoring one – both responding to traditional gender roles. Several women questioned how beneficial these projects would be economically, complaining that the leaders always ended up having their way. In spite of some training, these projects never materialized. Instead, both communities received a project of laying hens, which would generate income through the sale of eggs. Both groups, however, complained that they were not provided with the promised inputs to make the project profitable, and that, almost immediately, they had to pay for the chickens' food out of their own pocket. Even afterwards, the money made selling the eggs was only just sufficient for buying the food for the chickens, but did not generate a profit. This was at least what most women believed, since there was little transparency about the projects' finances. Although the projects did in fact make a small profit, which in the long run could have enabled their expansion, many women were disappointed by the lack of quick results. Several women quickly lost interest because they required the time to go to another part of the community to care for the chickens, since chicken pens were built in specific places for small groups of women to look after. Others admitted they sometimes forgot to do their turn at taking care of the chickens, causing frustration and additional work for the women in whose patios the pens were located. Both women's groups ended up dividing the chickens instead of continuing to work collectively, arguing that, in the future, they would prefer individual rather than group projects, so that they could work from their own homes without losing time for their household tasks.

This shows how projects that are not well designed or for which women are not well instructed can end up having counterproductive effects: making women disillusioned and weakening their already fragile organizational process. It also demonstrates how organization and accountability among women is crucial for the success of these projects. This aspect is often omitted in the interest of providing quick support. Furthermore, as an interviewee of a Colombian women's organization pointed out (Interview, 23 May 2017), projects to improve women's economic situation do not necessarily improve their quality of life, since if they are not accompanied with efforts to change the division of household and caring tasks within the family, they will most likely end up producing an additional burden for women. This can cause stress, which might outweigh the intended benefits of the project. Similar experiences are seen in other post-conflict contexts, where women's projects are offered as a quick solution to complex problems, often leading to little economic benefits for women (Coulter 2009). To really provide the redistribution envisioned in Nancy Fraser's view of transformative justice, more is needed than just a 'project for women' which does not structurally change their economic situation or address gender relations in a broader sense.

During one of my visits in 2019, I learned that the United Nations Food and Agriculture Organization (UNFAO) was planning to give the women's group in La Pola a new project: they would finally receive a bakery. The women received training, this time also on accounting, and an oven. In early 2020, I received a WhatsApp message with images of the bread the women were baking. Nevertheless, the process of setting up the bakery had not been easy. The UNFAO told the women that the bakery would be built in the area of the cooperative, and that the materials would belong to the cooperative if they were no longer used. Several women therefore decided not to join the project out of suspicion caused by an earlier incident between the cooperative and the women's group, discussed in the next section. The UNFAO were aware of the time constraints of many women due to their caring tasks. Patricia told me that the UNFAO representative had told the women that those who did not have time should not join the project at all. Since Patricia took care of her grandchildren while her children studied, she decided not to participate. Apparently, the UNFAO preferred not to address obstacles to women's participation, even though these could exclude many women and were key to overcome in order to transform gender inequality. Furthermore, it was unclear to me why this bakery project, in contrast to the laying hens, was going to be profitable. Although UNFAO had allegedly undertaken a market study, and several women assured me that a bakery would be profitable since many people in the communities ate bread, I had hardly ever eaten bread there, since yucca and rice constitute the most common staples. Furthermore, with the repeated droughts in recent years, people often complained about their struggles to make ends meet, making it even more unlikely that they would buy a relatively luxury product as bread. Finally, several women told me that a bakery needs electricity, which was not a stable factor in La Pola. To me, this project seemed yet another case of 'doing something for the women', since the UNFAO was about to finalize a years-long process of working intensely with the male cattle farmers. This resembles Berry's (2018) description of 'women's projects' in Bosnia and Rwanda. These often consisted of little profitable and gender-segregated work, which was not well adapted to women's skills and knowledge. The women in La Palizua never received a project at all, according to some of them because the women there were too lazy, and did not even show up when being promised a productive project.

The apparent lack of well-designed projects was also evident in Pondores. The clearest example of this is the restaurant that the gender committee runs. Not a project formally provided by any donor or state agency, it is admirable that the gender committee has taken it upon itself to develop this restaurant, which used to be run by the cooperative but had been abandoned. Mónica explained to me that they had made slow progress, starting off with nothing and gradually making more profit so that they could pay one or two women to work there. She explained that it was hard, since buying groceries in Fonseca required them to pay for transport fees, but the low price of a meal in Fonseca meant that raising the price to cover transportation costs would make them lose customers. The cooks working in the restaurant were therefore paid not even half of the minimum monthly wage, working six long days a week, dealing with frequent complaints from customers. On Sundays, the cooks' day off, the women of the gender committee cooked two or three meals, but they often struggled to get the amounts and portions right, leading to further complaints. This shows how difficult it is to make a project profitable and successful without specialised training and in difficult conditions like being outside an urban centre and in conditions of poverty. Furthermore, running a restaurant reconfirms women's traditional gender role, without the economic benefits to make women more independent economically. On a positive note, the women in Pondores did continue with this project, investing the little profits in improving the restaurant, rather than giving up and dividing the project, as the women in Chibolo did.

Another example of how women's projects reconfirm gender roles is the project provided by the British Council/ARN. Called 'Active Citizens', this project combined training on sexual and reproductive rights with an attempt to create a women's political agenda and a productive project. More details about this project will follow in the next section and the next chapters, but for now it suffices to indicate that the productive project selected by the women was a mobile kitchen, which would enable the gender committee to move a van with a small kitchen around the area to sell food at events. This project again confirmed women's caring role, while it was unclear whether there was a demand for such a service in the region. The project had not been delivered by the end of my fieldwork, making it hard to gauge its actual impact. The other project on its way to being implemented by the gender committee in Pondores was the already described United Nations Development Programme (UNDP)-funded nursery for plants. Again, the economic potential for this project, and whether this had been analysed, was unclear to me. Indeed, in March 2022, Rebeca told me that, although the women continued working on this project, they struggled to find ways to commercialize their produce (Informal conversation, 28 March 2022). Although it is certainly positive that this project was designed by the gender committee itself, and thus not imposed by an outside donor, uncritically following communities' ideas is not necessarily a recipe for success. The UN should know this, as early on in the reincorporation phase, it decided to donate projects to several ETCRs. In the case of Pondores, support materialized in the form of a plantain production project. Nevertheless, as La Guajira is one of the driest departments in Colombia, drought ruined the first harvest of the plantain project, making the new peasants lose a year of work. In 2022, Rebeca told me the project had failed completely, for lack of water for irrigation. They were then about to start a cattle project, although not everyone seemed to be enthusiastic about this and Rebeca doubted the project would be successful (Informal conversation, 28 March 2022). As a representative of a think tank working on peace-related research explained:

> 'Clearly, there was a hurry to start, and one could say a number of projects were approved more for security reasons. ... To start to occupy the people was important, especially in those first two, three years of the process, so that the people effectively start to feel that all of this is going to work and that there will be a real life outside of illegality. So for sure there have been projects of which it was known that they were not going to be feasible.' (Interview, 8 May 2019)

The risk of such non-viable projects is that they create disillusionment when high expectations prove to be unrealistic.

Something similar seemed to happen with the UN-supported gender project, as in addition to the nursery, the gender committee hoped to expand this project through the acquisition of a recycling plant with which they could convert PET bottles into poles for agricultural use. This would serve the ambitious goals of recycling, preventing deforestation and generating income. Mónica explained to me that for this, they would need, in addition to the recycling plant, a storehouse and a van to transport the poles. The plan seemed quite unrealistic to me, and to the regional UN Mission representative, who agreed that in a poor region like La Guajira, most peasants would rather cut down their own trees to make poles than to buy recycled ones. Nevertheless, on a visit to Bogotá, facilitated by UNDP, the gender committee were taken to a few companies to examine different recycling plants. They were not actually given one, at least not during my research period, but that a large part of the visit was dedicated to this was encouraging for the gender committee, and raised their expectations and hopes. The UN Mission representative was not aware of this trip, nor of the potential project, and critiqued how donor agencies often failed to coordinate among themselves, and raised expectations out of a genuine desire to help, which when frustrated could in fact backfire (Interview, 7 November 2019). Previous DDR processes in Colombia have also provided lump sums for productive projects or small businesses, most of which have failed, since developing business skills and plans takes time, trial and error (Carranza-Franco 2019). The short timeframe for projects that NGOs tend to have (de Waardt and Willems 2022) means that there is often no time and space for this, nor patience due to highly raised expectations. As a result, these 'women's projects' do little to bring about the redistribution of roles and resources envisioned in Nancy Fraser's (2008) model of gender justice.

How good intentions can have unintended consequences

That good intentions can be unsuccessful or even end up producing counterproductive results is apparent from the plantain project in Pondores and the chickens project in Chibolo. Unfortunately, these were not the only examples. I already alluded to an incident that happened in La Pola (Chibolo), which created divisions not only within the women's committee but also between the women's committee and the cooperative. In spring 2019, many women commented on this problem, caused by the Victims' Unit, which, according to some women, had promised a small truck to the women's committee as a reparation measure. These women believed that the women's committee would then rent the truck to the cooperative, which would use it to transport milk. The then leader of the women's committee arranged all the paperwork to receive the truck, and was utterly disappointed when the cooperative claimed it. She and others eventually stopped participating in the gender committee, as they believed the "women should not be fooled again" (Informal conversation, 10 May). Other women, however, argued that it had always been clear that the women's committee would receive the truck, for legal reasons I did not entirely understand, but that it was never meant to be for this committee. Carola, another female leader, argued that the problem was that the VU never communicated this clearly. According to her, the VU representative told the women "*Mujeres*, you will receive a truck", to only later explain how things really were. By then, the women no longer believed her (Informal conversation, 25 October 2019). Her actions caused a great deal of confusion, and raised the suspicion among several women that the cooperative tried to usurp the support for the women's committee. When the UNFAO then made the reception of the bakery project dependent on it being located within the cooperative's installations, many women preferred not to join. Cecilia also stopped participating in the committee, since she believed that to join the bakery project, one had to be a member of the cooperative, and since she did not own land, she preferred not to, as she did not want to pay the cooperative membership.

This anecdote shows how miscommunication and the way in which projects are delivered and designed can have unintended effects, in this case creating divisions, a lack of trust in state institutions and other community organizations, eventually causing women to stop participating and organizing. Cecilia, for example, believed it was better to work for one's own interests and family, rather than waiting for projects to arrive (Weber 2021c). As a result, such well-intentioned projects can in fact undermine citizenship practices, as women lose trust in the power of participation and collective action to change their lives, and instead prefer to look after their own needs only. This means an important building block for citizenship practice is undermined, thus weakening the possibilities of collective action and organization which could produce more transformative change to people's lives. As other researchers have also showed, post-conflict support which is merely focused on development or technical skills can damage social cohesion rather than promote peace and security (Firchow 2018). Instead, more attention is needed on 'softer' issues such as organizational strengthening, psychosocial accompaniment or trust and relationship building.

In Pondores too, unclear communication caused disappointment and tensions, weakening avenues for collective organization and action. This was especially true for the project delivered by the British Council and ARN. This was a so-called community project, with which the ARN aimed to improve relationships between ex-combatants and the surrounding communities. The involvement of the community of Conejo was, however, not clear for the female ex-combatants. Leader Anita told me that it was quite a surprise to see the community women in the first project meeting, and she felt uncomfortable because the ex-combatants could not publicly say they were not interested in a joint project, as that would harm their reputation with the community women. Anita said they felt fooled, as they were promised a mobile kitchen for themselves, and were not keen to share it with the women from Conejo, who, moreover, had their own coffee association, making the ex-combatants worry that they would be mainly interested in strengthening their association. Anita therefore decided not to join this project. Indeed, the meeting in which both groups were finally able to discuss the project in more detail was somewhat tense. Deciding on a name for the mobile kitchen proved challenging, as the ex-combatants insisted on the name bearing some semblance to the FARC acronym, which the community women did not seem keen on, although they were diplomatic enough not to say so. The decision about the formal location of the project was even more difficult, since the community women wanted it to be in Conejo and the *farianas* in Pondores, since they insisted it was originally an ex-combatant project.

The participants in this project experienced further disappointment when it became clear that the budget for the mobile kitchen was quite limited, and insufficient to buy a van to actually make the kitchen mobile. Especially the leaders of the gender committee spoke about the project quite negatively. Mónica at some point even told the other members of the committee that she and Anita felt fooled and believed that the British Council was using this project to steal money for the peace process. They believed that much of its budget was spent on staff, travel costs and the numerous trainings, rather than on material support. This is a complaint also heard in other post-conflict situations, where it is believed that interveners lead comfortable lives while violence persists and the local population continues to struggle (Autesserre 2014). Trust with the Conejo women was never really established either. Even though both groups of women were meant to implement joint educational and political activities, each group worked completely separate from the other, while the materials for the kitchen were divided between the two groups. The project coordinators failed to put in place a mechanism to encourage or facilitate collaboration. On several occasions, I heard the ex-combatants make negative comments about the community women, especially in relation to their leader, whereas the community women showed little enthusiasm to collaborate with the ex-combatants. For community integration and reconciliation, clearly more was needed than a poorly communicated and implemented project. The ARN official involved seemed to realize some of these issues. She made sure the budget increased, although it was still insufficient for the desired project. This also raises questions about how best to design a project to begin with, and shows how encouraging people to 'participate in an asking free-for-all' can result in unrealistic expectations (Peñaranda Currie 2020). The ARN official finally explained to me that she had spoken with the community women, who now understood that the project was delivered because of the ex-combatants, something the *farianas* insisted on. This shows, however, that civilian and ex-combatant identities remained firmly established and separate, a joint and future-oriented citizen identity still absent. As a result, cross-group organization remained a faraway reality, limiting prospects for an overarching gendered citizenship practice that could unite women to lobby for greater gender equality for all.

These cases illustrate the importance of clear communication and expectation management, but also that those providing support and implementing activities often struggle to understand local dynamics, sensitivities and tensions. This is because, although most of the TJ and DDR interveners I spoke with were committed and capable, most if not all of them came from and lived in major cities, and many did not seem to fully understand the local context in which people lived. They might have been women, but not *campesinas* like the women in Chibolo and Pondores, highlighting the need for an intersectional perspective. Apart from the examples given, there were many other occasions throughout my research in which well-intended actions, for example, to speed up the provision of support, did not match the needs and preferences of community members. The mismatch between gendered policy frameworks on paper and beneficiaries' everyday realities and needs is also apparent in most WPS NAPs in Latin America (Drumond and Rebelo 2020). As a result, gendered policies like TJ, DDR or NAPs often end up being a disappointment. The genuine concern and serious attempts by many interveners are not able to overcome historic patterns of inequality and exclusion based on class and place (Bueno-Hansen 2015). This inequality is not lost on the research participants either. Ex-combatants frequently complained that the government hired many people for implementing the peace accords, but hardly any ex-combatants. Similarly, Jonathan, a young community leader from Conejo, explained:

'Let's say that the peace process has brought little employment here. I mean, because the state does come with its institutional offers [of employment], but few of the consultants they hire come from the community. … Perhaps that is because here they don't have university degrees, they don't have the capacity to manage those issues and this is what I was telling you, it's because the community has no access to professional education. Without access to professional education, of course it's not going to have access to those institutional job offers which need strong knowledge on different social issues. ... Perhaps because the peasant, the leader, doesn't have a professional degree, they don't trust his capacities.' (Interview, 8 October 2019)

Jonathan's comment illustrates that this tendency to prioritize hiring staff with 'technical expertise' over staff with 'local knowledge' (Autesserre 2014, 69) not only causes the unintended negative consequences described earlier but also maintains inequalities between the national and regional, urban and peasant backgrounds, and between state institutions and 'beneficiaries' – a term which in itself signals inequality (Autesserre 2014) – by making the latter feel that they are not capable enough. This has even stronger gendered effects, as grassroots women are less likely to have professional, let alone university, degrees.

At the same time, staff of TJ and DDR institutions are often not treated as well as community participants believe. For example, a researcher of the National Centre for Historical Memory explained that most of the staff in the Victims' Law institutions are given temporary contracts, providing them little security and making it difficult to accompany communities on a continuous basis in a long-term process. Two female officials of the ARN once told me about their situation, which was hardly better, even though they did have permanent contracts. As they were not from the region, they had to move to Fonseca, the closest municipality, leaving their families – in the case of one of them, a small child – behind in their places of origin, only being able to see them once a month. Furthermore, they did not receive a budget for travelling between Fonseca and Pondores or other locations, and thus had to catch rides, since otherwise, travelling to work would become very expensive. They told me this while waiting for a ride in the ETCR, obviously making it hard to make tight daily or weekly planning.

The treatment of staff thus often goes hand in hand with ineffective and inefficient peacebuilding processes, raising questions about the state's real intention. This is hard for those interveners who are genuinely committed to making a change to the communities they work with. A LRU official once told me how hard she found it to do her job; working with the corrupt local government institutions in Magdalena made her fall from one deception into another. She said she had to start taking better care of herself, eating well and doing sports, because the stress and anger gave her sleeping problems. The regional coordinator of the ARN office also confessed how tired he was after 11 years of doing this work, often being regarded with suspicion by the different groups he worked with – ex-guerrillas, ex-paramilitaries and communities. Hiring more permanent and more local teams would offer a solution to overcome some of these problems. It would help to prevent misunderstandings and mismatches between needs and support, enabling greater trust between communities and officials, and towards the state, because people would see that 'their own' are hired for peacebuilding jobs. It would also enable the building of longer-term local technical, thematic and organizational capacities, and generate jobs in communities. If an equal number of men and women were hired for these local functions, this strategy could, furthermore, prove more gender-transformative than the currently ineffective attempts to provide women with projects, and actually help to redistribute access to economic resources, in Fraser's model of gender justice. This in fact responds to what most women want: to find a job, gain more independence and work to make their family '*salir adelante*', as the final chapter shows.

Conclusion

This chapter has shown what the differential perspective of Colombia's reparation and reincorporation processes looks like in practice. In spite of its progressive and transformative discourse, in reality, most efforts are directed towards actions aimed at women, often as an afterthought instead of designing policies and programmes based on a thorough gender analysis with the goal of transforming unequal gendered power relations. TJ and DDR programmes tend to hold traditional views of femininities and masculinities, and, as a result, the 'women's projects' they implement to compensate for their otherwise gender-neutral programming do little to structurally transform women's positions, either economically or in terms of decision-making positions. Although, more recently, the differential perspective has started to include terms like masculinities and LGBTQ rights, not much of this discourse has trickled down into policies and activities, or into changing perceptions at the local level. Apart from maintaining the gendered status quo, such ineffective programming, especially when combined with unfortunate communication and unsuccessful expectation management, can actually do harm by fragmenting organizational processes and creating divisions and suspicions among community members and between them and the state. TJ and the institutions supporting and promoting it – including international donor agencies – need to rethink how they implement the gender and other perspectives they ambitiously talk about. This involves taking a more critical look at their own practice. Better listening and responding to local gendered needs, while maintaining a balance between what is desirable and what is feasible, will be key for this, as is better involving local communities through engaging them in genuinely participatory decision-making and project design processes and giving them more formal roles, as truly equal citizens. Furthermore, as the next chapters show, there might be more (cost-)effective ways to promote gender equality than the generic women's projects that seem to be intended more to be *seen* to be doing something than to actually make changes in the distribution of resources and power, and to increase women's representation in and beyond TJ and DDR.

5

Gradations of Citizenship: Of Radical Agrarian Citizens and Transitional Justice Bureaucracies

The previous chapters have described different aspects of why reparation and reintegration have failed to transform gender inequality, including essentialized views of gendered harms, persistent victim–perpetrator binaries and the tendency to 'do something for women' rather than transform gender relations. Although, in different ways, these elements are all related to aspects of citizenship, in this chapter, I focus more specifically on the practices of citizenship of the women in Chibolo and Pondores and how these are reinforced or weakened by reparation and reintegration. The chapter thus focuses on the second part of my research question: do current reparation and reintegration laws and policies enable communities to '*salir adelante*', or move forward? Citizenship might seem a very abstract concept, based on a combination of formal rights and obligations, but it also entails a practice, which can be more or less active, in which individuals demand their citizenship rights as part of a shared political community in which they participate as equals, based on a sense of political autonomy (Mouffe 1992; Taylor 2004; Kabeer 2012). Since citizenship essentially is about people's relationship with the state – and each other – it is in fact very relevant to local, everyday experiences of peacebuilding and integration of both survivors and ex-combatants in society. Based on the previous chapters, it is perhaps not surprising that people both in Pondores and Chibolo describe, either explicitly or implicitly, their sense of not being treated as full citizens by the state, as I explain in this chapter. I also describe how their citizenship practice changed from active or even radical to passive. I then look at how reparation and reintegration processes reproduced clientelist and 'assistentialist' tendencies which make people passive recipients rather than active citizens, thus diminishing the transformative potential of these processes and instead making people dependent on an ineffective state.

Experiences of citizenship

In Chibolo, the feeling of not being treated as full citizens by the state was the result of the state's failure to deliver upon promises about reparations, restitution and the corresponding improvements in basic social and infrastructural services. Cecilia expressed the feeling that internally displaced persons (IDPs) were being treated as second-class citizens, or what Gibney (2006, 3) describes as 'stunted citizens', who enjoy formal equality but, in reality, are unable to exercise their rights due to factors such as racism, sexism or economic deprivation: "Well, the government should take us, as displaced persons, a bit more into account and help us with those things, those needs that we endure. But nothing, I don't know, they say they will bring projects but we never hear anything" (Interview, 23 January 2016). Claudia agreed: "Well, for me, I say that the government should look and take us into account as displaced people, because we really need it" (Interview, 5 October 2015). Also, Luz described feeling abandoned by the government:

> 'The government should be more interested in the displaced persons. They say they are repairing the displaced but we don't see it. ... We left without anything, we returned without anything and we are in the same position still. They give assistance, of course they do. But that's not a reparation; I mean, a just reparation, so that one can have a dignified life. Here, for example, there is no electricity, there is no water, there is no housing.' (Interview, 29 March 2016)

Clearly, reparations in Chibolo are not effective in achieving their goal of turning victims into equal citizens, since not only are reparations slow to arrive but also the basic conditions needed for a dignified life are not met. These comments show that for people to feel like full citizens, more is needed than a symbolic message of the state's commitment with survivors, which is sent in the form of a 'dignification letter'. Survivors need to actually see this commitment materialized in terms of the improvement of their living conditions. This shows that the often assumed division between material and symbolic reparations does not exist (Moon 2012). Whereas material reparations send a symbolic message of recognizing survivors as equal citizens (Hamber and Wilson 2002; De Waardt 2013), the opposite is also true: symbolic reparations lose much of their meaning and purpose if they are not accompanied by material reparations that demonstrate this equality. Participants in Chibolo do not only desire formal recognition as equal citizens but especially to enjoy the protection of their basic rights as citizens, including to health, education and social and infrastructural services. It should be pointed out, however, that many people who did not experience violence or displacement during the conflict might describe their situation in relatively similar terms, as they also find themselves in a marginalized situation with little access to basic state services or citizenship rights. Unfortunately, in Colombia, there are still many regions, especially in rural and isolated areas, with little government presence. The territorial development plans (PDET) should change this, but they only cover selected areas – excluding Chibolo – and their implementation is so far slow in many places.

In Pondores, the reasons why several people describe the feeling of being treated as second-class citizens are slightly different. In part, they are related to the way in which reincorporation is being undertaken. The reincorporation process all in all lasts eight years, a period during which ex-combatants are in close contact with the Agency for Reincorporation and Normalization (ARN) through periodic monitoring meetings which involve the signing of registers to confirm the attendance of trainings, meetings and other activities which are meant to help them transition to civilian life. In the first phase of the reincorporation process, the territorial spaces for training and reincorporation (ETCRs) were called 'Transitory Community Zones for *Normalization*', signalling this process of transition to a 'normal', civilian life. In fact, in previous reintegration processes, ex-combatants would receive citizenship skills training, and after the eight-year reintegration process, they graduated in a process that marked their inclusion as a specific kind of citizens: reintegrated ex-combatant citizens (McFee 2016; Carranza-Franco 2019). The close accompaniment by the ARN is experienced by some people as an infringement to their citizenship. Roberto, for example, complains:

> 'Until now, we depend on the ARN for everything, everything. For example, when I go to work, whatever type of work, like community work, they will be there. They go and immediately check who is there, they are monitoring. We really haven't made the step … we are not real citizens. We aren't, because if we want to move from here, we have to tell them where we go. … We are in a sort of prison, this is like a prison.' (Interview, 24 September 2019)

The ex-combatants in Pondores and other ETCRs feel limited in their free movement, because to benefit from the collective reincorporation process, they have to be in the ETCR and participate in the activities that the ARN organizes there. This means that they cannot move to other places, or be with their family elsewhere. Judy, for example, said she would like to move to Medellín to be with her family and find a job, but this is impossible as the periodic travelling to attend ARN meetings would be too time- and resource-consuming. It is, however, not necessarily the ARN that imposes this restriction on them. As explained in Chapter 1, ex-combatants are free to move elsewhere and reintegrate individually (rather than reincorporate collectively). It might be the strong influence of the previous collective spirit, the influence of the ETCR leadership and the continuing discourse about the need to commit to the collective political project that keeps people in the ETCR. Another factor in this decision is safety. Since the signing of the peace accords, over 250 ex-combatants have been killed. For Judy, this is the main reason to stay in the ETCR, because being together gives a sense of safety. Tania also stressed the importance of safety, and its connection to citizenship and feeling protected by the state: "The important thing for us is at least to ask, well, not to ask, that they respect the life of the people, since we are also citizens and we deserve respect, that they don't massacre us, because lately, they have been massacring many, many people" (Interview, 18 October 2019). Some people have decided not to fully comply with the spirit of collective reincorporation, while still formally following the rules. They have moved to communities surrounding the ETCR, sometimes close by but, in other cases, hours away, where they have acquired pieces of land or are sharecropping. They come to the ETCR once a month, for the cooperative assembly or the ARN meetings, and to sign the ARN register. These people tend to emphasize that they did not want to sit and wait in the ETCR to receive government support, and rather opted for remaking their own lives. It is, however, easier for men to adapt to the hard farming life on their own, whereas for women, it is harder to make a living that way. Most people in the ETCR find it hard to make autonomous decisions to take such initiatives, or to abandon the collective project, and rather sit and wait for support to come, while constantly complaining about its slowness and incompleteness.

From active to passive citizenship

This passivity is quite a contrast to previous practices of citizenship in both contexts. In Chibolo, the communities of La Pola and La Palizua were formed through land occupation in the 1980s. Land occupation can be seen as a form of 'radical citizenship', described by McEwan (2005) as spaces which originate as a result of popular mobilization around common goals, often linked to social movements. It is an expression of 'agrarian citizenship', in which peasants challenge traditional power dynamics in a collective struggle for well-being, and which has historically been strong in Latin America, with Brazil as a key example (Wittman 2013). Women had a leading role in such land occupations, even though they did not acquire corresponding leadership positions in peasant organizations like ANUC. Women also enacted clear resistance during the time of the conflict. Since men were seen as the main targets of violence, women often stayed on the land to defend it, only fleeing once they were directly targeted too (Meertens 2019). Pablo's wife Alicia, for example, had a traumatic experience when she was looking after their farm while Pablo was away – in fairness, he was not fleeing the paramilitary but spending time with his two girlfriends, showing how *machismo* can produce physical risks for women during conflict. One day, the paramilitary came to look for Pablo and only found Alicia, who they tied up, interrogated roughly and forced to cook food. They eventually let her go, and she left the village the next day, seeking refuge with family. The anecdote shows how women, from their gendered role as those responsible for the household, became protectors of the household, an agency which is not sufficiently recognized. The communities' post-conflict return to the land after displacement is also an example of active agrarian citizenship, the result of their own organization and resistance to paramilitary occupiers and even attempts at forced eviction by the police. Although most women did not return in this phase, some did. Palizua's leader Josefa was in fact crucial in the community's return after displacement. She frequently remembered how they had occupied the land for months in makeshift huts, enduring rain, heat, hunger and mosquitoes, whereas most women only returned when the resettlement had been secured. Even so, women and men together worked hard during the process of readapting the land for cattle farming.

Nevertheless, in Chibolo, this radical, agrarian citizenship has given way to a more passive attitude built around the conception of victimhood and its related entitlement to reparation and restitution. Although in other contexts victimhood has provided spaces for radical citizenship, Colombia does not have many strong victims' movements. Although there are some iconic victims' groups, often with a strong female presence such as groups of mothers of victims of extrajudicial execution and some strong groups of displaced women, less than 7 per cent of survivors belong to one of 3,000 victims' organizations. This shows a dispersion among organizations which makes it hard for survivors to produce collective action and demands (Rettberg 2013). Furthermore, as I have described elsewhere (De Waardt and Weber 2019; Weber 2021c), the Victims' Law's reparation process has created a large number of spaces for victim participation, which gave survivors hopes of being able to influence reparation policy and the contents of their collective reparation plans. Hopes, however, turned into frustration when reparations and other support were slow to arrive. This ineffective form of participation, facilitated and prescribed by the state in 'invited spaces', risks weakening 'popular spaces' of community organization, as I illustrated in Chapter 4 (Cornwall 2004). Echoing contexts like South Africa, it is not clear if these 'invited spaces' are created with real emancipatory intention, or whether they rather intend to 'domesticate' participation and deflect attention away from other, more political forms of action that survivors could take (McEwan 2005). Furthermore, those participating most actively in these invited spaces were men, as described in Chapter 4. This was even more the case for meetings and workshops held in major towns such as Cartagena or Bogotá, where participation was generally limited to the same few women who had obtained their husbands' permission to travel or who felt secure enough to leave their household tasks for a couple of days. Women with young children were therefore generally excluded. Popular struggles for rights through active citizenship – land occupations – have thus been turned into appeals for human rights from the state through a passive form of citizenship organized around victimhood, which does not challenge power relations or structural inequality (Neocosmos 2006). The loss of women's conflict-era gendered agency, described in Chapter 2, can also be seen as an example of how citizenship can fluctuate, and is eventually curtailed by structural inequalities of power, in this case, gendered ones.

In contrast to the passivity of many ex-combatants described earlier, the FARC have also historically been characterized by active citizenship. Their struggle for a more just and equal society in Colombia – their official goal, at least initially – can be seen as an example of radical citizenship, in which citizens decided to actively demand their rights, albeit in a violent way. As described in Chapter 2, although initially women accompanied the FARC only as their husbands' helpers, in charge of cooking and other activities but without carrying arms, from the late 1970s onwards, the FARC started to accept women in their ranks as part of their transformation into a more formal guerrilla army, and women were formally accepted as equals in 1985 (Herrera and Porch 2008; Gutiérrez Sanín and Carranza-Franco 2017). To gain strength to achieve their goals, the FARC constructed a large collective with strong internal cohesion and discipline (Ugarriza and Quishpe 2019). Participants like Roberto liked to stress that the FARC had excellent female commanders, although it is hard to agree that gender equality did reach all levels of the organization. A look at the Secretariat suffices to counter this, as all members are men. The FARC's military force gave it political power, enabling it to negotiate the end of the conflict and their own terms of reincorporation quite successfully. This political agency to actively negotiate their reincorporation conditions was also apparent in Pondores, where the leadership obtained international funding for housing and agricultural projects, and negotiated the conditions of this support. The FARC party's gender commissioner highlighted a similar process among female ex-combatants in other ETCRs, where female ex-combatants obtained funding for 'gender projects' (Interview, 1 October 2019).

This collective political agency contrasts with the lack of individual agency to take control over and improve their lives which I saw among most ex-combatants in Pondores. This is perhaps unsurprising, since although the FARC as a collective was a strong military and political actor, the movement was characterized by strict hierarchy and discipline, meaning that most people simply followed the orders they were given. In return for this, people received food, clothes and other essentials like soap. This resembles a clientelist system – a phenomenon I explain in more detail in the next section – in which people lack individual agency. Since many people were part of the FARC for a long time, sometimes 20 years or longer, they interiorized this system in which needs were fulfilled in return for compliance with rules and orders. Undoing this habit is not an easy process. Cristina explains why even the apparently attractive housing project, in which ex-combatants pooled their individual productive projects to build their own houses with additional EU support, is not successful:

> 'People are exhausted. They no longer take on collective work because they are tired of working and not receiving a remuneration, and that complicated things. Because there are too many needs, in contrast to when we were in the guerrilla movement: everything was given to us, we only had to open our mouths. We were better off than we are now.' (Personal communication, 16 March 2021)

Andrea explained that she found it hard to adapt and become a leader of the tourism team and participate actively in different spaces:

> 'I think that this step has been a bit difficult, because in guerrilla life, we had guidelines, regulations, statutes which said that one simply was a soldier who complied with orders. … So in that time, we knew very clearly what to do and how to do it. This moment of transition to civilian life has been very difficult for me because there are really so many things that one doesn't know what they are, what to do. … The legalization of the project has been very difficult, because we had never been involved in that legal aspect of the laws and norms and all that. So it has been a very difficult process because one doesn't know even about technology, computers, telephones.' (Interview, 5 November 2019)

Although Andrea managed to overcome this difficulty and has taken on a leadership role, albeit frequently struggling, it is important to mention that she might have had an advantage over other women. For a long time, she was the partner of a former commander, which probably gave her a higher status and more agency and autonomy than other women. As I described in Chapter 2, those women who were partners of guerrilla commanders frequently had more privileges and a higher status than other female combatants (Barrios Sabogal and Richter 2019). Others, both men and women, simply continued their previous role of receiving orders rather than actively planning their own future. This was clear also in the local elections held in the autumn of 2019, when the ETCR leadership decided which candidates the ex-combatants could vote for, with the gender committee collectively supporting a female candidate for the municipal council. Many people, like Maricela, Jorge and Mónica, complained about the passive attitude of their peers, who they saw as simply waiting for the government to give them things without thinking about the future. Like the FARC leadership had fulfilled their needs while they were guerrillas, now the government had taken on this role.

Clientelism and 'assistentialism' as obstacles to citizenship

Before delving deeper into how the reparation and reintegration process undermines active citizenship, there is an underlying obstacle to active citizenship which is relevant to briefly explain: clientelism. Clientelism as a system has historically been strong throughout Latin America, including Colombia (Taylor 2004). In this system, the population is not seen as full citizens but as 'client-citizens' who obtain resources and favours in return for political loyalty to often authoritarian and populist leaders (Pearce 1990; Jelin 1996; Taylor 2004; Grupo de Memoria Histórica 2010). This contrasts with citizenship, which is based on the notion of rights that can be claimed through autonomous political agency. Clientelism was historically strong in *La Costa*, also being exploited by armed groups in a phenomenon called armed clientelism in which resources, services and positions were provided based on support for these groups (Eaton 2006; Tate 2018). In a way, even within the FARC, something similar to clientelism was experienced, as María explained: "we had our arms and we didn't lack anything. The commanders looked after our health, our food, the logistics" (Interview, 8 October 2019). As combatants, they simply had to follow their superiors' orders, like many civilians followed their local political leaders, often based on personal relationships (Tate 2018).

I frequently experienced how this clientelist system was still in place both in Pondores and Chibolo, particularly during the time of local elections in 2015 and 2019, in which politicians frequently visited the communities, organizing all sorts of activities. The mobilizations and marches through the municipalities that were held in election time gave people a feeling of agency. The many promises made by politicians made them feel taken seriously by a state that was finally on their side (Taylor 2004). Like in many Asian contexts (Kent 2016), the often weak state presence in large parts of the Latin American territory results in a particularly weak understanding of citizenship in rural areas like Chibolo and Pondores. People often prefer the tangible benefits promised by populist politicians over uncertain long-term transformations made by unrepresentative and weak political parties, in whom they have lost trust (Taylor 2004; Domingo 2009). Although people frequently use a rights discourse in Latin America, this is not translated into a more active citizenship or a practice of demanding rights (Jelin 1996).

This clientelist social system resonates with the paternalist welfare programmes which are popular in Latin America, such as conditional cash transfers which hand out cash or goods, generally to mothers, in return for complying with medical check-ups or school enrolment for their children (Lloyd-Sherlock 2008; Farah Quijano 2009). These programmes were also implemented in Chibolo and Pondores. In Chibolo, for example, there was the PAIPI[1] programme in which young mothers received food and household products in return for regular medical check-ups of their babies and toddlers. Josefa often complained how the young mothers in La Palizua did not participate in the women's committee, but never missed a single PAIPI meeting. In Pondores, I attended a meeting of a civil society organization which, according to their vests, worked together with the state institution responsible for child well-being. The meeting consisted of a prayer, some physical exercise and the exchange of sweets because of the annual 'day of love and friendship'. The attendants then received bags with food for their children, depending on their age and weight, which was measured after the meeting. Although the meeting was not strictly meant for women, practically all participants were women, and no effort was made to explicitly invite men, or counter the stereotype that it was logical that meetings about children were mostly attended by women. The participation of most women was not very active, and, in spite of the exercise that was used as an icebreaker and a way to show women the importance of physical well-being, the actual elements of the meeting that focused on children's education were barely audible because of the shyness of the employee.

This sort of programme mainly focuses on the handing out of support, mostly to women and aiming to promote child well-being. In addition to targeting women over men, and thus reinforcing women's roles as mothers who are in charge of taking care of their children, they result in only 'doing a bit more for the poor' (Lloyd-Sherlock 2008), without disrupting the long history of inequality and social injustice. Such programmes are therefore described in Spanish as '*asistencialismo*', which can be understood as a way of giving short-term aid which ends up making people dependent on that aid rather than reinforcing their self-reliance. Women's organizations, for instance, critique the assistentialist perspective in the implementation of the peace agreement, which prioritizes handing out support over transforming inequalities (Cardoza Sanchez et al 2022). Such practices risk weakening political agency by forcing people to dedicate considerable time and energy to accessing limited welfare support, while competing with other poor people for scant resources (Lemaitre and Sandvik 2016). They,

---

[1] PAIPI stands for *Programa de Atención Integral a la Primera Infancia* – Programme for Integral Attention for Early Childhood.

furthermore, suggest that simply attending a meeting will solve the most urgent problems, instead of developing women's agency. This is related to a culture of poverty, in which a passive attitude is a way of coping with a feeling of hopelessness in a world characterized by injustice (Martín-Baró 1994). In this way, structural violence and poverty caused by structural inequality can have strong impacts on self-respect and personhood (Bourgois and Scheper-Hghes, cited in Farmer 2004). For many marginalized groups in Latin America, their position of subordination has thus become 'normal' in the predominant social hierarchy (Jelin 1996). Instead of giving people the tools to overcome their poverty and combat injustice, clientelist politics and assistentialist social policies reinforce people's dependency on the state for short-term support, and their expectation that favours will be done in return for political loyalty or simple requirements like attending meetings or medical check-ups for children. A practice of active citizenship would instead enable people to become owners of their own lives. I do not mean this in a neoliberal way, where citizenship is often understood and promoted in terms of creating empowered, entrepreneurial citizens who are self-reliant and do not depend on the state (Lazar 2013a). I refer to an active and even radical citizenship in which communities and social movements mobilize and take actions to demand their basic human rights from the state (McEwan 2005; Rosaldo 2013).

Reparation and reintegration bureaucracies and citizenship

I now turn more specifically to how reparation and reintegration support, provided both by the government and civil society and international organizations, reinforce a sense of passivity and lack of agency and autonomy among IDPs and ex-combatants. I will explain two specific patterns in their mode of functioning. The first one is a focus on material support, rather than the building of skills or capacities. The second one is the requirements for and process of receiving this support, which reinforce a passive attitude. The failure to provide longer-term processes of capacity building shows how development aid and other forms of support are often a way to manage poverty and inequality, rather than to eradicate and prevent them (Farmer 2004). As described in Chapters 2 and 4, most women in Chibolo were only interested in participating in the communities' women's groups when they believed the chickens project was profitable, whereas their interest in regular meetings waned in the absence of clear short-term material benefits. Many then saw the meetings as a waste of their time, rather than as an opportunity to discuss shared concerns and thus increase solidarity. The male community leaders too saw women's organization as a way of receiving material benefits – they were even less interested in women's increased awareness, solidarity and self-esteem. There was no awareness among most women of the fact that making projects sustainable, or undertaking lobbying activities to obtain additional projects, would require a longer-term process in which they all had to play an active part, and which required particular skills to be successful. The lack of this awareness is not the responsibility of these women, who are consumed by their everyday struggle to make ends meet in a political economy that has historically marginalized them. Such long-term marginalization unavoidably affects the consciousness, since the 'social machinery of oppression' makes it hard to look beyond the immediate future (Farmer 2004, 311). Building such awareness is the responsibility of those who provide support.

According to a similar pattern in which historical oppression constricts the agency and autonomy of those suffering it, the FARC ex-combatants also prioritized receiving material support over capacity building. For example, complaints were constantly made about the government's reduction of bi-weekly food supplies, while, instead, most people showed little interest to work on the existing collective productive projects – with the exception of a small group of women working enthusiastically in the tailoring workshop and tourism project. One of the projects that the gender committee received, delivered by the British Council/ARN and called 'Active Citizens', did, however, contain aspects of capacity building, on sexual and reproductive rights. It also included the design of a political agenda for women. Nevertheless, the women were not very interested in the quite poorly delivered trainings on rights. Several women even threatened to stop participating in the project if it did not soon provide the material support promised: a mobile kitchen, which was only discussed in the last few meetings. As part of this project, some women organized an event on masculinities. To be fair, very few of those who originally committed to organizing it actually did so, making most of the organization come down on young Maritza, not even an ex-combatant herself, but one of the Venezuelan migrants living in the ETCR. The event was, however, well attended and valued, both by the participants and the ARN. Nevertheless, when the project ended and the women were in charge of spending a small budget on their 'political agenda', gender committee leader Mónica suggested spending it on a Halloween party with sweets for the children. Although the women in charge of organizing the activities eventually decided to organize an event for children about climate change and the environment, there was no apparent interest in more political and strategic activities to improve women's own rights and position, and most attention was focused on purchasing the mobile kitchen. Again, this seems to confirm the way in which structural violence and poverty constricts the agency of those experiencing it, limiting their options and dreams and making them dependent on the support most easily at hand.

The effect of the focus on direct benefits over longer-term capacity building was also apparent in how people evaluated meetings and workshops. Numerous times I heard that a meeting had been excellent because participants were treated well with lunch, snacks and reimbursement for transport costs. For example, everyone attending the British Council workshops, half of which were held in nearby Conejo, received quite generous transportation fees, even though the women were brought to and from the workshop location by the ETCR's collective cars, and therefore did not have to pay for their own transportation. The UN also followed this pattern, organizing visits to recycling plants in Bogotá and exchange visits to plant nurseries on the coast of La Guajira, which women enjoyed mostly because they found the short trips and the food and accommodation provided '*chevere*', in leader Anita's words. Vice versa, I heard people, including female leaders like Andrea, question why they would attend trainings if they were not given money for food and transportation. Many of the ETCR leaders, like Mónica and Anita, frequently mentioned that they did not desire any more workshops, and instead wanted to receive projects which would allow them sources of work and income as a collective. It was, however, my – and several stakeholders' – perception that the FARC continuously seemed to overestimate their own capacity to implement and maintain the productive projects that they negotiated. For example, only a handful of people regularly worked on the collective farm and a collective yam-growing project, which, as a result, were little profitable. I wondered how they would manage even more projects. I, however, also wondered why those providing support in both locations did not realize this, and why they failed to invest more time in working with the participants to thoroughly reflect on their needs, dreams and the steps that were needed to actually change their situation. Instead, they offered quick solutions that were unlikely to have profound long-term effects. Of course, short-term needs must be addressed too, but *only* focusing on those short-term rather than also on more strategic needs will prove disappointing and little effective in the long run.

An employee of the United Nations Food and Agriculture Organization (UNFAO) who accompanied the communities in Chibolo who I spoke to in 2019 formed an exception. He said it was hard to work there because people saw the UNFAO merely as a source of funding, but were less interested in receiving training to develop capacities to make the projects sustainable and profitable. Yet simply receiving a project is not enough if there are little skills or willingness to actively dedicate time and effort to make it work. The UNFAO resolved this problem by maintaining a long-term presence with frequent visits over a number of years, which enabled the building of trust. This motivated people to invest energy in return for receiving support, for example, by improving their *finca*'s facilities to milk their cows. Similarly, the ex-combatants running the tailoring workshop received an intensive training programme by a tailoring company, consisting of technical, marketing and administrative skills and involving almost daily accompaniment over several months. More continuous accompaniment in relation to projects and topics that are actually of direct and practical interest to their recipients is more effective than the currently common short-term and incidental training sessions on abstract issues such as gender or human rights. This, however, requires a long-term commitment and sometimes personal sacrifices – long working hours in difficult conditions – by the supporting institutions. Moreover, it requires a shift towards measuring the impact of support in a different way, as I will describe in more detail in the next section.

The participants' interest in material gains sometimes complicated my own research too, since several people, including Mónica, made it clear to me implicitly or explicitly that they were not interested in any activities that did not bring them tangible results. I did not even try to explain to them the potential long-term benefits that academic research can have on how reintegration is approached. Cristina explained:

'What we really want is not for somebody to come, do some research and make a video. No, we want this to get known to the world, so that donations can come, so that a project can come, for the women or for everyone. We don't really want something that stays on paper, an investigation and that's it. No, we want to really have good things arriving here in Pondores, here to the farm where I live.' (Personal communication, 16 March 2021)

This was difficult, because as an academic researcher, I knew that my capacity to attract funding for the ETCR was limited. Eventually, the video and podcast we produced collaboratively, and the equipment which I donated, were considered a useful contribution to the reincorporation process, at least by some. In addition, I did my best to make connections between the ETCR and the Dutch Embassy, leaving the actual negotiation of collaboration to the cooperative. Yet, as I have also described in Chapter 2, the balance between the long-term benefits of academic research and the immediate investment of time and energy it takes for participants is a difficult one to strike. I reflect on this further in the Appendix.

Transitional justice and audit culture

Although people are correct in believing they have a right to directly receive the benefits of reparation and reintegration, and basic state services, the concept of citizenship relies on a balance between rights and duties or obligations. In the passive attitude I have described, rights and privileges are prioritized over duties and responsibilities (Pailey 2016), not only by survivors and ex-combatants but also by the supporting state and civil society institutions, in spite of their strong emphasis on training and workshops, described in the previous chapter. This is because, in the case of most of the workshops and meetings I attended, more attention was focused on the mere act of participating than on the quality or degree of this participation, and on whether participants actually learned what they were meant to learn. For example, in the British Council project meetings, I never saw anyone taking notes, or even paying considerable attention, whereas the trainers never provided detailed feedback on the discussions or exercises. Also, other trainers, who often suffered with the heat, seemed keener to finish their workshops quickly than to make sure that people actually acquired new knowledge.

This is related to what has been described as an audit culture in and beyond transitional justice (TJ). Audit culture refers to the way in which state and other institutions place a strong emphasis on monitoring and reporting the effectiveness of their work, using auditing techniques. In this process, only those things which can most easily be quantified get measured and become visible, to the exclusion of other things. Auditing techniques thus become an organizing principle, part of a wider neoliberal culture in which terms and values like efficiency, effectiveness, value for money and managerialism are prioritized (Shore and Wright 2015). This leads to a greater interest in giving trainings, providing material support and undertaking activities than in identifying the impact they have on the participants (Lazar 2013a). The quantification of material support in the form of projects, compensation cheques and lists of executed activities are deemed to show the progress made and benefits offered, thus creating a 'mirage of substance' (Purdeková 2015, 155), which, nevertheless, says little about the actual impact of these benefits and the extent to which they have changed survivors' lives (Buchely 2015). This shows how structural violence is built into the functioning of bureaucratic systems, as they are designed to manage rather than transform inequality (Kirmayer, cited in Farmer 2004).

Since people's presence is more easily registered and quantified than the quality of their participation or learning, TJ and disarmament, demobilization and reintegration (DDR) bureaucracies revolve to a large extent around monitoring participation through the signing of attendance sheets (Krystalli 2020a). The filling out of different forms and registers, also apparent in other post-conflict processes in Colombia such as psychosocial support, in turn reduces time for actual work, and for building trust or simply listening to people's experiences (Moreno Camacho and Díaz Rico 2016). Keeping such registers can generate anxiety for state officials, who always need to make sure their work and presence is registered to maintain their institutions' legitimacy. Vice versa, it also influences the attitude of those participating, who interiorize the need to sign the attendance sheet and prioritize this over the actual goal of the activities. The effect of this was palpable in the women's groups in Chibolo, as Ligia's comment makes clear:

Ligia: You have to attend the meetings, because we have been told: you have to attend the meetings. If one doesn't attend the meetings and doesn't sign the, how is it called?
Sanne: The register?
Ligia: The register, you have to sign it. Otherwise, they don't tell us when the help comes. (Interview, 15 December 2015)

Among ex-combatants, the signing of attendance sheets also took on a meaning of its own. As described, various people decided not to move elsewhere and find a job, since this would not allow them to sign the ARN register on a monthly basis. During the meetings I attended of several projects, leader Mónica made the effort of personally taking the attendance sheet to every participant for them to sign it. This not only sent a message about the importance of the attendance sheet but also suggested that the other women were incapable of signing the sheet without Mónica's explicit instruction. This reinforced dependency not only on the supporting institution but also on Mónica as a leader, inviting people to simply wait until they were told to sign a register or attend a meeting. The nurse who was employed in the ETCR on a permanent basis, though taking her task of caring for the ex-combatants and especially the women very seriously, performed a similar hand-holding role. She repeatedly told me how she used to call the local hospital or the health insurance to make appointments for the women, and informed and reminded them of their appointments. Like Roberto's evaluation of how the ARN does not treat them as real citizens, the attitudes of Mónica and the nurse also fail to treat the female ex-combatants as full citizens, capable of making their own decisions about their lives.

The effect of this audit culture with its emphasis on attendance registering is a 'wait and see' attitude in which people perceive that attending a meeting and signing the attendance sheet is all that is needed to receive benefits. Irene's comment illustrates this: "The government says we are deserving of a decent house and, well, of many things, so we have to wait for what the government will give us. What it gives us, we will receive" (Interview, 5 October 2015). Even Palizua's leader Josefa, who insisted on the need for women's organizing, showed this passive attitude. She repeatedly insisted that there was no need to lobby for infrastructural or women's projects, since these would arrive automatically with the land restitution sentences. Most of this support, however, never materialized in all the years that I followed the communities. Carmen, one of the older women in La Pola, had been active in the pre-displacement women's committees. She told me that she disliked how the women nowadays only came to a meeting when someone from outside the community organized it; otherwise, only a couple of women would show up. She said that before displacement, they always met up with all 20 women of the committee. They would send delegations to Chibolo on donkey, since back then there were no motorbikes. They managed to obtain different forms of support, such as a school and health centre. She believed that the younger women lacked this sense of urgency to actively try to improve their own lives. The frustration among the community members about the time spent in the different participation spaces created for the Victims' Law, which had little tangible impact, probably explains part of this passivity. The assistentialist focus of reparations and other support programmes reinforced this.

A similar tendency was apparent in Pondores, where Pedro, a disabled ex-combatant, was trying to form an association for disabled and other marginalized people in La Guajira, to lobby for better government policies. He struggled to generate interest, telling me that the difficulty was that people had become used to meetings where they would receive something, and therefore showed little interest in joining insecure lobbying processes which might lead to nothing. At first glance, this assistentialist attitude seems easy and comfortable. It only requires signing attendance sheets and attending meetings in order to receive the reward of a project. But this pattern of passive participation eventually depoliticizes citizenship attitudes (Lazar 2013a). In the long run, it makes people passive recipients who are dependent on a state that is not really interested in structurally improving their situation, while they have forgotten the habits and practice of active citizenship that enabled them to make gains in the past. This makes it harder for people to guarantee a better future for themselves, once support projects have finished. Even though passive citizenship attitudes are visible among women and men, for women, their effects are even more serious, since they face additional barriers to full citizenship, based on gender inequality. Furthermore, whereas men tend to be engaged more in support projects as agricultural workers or even armed security guards, as described in the previous chapter, women are more often targeted by 'assistentialist' aid centred around their motherhood and caring role. Such aid reinforces women's roles as mothers who receive support to look after their children, putting them at an even greater disadvantage for equal citizenship, with the risk of turning them into housewives, as Natalia complained in Chapter 2.

Conclusion

In this chapter, I have described how both survivors in Chibolo and ex-combatants in Pondores believe that the government treats them like second-class citizens, whose rights are not being protected. I have also described how, in spite of their prior practices of active and even radical citizenship, most people within both groups in fact have become passive citizens, used to receiving the rights and privileges of citizenship while forgetting about its duties and responsibilities. The support involved in reparation and reintegration processes, implemented by the state, civil society and international organizations, does little to disrupt such passive citizenship attitudes, since they make people dependent on material support, with seemingly the only requirement to attend workshops or meetings and sign the attendance sheet. Often this support reinforced gender stereotypes, which portray women mainly in their role as mothers, or at least it does little to counter this perception. Unfortunately, supporting institutions show little interest in the actual impact of their support on people's lives. In the next chapter, I argue why the promotion of organizational and leadership skills, in a broader process of citizenship building, is crucial to make sure that reparations and reintegration actually have an impact on the transformation of women's lives and gender inequality.

6

Overcoming Obstacles to Citizenship: Imagining Post-Conflict Gender Equality

Having focused in the last chapter on how the functioning of the reintegration and reparation processes weakened participants' citizenship practices by reinforcing prior tendencies of clientelism and paternalism, in this chapter, I describe how I believe those obstacles could be overcome to help women achieve a better future in a more sustainable way. While my main research question asked what the gendered dynamics of current reparation and reintegration laws and policies are on the ground and whether they effectively transform structural gender inequality, thus enabling communities to move forward, this chapter looks at what this 'moving forward' means for the women in the communities where I worked. What are the hopes that women themselves hold for their future? Are these ideas similar or different for survivors and ex-combatants, and how do they contrast with their current situation? These were questions that we explored through the photovoice process with the women in Chibolo, and through video recordings with ex-combatants in Pondores. Women's ideas about this, which describe their hopes of *salir adelante*, form the starting point of this chapter. I then contrast these dreams with reality, where persistent gendered roles and stereotypes prevent the active citizenship that would enable women to realize their dreams. Finally, I return to organization and participation among women, which I already touched upon in Chapter 2. Being organized can promote collective action, which is a key element for women's citizenship practice and can help them to demand changes to fulfil their citizenship rights and overcome gender inequality.

Gendered dreams for the future versus reality

As I have described elsewhere (Weber 2018), women in Chibolo had quite a clear idea of what they wanted their future to look like. Although they

Figure 6.1: The need for basic services. "We need something like a water tank, because when the water of the wells gets bad, we don't have anything to drink."

Source: Interview, 18 January 2016; photograph by Julia, December 2015

did not use the feminist jargon of agency and citizenship, they clearly had visions of emancipation. One key element for this was to overcome poverty and alleviate their time-consuming household tasks through basic services such as water and electricity. Many women took photographs of their daily task of fetching water, the bad quality of this water and the lack of electricity which forced them to cook in the dark at night (see Figures 6.1, 6.2 and 6.3). As in other contexts, such intensive household tasks left them with little time for participation in other spheres of life (Moosa, Rahmani and Webster 2013).

María José, for example, described: "That is why we want there to be electricity, so that one can buy a washing machine. ... With a washing machine, one can do one task and do the other and advance with both tasks" (Interview, 5 March 2016). Women, however, did not just want to alleviate these tasks to have more free time, but expressed a clear desire to become 'more independent of their husbands' (Meeting notes 10 September 2015). Many of them believed that education would be a key step for gaining independence and the self-esteem needed for this. Being able to read and write would give Ana more confidence to participate in meetings, whereas Dina stressed that "being a woman, one is also capable of learning many things" (Interview, 10 March 2016). Self-esteem, which can be gained

Figure 6.2: The need for basic services. "We see a dark kitchen, exposed to many things."

Source: Caption in Photovoice booklet, April 2016; photograph by Celia, January 2016

Figure 6.3: The need for basic services. "We don't have access to good public services. We want a dignified house and access to water, electricity, roads and health care."

Source: Caption in Photovoice booklet, April 2016; photograph by Dina, March 2016

through education, is a crucial element for agency and citizenship (Lister 2003). In addition, higher levels of education can create a stronger awareness of how political processes work, thus increasing possibilities for lobbying for better conditions for women (Moosa, Rahmani and Webster 2013). Women also considered education important because of their desire to secure a better life for their children. Patricia, for example, said:

> 'I wish that, in a future, my children were professionals. I mean, that they would have whatever they wanted. Like Paola, she wants to be a teacher, a qualified teacher. And my boys, I wish they could finish their studies so that they got a qualification too, in whatever they would like. I wish we were no longer struggling to keep our head above water, but that we'd have a comfortable life.' (Interview, 15 October 2015)

This emphasis on their children's situation, echoed by other women, reflects a 'maternalist' ethics of care, in which women's main concern is the responsibility for their family and children (Lister 2003). At the same time, Patricia's remark shows how the situation of parents and their children is intricately connected in Latin America's 'familistic' culture, where blood ties are a crucial way of uniting generations and transmitting relationships of care. In 'familism', family relations and the resulting responsibility and obligations are the key resource for solving daily problems (Jelin 1994). Children are seen as a safety net for old age, since they will take care of their parents (Jiménez Ocampo et al 2009). Therefore, in addition to building women's self-esteem, education is seen by many as a step towards overcoming poverty for both them and their children.

Increased self-esteem is important too because of the second element in women's desires for the future, which is to become more independent economically, and thus less dependent on their husbands. In Eloisa's words, women's current position is to "wait for the husband to receive his project, since he is who sells the little bit of milk, he is who brings in the material things, and she is just there, like it has always been" (Interview, 31 March 2016). At the same time, economic independence would enable women to better perform their ethics of care by contributing economically to the well-being of their families, as Carola explains:

> 'I think it would be good to receive training and that there'd be a project for women, so that we can also get by in other ways. So that we learn about the countryside, but also learn other things, to help ourselves in different ways. ... With other ways of generating income, so that it is not just the income of the cattle.' (Interview, 3 March 2016)

Figure 6.4: Chickens project. "Chickens are important for us women, because we eat them and their eggs and they reproduce. We can sell them to have some income."

Source: Caption in Photovoice booklet, April 2016; photograph by Ligia, December 2015

Women expressed several ideas for small women-led businesses, in which holding animals and other agrarian activities played an important role, as was reflected in the photovoice pictures (for example, Figure 6.4).

Nevertheless, also non-agricultural ideas, for example, about a tailoring or bakery project – the latter implemented in La Pola – were mentioned. Josefa was one of the proponents of a tailoring project (for example, Figure 6.5): "Women's groups can set up a small business here, of dressmaking and selling outside, or even here [in the communities]. One generates income and generates work. Income and production" (Interview, 19 November 2015). Claudia also expressed the preference for a small business over a more informal project: "Because if one aspires to have a bakery, one would no longer be working alone, but it's a source of work for others. I would like that" (Interview, 5 October 2015). Both women emphasize the importance of generating sources of income in the remote countryside of Chibolo, where most people rely on the income generated through their family farm, with little space or recognition for women's agricultural activities. Furthermore, they stress the importance of the collective in this. This is, however, not altogether unproblematic, since Chapters 2 and 4 have described the challenges in generating and maintaining women's organization and their participation in collective projects. The final section of this chapter will return to this issue.

Figure 6.5: Tailoring projects. "Sewing machines can help to form a business, an important project. We want to lobby for training to start our own micro business and to produce clothes to have our own income."

Source: Caption in Photovoice booklet, April 2016; photograph by Josefa, November 2015

The desires of the female ex-combatants in Pondores are quite similar. Many women stress the importance of education, since most ex-combatants joined the FARC at a young age, and often from a situation of great poverty, and therefore had not finished secondary or even primary school. An interesting option in this regard, which was also successfully implemented in other reintegration processes such as the one in Guatemala (Weber 2021b), is a process called 'homologation of knowledge', which allows those who gained specific practical experience in the guerrilla movement, especially in terms of health and education, to validate this knowledge and receive a certificate which allows them to find a job (Consejo Nacional de Política Económica y Social 2018). This aids the reincorporation process by valuing experiential knowledge, although it requires participants to have finalized secondary education. Women like Tania, Gloria and Judy expressed an interest in this, because it would be the most concrete and feasible option to find a job, as María explains: "In the future, I would like to study nursing, through a homologation process, but for this, I first need to finish grade 10 and 11" (Interview, 8 October 2019). This shows the importance of education here too. Andrea says: "Most of us have wanted to study, go to university, because we all have a dream and we said, 'We are going to make that dream a reality.' But many of our comrades have quit along the way" (Interview, 5 November 2019). Andrea refers to the fact that many people, both men and women, initially felt ashamed or too old to study, and were therefore reluctant to enrol in the primary and secondary school catch-up programme provided by the Agency for Reincorporation and Normalization (ARN). It was not until people realized that they had to study to receive reincorporation assistance, and that they needed to finish secondary school to be able to enrol in knowledge and skills validation programmes, that they decided to resume their education. In part, this reluctance to study speaks to the overall sense of self-esteem, sometimes bordering on arrogance, which I experienced in the territorial space for training and reincorporation (ETCR). People often repeated that they did not need any training since they had learned many skills in the FARC, the world's largest guerrilla force after all, such as subsistence farming, cooking and nursing. They believed that the many workshops offered by accompanying institutions suggested that they did not have any skills, and, instead, they preferred aid budgets to be spent on material support or on paying for people's work on projects. Although they are probably right in stating that every supporting institution or organization comes with its own ideas for workshops and projects, which might not always correspond to the needs and interests of the beneficiaries, their attitude fails to recognize that running a guerrilla army, and the organizational skills needed for that, are very different from the skills and knowledge required to manage agricultural and other businesses, or become health professionals in the post-conflict scenario. Specialized and additional training is needed to make projects sustainable.

On the other hand, the significant and often long-term practical experience gained by many ex-combatants also means that bureaucratic requirements like a secondary school diploma could have been waived in specific cases. This would have made economic self-reliance a more likely possibility in the near future, aiding reincorporation, and would have enabled many women who worked as nurses to gain a stable and well-regarded job. Furthermore, the insufficient acknowledgement of experiential knowledge is demotivating for many people, which does not help the rebuilding of trust in the state. The process of finishing secondary school before enrolling in a homologation process is too long for many, making them prefer other options instead. Gloria, for example, who had been a nurse in the FARC, told me that she would have liked to study nursing, but, in the end, decided to join the tailoring workshop, since she could only do one thing at a time, and she could not wait forever for the nursing course to start. Nevertheless, she was not altogether happy with her current job either, since the tailoring project was not yet profitable, and they often had to work in evenings and at weekends without regular pay. Other people in the tailoring workshop agreed that they struggled, not being aware of the adequate pricing, tax rules, marketing and communication strategies. This proves the point that specialized training is indeed needed, since the skills acquired during conflict, of which tailoring guerrilla uniforms and backpacks was one, is not sufficient to guarantee a profitable and sustainable business.

Nevertheless, Gloria's decision reflects how many women in the ETCR, like those in Chibolo, insisted on the need for businesses and projects, and work in general. Silvia has placed her hopes on the plant nursery in this regard:

> 'In the nursery, many women will find a job. Because you know that now in the reincorporation process, most women are without a job. ... So there we will have work, women and men, and we have children that we will teach, children of the ex-combatants, that we will teach little by little how to look after fauna.' (Interview, 20 October 2019)

Also, Natalia stresses the need to have projects, to gain an income:

> 'In the future, we hope to have some projects, so that we can depend on those at least for our basic subsistence, you see? So that at least we can work a bit more comfortably, and that I can say: I will sell this product, or whatever we have in mind. And that we will gain resources to survive, because right now, we don't have them, no resources whatsoever enter here.' (Interview, 9 October 2019)

Gloria agrees on the need for work and income, also from a maternalist perspective: "We want to generate employment, so that we have a means to work, because many people here don't have a place to work. So we need that to survive, because we have children too" (Interview, 20 October 2019). Even though, at this moment, the ex-combatants are still receiving a monthly stipend, for many, having a job is a main concern for the future.

Between moving forward and getting stuck

The end goal of these emancipatory processes of education and employment that both groups of participants have is to *salir adelante*, or to move forward, which they understand as generating a better, more comfortable life with less poverty for themselves and their children. In Chibolo, for example, Elizabeth describes her dream like this: "Lord, I want to improve my life. I want my children to keep moving forward, for them to continue studying and become professionals. Even if they don't become professionals, I want my children to move forward" (Interview, 8 March 2016). In Pondores, Tania describes her hopes for the future this way:

'What we want to achieve is, well, to see a better future for our children. Because all that we want is for our children, because they are the future, the future of Colombia, and what we need is that our children do not suffer the consequences that we have had, that they will have a better Colombia.' (Interview, 18 October 2019)

Natalia says: "With this process that we are building, which is peace, we can move forward with the support of many others. We want to have projects for our benefit" (Interview, 9 October 2019).

What women's different visions and dreams have in common is a better socio-economic future, based on education and work, and also a tendency to connect this better future to the situation of their children. These emphases are problematic in two ways, related to the specific idea of moving forward economically through entrepreneurial strategies, and the connection between moving forward and motherhood. In the first place, the focus on moving forward through projects and small businesses aligns with neoliberal visions of development, which rely on the 'empowerment' of individual citizens to take responsibility for their own well-being through entrepreneurial skills in the neoliberal free-market economy (Lazar 2013a; Gutiérrez and Murphy 2022). Although taking control of one's own life and future is indeed positive, the entrepreneurial aspect of this specific vision is problematic because it deflects attention away from the state's obligation to guarantee the basic conditions for such enterprises to be successful and provide a safety net in case they are not. In this way, overcoming poverty becomes the responsibility of the poor themselves (Wilson 2010). The promotion of empowerment and (individual) agency risks becoming an alternative for the transformation of unjust political and social institutions and structures, while both strategies are needed (Destrooper and Parmentier 2018). As described throughout this book, basic social and infrastructural conditions are largely absent in the marginalized regions where my research took place, which are frequently hit by drought, have unstable electricity provision, inadequate access roads and few options to market and sell goods. At the same time, participants have lost the habits to demand these basic rights as active citizens. An official of a peacebuilding organization reflected on the FARC's tendency to start businesses, and their reluctance to become employees managed by others, a reflection that also applies to the situation in Chibolo:

'Having ambition and aspirations is important, it's good. But if you look at the reality, it's a process that will hopefully be successful, but it is going to last many years and they will have to see what the level of success is that many of those businesses will have, and how they consider the fact that a good number of these businesses will not survive after three or four years. … The people are still in rural areas and there is a number of challenges there. Today, the situation of peasants in Colombia, the economic situation of rural areas in Colombia is very critical: a lack of access to public services, lack of infrastructure. In short, a series of conditions that prevent the promotion of development in rural areas, and that is the same situation that they [the FARC] will encounter.' (Interview, 8 May 2019)

Nevertheless, people are easily seduced by the idea of starting a business as entrepreneurial citizens. For example, during my fieldwork in 2019, many ex-combatants in Pondores were following construction courses, initially to build their own houses, but with a view to creating longer-term employment by starting a construction company to build houses in the region. Nevertheless, the likelihood of a construction company in a marginalized and poor region like La Guajira becoming profitable seems very low, even more so with the influx of Venezuelan migrants because of the crisis in the neighbouring country. In 2019, I even met Venezuelan construction workers in the small villages in Chibolo, since they offered cheaper labour than the local builders. This contrasts considerably with the FARC, whose construction project halted with the first 'model house' in 2021, because people were tired with the little progress of their unremunerated work. Furthermore, it is questionable how many women would be employed in this construction company. Even though several women participated in the construction course, construction is not a field known to employ many women, because it requires considerable physical strength. In Pondores and in Chibolo, there seemed to be little reflection about what sort of businesses would actually be profitable, and what conditions were needed for success in terms of skills, capacities and other conditions. Supporting organizations in transitional justice (TJ) and disarmament, demobilization and reintegration (DDR) processes are keen to give material support, often without a proper market analysis, following the audit culture logic of showing quick results (MacKenzie 2012). Although, of course, people have urgent needs which must be fulfilled, this should be done based on an in-depth assessment of which projects can indeed help to alleviate these needs. This should, moreover, be accompanied by longer-term processes in which people reflect on which structural conditions are needed for projects and businesses to become successful, and devise strategies to lobby the government for this. One can even wonder whether the setting up of small businesses is the way to 'move forward' or whether there is instead a responsibility for the government to create the conditions for or stimulate more formal employment in these marginalized regions, through their broader development.

The second problem with women's visions of *salir adelante* is the connection between moving forward and the future of their children. This is because, although having children is an important motivation for women to move forward, it simultaneously presents an obstacle for their success as entrepreneurial or otherwise active citizens. In spite of the gender role changes described in Chapter 2, motherhood continues to be an important way for women to fulfil their sense of self and identity. In a way, motherhood is understood as an element of being a good citizen for a woman. This is also apparent from the so-called baby boom in the FARC, since women took the prospect of peace as a new starting point, where it was suddenly possible to realize their postponed life plans. Motherhood gave their lives a new purpose and direction. Having children illustrated their hopes for a peaceful future, and became a symbol of peace (Giraldo-Gartner 2020). At the same time, the baby boom illustrated that gender roles remained similar in spite of temporarily changed gender roles in the guerrilla movement. The end of war signalled the postponed start of women's natural gender role thanks to the 'liberation of their reproductive capacities' (Barrios Sabogal and Richter 2019, 771). This is not unique to Colombia; after conflicts such as the ones in El Salvador and Guatemala, many ex-combatants decided to have children too, since motherhood for many women continued to be a significant aspect in fulfilling their life plan (Vázquez 1997; Nodo de Saberes Populares Orinoco-Magdalena 2018; Weber 2021b). For some, like María, who recommended me to have children of my own, having children is important since "they are the only ones who will look after you when you need it" (Informal conversation, 26 August 2019).

In Chibolo too, a baby boom had taken place in the years after I started working there, albeit a different baby boom: one of teenage mothers. During my visits in 2019, I was shocked to hear the many stories of girls as young as 14 and 15 who had children with boys often not much older. The case of Patricia's daughter was especially hard. Her oldest daughter Paola told me that Patricia had been very sad and angry to learn that her 14-year-old youngest daughter was pregnant. They decided to talk to the school psychologist who, rather than protecting the girl's right to education, advised Patricia to make her daughter keep the child, so that she would learn to become responsible. Around the same time, Juana's 12-year-old niece had been 'stolen' by her 17-year-old boyfriend, who was in fact the son of one of Juana's cousins who lived in the same village. After a week, they returned to the village and moved in together. The family was upset but seemed to believe that there was nothing to be done about it. Even female leader Carola told me that one of her daughters got 'married' aged 15, and that even though Carola did not agree, she did not protest either, knowing that her daughter would find herself a husband anyway. Fortunately, the marriage broke down before they had children. Teenage motherhood reflects a wider trend in and beyond Latin America, where girls have children at a young age for lack of something else that gives them a sense of purpose or meaning, and since they see little direct or tangible benefits in alternatives such as education (Barker 2005; Coulter 2009). Yet, rather than providing a safety net for old age, these children in fact made the situation of their families more complicated: while teenage mothers struggled to finish their education, their grandmothers often stepped in to look after their grandchildren, thus preventing them from joining productive projects or women's meetings. These shocking cases contrasted with a few hopeful ones, of young women continuing their education and postponing their plans to marry and have children, described in Chapter 2.

Yet whether women had children inspired by their hopes for a peaceful future, or for lack of hope for a better future, in both cases, their children prevented them from studying, finding a job and doing the other things that women identify as important to move forward. It is striking, for example, in Pondores, that those women who decided to really focus on their own life plans, making autonomous decisions to take on new roles and jobs, like Andrea and Maricela, had also consciously decided not to have children. They instead insisted on the importance of finishing their secondary school to continue studying and find a job or other life project. Overcoming this problem is not an easy feat, as it would be impossible and undesirable to discourage women from having children – although it would be advisable to strengthen reflection processes with (young) women about the impact of having children on their life plans and opportunities, and strengthen education about sexual and reproductive health and rights. It is a fact that many women in and beyond Colombia, both survivors and ex-combatants, have a strong desire to be mothers, perhaps for some even in response to the changed gender roles during conflict (Ketola 2020). What is problematic, however, is that these women, as well as supporting organizations and institutions, and the general imaginary, adopt a form of maternal citizenship, which centres women's role as mothers whose main responsibility is to secure a better future for their children (Lister 2003; Rayas Velasco 2009). Yet rather than trying to remove the maternal aspect from women's citizenship altogether, it is key to at least decentre it so that women, and especially young women, also consider other options.

Women's citizenship, moreover, contrasts with the hegemonic peasant and insurgent masculinities embodied by men, which do not centre the caring aspects of fatherhood. Therefore, it is crucial to incorporate fatherhood more strongly in men's vision and practice of citizenship, and promote models of 'caring masculinities' (Elliott 2016). This would involve men more actively in family life, and might make them reconsider the decision to have children at a young age or with different women, as is common in both Chibolo and Pondores. Furthermore, there is a need to redistribute caring responsibilities among men and women in a way that enables women to be more active beyond their motherhood roles, allowing both men and women to develop as active public citizens (Lister 2003). Public education can play a role in this, whereas reflection and discussion spaces among (young) men have also proved successful elsewhere (Barker 2005). Men tend to be concerned with key aspects defining their manhood, such as work and fatherhood. These are principal axes of hegemonic models of masculinity (Olavarría 2006). Discussing these issues, for example, by stressing how women's increased economic participation could improve their families' economic well-being or their children's future, could be a way of engaging men in these longer-term processes of transforming gender relations, and the need for their increased involvement in caring and household tasks. The use of male role models, like former nurse and committed father Henry or Mónica's husband in Pondores, or Carola's husband in Chibolo, could also help change imaginaries. In order to push for those shifts, and for the basic conditions needed for women to move forward through their desired projects or businesses, women need to start demanding these citizenship rights from both their male peers and the state.

Collective action and 'disruptive politics' are important strategies to demand changes from the government or women's families and communities to transform structures of inequality, hold states and communities accountable for them and disturb the silence, ignorance and complicity that maintains these structures (Goetz 2007; Green 2012; Hayward 2017). Such disruptive politics could take place on a small scale, at the community or family level, forcing men to rethink their gender role, for example, by going back to the described 'insurgent masculinities', or at a broader, national level. Protests, occupations of streets or buildings, social media strategies and performative actions are examples of ways in which oppressed groups can exert political power (Gready and Robins 2017). Women's collective agency is crucial for this. Organization among women can increase their self-esteem and help them to see themselves as political actors. Organization is therefore a building block for their citizenship practice (Lister 2003). In this way, they can actively push for the changes they need, either from their partners and communities or from the state, instead of waiting for support to come simply after signing an attendance sheet. Organization is thus a crucial aspect to guarantee the representation of women in and beyond TJ and DDR, in Nancy Fraser's approach to transformative justice.

Participation, organization and collective political agency

Nevertheless, as described in Chapters 2 and 4, women's organization has been complicated in both Chibolo and Pondores, to a large extent thanks to the passive citizenship practice described in the previous chapter. Many women in both communities are, however, aware of the need to organize to make change possible. In Chibolo, Claudia emphasized this: "This is what I would like, that the other women would be eager for this. Because all together, we can really achieve something" (Interview, 5 October 2015). Ana too expressed her desire for organizing: "That's what I say to these women: aha, what are we going to do? We have to do it [organizing] soon, to see what we will achieve, because if we are like this [unorganized] we are doing nothing" (Interview, 21 January 2016). Yet four years after these remarks, the women's committees in both communities were still weak. Many women had stopped participating in them, partly because of the divisions created by the Victims' Unit, described in Chapter 4. Elena told me in 2019 that she was not sure whether she would continue in the group, because many women did not attend the meetings regularly, and they did not even want to pay the small monthly fee that they had agreed on. The lack of solidarity and interest of many women demotivated others to continue as members of the committees.

In Pondores, several women also stressed the importance of organizing among themselves. Tania, for example, said: "Well, for me, the importance of the gender committee is to continue working, fighting so that we defend ourselves as women, so that they comply with our rights as women. We have a strong commitment with all of these things" (Interview, 18 October 2019). For leader Mónica, the importance of organization lies in "starting from the family upwards, to reconsider and replicate what we did in the mountains, and for us women to have influence. Let's be participatory women, communicative and entrepreneurial women" (Interview, 29 October 2019). During a meeting of the gender committee, Mónica told the women that they used to be strong during the conflict because of their unity, and that they now had to maintain this unity and be organized. Lisa said that "we would like to call on all other ETCRs, all the community, to organize. And we need to organize more widely" (Interview, 2 November 2019). Lisa's comment shows that she is aware of the need to strengthen the organizational capacity in Pondores, even though the gender committee here is clearly more active than in Chibolo. Their leader Mónica takes initiatives for regular meetings, which generally have a good attendance. It should be mentioned that women's organizing in Pondores is facilitated by the fact that almost all members live very close to each other, making it easier to communicate and to attend meetings, whereas in Chibolo, some women live very far away and isolated, making it a logistical challenge for them to attend a meeting, as they might need to walk for half an hour or more in the burning sun if they do not find someone to take them to the village centre by motorbike. The gender committee in Pondores is often applauded for its organizational strength, for example, by representatives of supporting non-governmental organizations (NGOs) and the UN that I interviewed. Mónica and Anita take an active stance in negotiating the support that the committee receives. They managed to change the format of the earlier-mentioned British Council/ARN project from a few intense training weekends to a longer-term process of a three-hour workshop each week, for which the trainers flew in from Bogotá on a weekly basis. They also actively negotiated the contents of a project by a Swedish organization. A representative of the FARC Gender Commission expressed her satisfaction at this attitude:

> 'Something which is very healing and that helps a lot to recover is the exercise of active citizenship, the experience of feeling part of discussions. ... They now go to scenes of local debates, with mayors, the health sector, whatever, and they are one more actor, and that is very, very important. This helps their emotional recovery, and I think it is a step towards reconciliation, an exercise of recognition and self-recognition that you don't achieve in any workshop.' (Interview, 1 October 2019)

Nevertheless, although this active citizenship is true for a number of women, it is striking that apart from female leaders Mónica and Anita and a few other more outspoken women, most women simply attend the meetings, listen to their leaders and follow the orders given to them. Andrea, who leads the tourism project, expressed her frustration with this:

> 'I was thinking the other day, that the people hear what one says: "we can do this, there is so-and-so here, and so-and-so there", but there are only a few women who do that and the rest, well, they are lying down, waiting for the husband to bring them food, give them things. ... And perhaps we can't blame anyone for that, but it's what I perceive because, aha, we can't lie and say, "here in the ETCR we all work". We work only when we are being pulled forward. ... Very few women have dared to take up that responsibility. ... One sees the little real commitment of the women in the ETCR.' (Interview, 5 November 2019)

On repeated occasions, women like María and Natalia told me that they would go to meetings or workshops outside the ETCR, since Mónica had asked them to. They, however, had no idea what these activities were about; they simply played their part in the gender committee, of attending meetings and doing what their leader decided. They kept doing what they were used to during the conflict, when orders were followed and critical opinions were not appreciated. Making autonomous decisions was not yet something they felt comfortable with. The fact that critical thinking and dissenting opinions are still not very much welcomed became clear in the earlier-mentioned period of the election campaign in autumn 2019, particularly in an incident in the gender committee, when Mónica explained that the civilian woman who worked as a cook in the restaurant had resigned because of disagreements. Mónica said that this was fortunate because, otherwise, she would have needed to fire her, since she wore a T-shirt of one of the opposing candidates for mayor, which she could not accept since they "only want people around them that support and love them, and support their political candidates" (Meeting notes 27 September 2019). In such a restrictive environment, it is not surprising that most women stick to what they know: following orders.

As a result, the foundation that the gender committees of Pondores and the other Caribbean ETCR in the Cesar department had created, and were still enthusiastic about during my first visit in May 2019, had already died a quiet death in the autumn of the same year. The training that the women received, both in Pondores and in Chibolo, did not focus on organization itself and how to manage this best, or how to maintain membership and rotate leadership. This would be an important avenue for future support, since other research has shown that once women have experienced a process of strong and effective organizing, this changes their consciousness, which makes them more likely to stay organized even in adverse conditions (Zulver 2021). Andrea explained that she did experience a change of consciousness when conflict was over, and that she considered peace an opportunity to change the previous pattern of simply following orders. She decided not to continue being a nurse, but to pursue her own life plan by leading the tourism project:

> 'Well, really back then it was a question that one had to help our comrades, and one was told "pack your bag and go, because you're going on a nursing training" or "get ready for a dentistry training" and so we did that. But, in this moment, it has been more like ... like I told you, that one is able to choose what she likes.' (Interview, 5 November 2019)

Yet this agency to make their own choices is limited to only a handful of women, whereas the others do not seem to have been able or willing to overcome their previous habit of following orders. This is, to a certain extent, even the case with female leader Mónica. She often mentioned that she implemented the projects and activities she was ordered to by the FARC Gender Commission at the national level, or by national FARC leader Victoria Sandino herself. For instance, she once explained that the gender committee in the ETCR would deliver meetings and trainings to the neighbouring communities, even though they had decided they would only accept projects that would give them material benefits. But since this project came from the national level, it had to be implemented. What is more, after the proposed content of the project was negotiated among the female leaders of two ETCRs, it first had to be approved by the general – male – leadership of these ETCRs before it was even communicated to or consulted with the gender committee members. A representative of a women's organization who works with ex-combatants in two other ETCRs describes it this way:

> 'If the top leadership do not give the order to attend a workshop, the people don't go out of their own will, because there is no political interest that you see in women's civil society organizations, to educate themselves to demand their rights. It is a whole process that these women have to go through to recognize themselves as political subjects.' (Interview, 12 November 2019)

In fact, even Mónica, now a leader of both the women's committee and the larger ETCR, explained that, for her, it had been a learning process to take on public roles. She only obtained a formal leadership position as a 'gender focal point' with the UN Monitoring Mission of the peace accords in 2017. Although she had some prior experience with leading meetings and commanding some activities in the FARC, she had never spoken to a large audience before and was initially really scared by the idea of using a microphone to talk in front of large groups, including the UN and the police. Gradually, she got used to it, and considered that other women could get used to it too if they were given the chance.

The promotion of the recognition of women as political subjects and actors is not something that TJ and DDR processes incorporate in their work. Even though some projects or trainings for women are provided, including about women's rights, the actual step from knowing what rights are on a formal level to actually interiorizing them and knowing how to demand them is missing. That several women, including Mónica but also national-level female FARC leaders such as Victoria Sandino, and female leaders like Carola in Chibolo, have made this transition to active gendered citizenship is something to emphasize and celebrate. This is partly to do with their prior leadership roles, but also with their family situations, since, as I described in Chapter 2, their supportive husbands participate – fairly – equally in the household so they have more time to develop their leadership capacities. This shows how time is a crucial resource for citizenship, and how enabling gender justice and gendered citizenship requires bridging the public–private divide and promoting 'caring masculinities' (Lister 2003; Goetz 2007; Elliott 2016). But it is not enough to be satisfied with these few examples of powerful female leaders, important though they are. Other women should also be supported to develop their citizenship practice in the public sphere, if they so desire. To achieve this, childcare facilities can be a short-term solution to deal with a direct, urgent problem. Yet to make lasting, more strategic changes, time and caring roles need to be redistributed, so that both men and women can participate in the public sphere. This requires working with men to change the elements of male citizenship and the ways in which masculinities are viewed and valued. Women can push for this through their collective strength and action, but for this, they first need to see themselves as political subjects and actors.

Therefore, leadership training and organizational and lobbying skills training are essential (Molyneux 2010; Kabeer 2012), to guarantee transitions from passive to active citizenship among women and to guarantee that leadership does not stay with a few already emancipated women, but instead can expand and rotate. These activities should become part of reparation and reintegration processes, to guarantee more effective representation in these processes, and eventually in broader political and economic life. Instead of a couple of workshops which produce few tangible changes in and for women, this requires a slower and long-term process of building skills and capacities, changing beliefs about gender norms and raising awareness about the possibilities of collective action (Green 2012). To be effective in the long run, a process of reflection and recognition is needed within and among women about the meaning of active citizenship, about the need to demand recognition for their roles in their family and community and to demand changes in the division of time, political and economic resources and agency. For their support to really become meaningful and transformative, accompanying institutions need to overcome their audit anxiety, and instead of donating money for ineffective projects or vague political agendas which only look good in annual reports, they should actually commit to a long-term accompaniment of women and their organizational processes – while, of course, also alleviating some of the most urgent needs, but based on an in-depth analysis of which support will actually be effective. This means that budgets are better spent on the hiring of local teams which can work intensively with groups of survivors and ex-combatants in a long-term process, combining the teaching of a diverse set of technical, organizational, administrative and political skills with a concrete form of material support. Such support should respond to women's ideas for the future, to make them motivated to invest energy in something they see the benefit of, rather than in abstract rights and gender training that has little connection to their immediate needs and hopes of 'moving forward' with their families.

Conclusion

In this chapter, I have described how survivors in Chibolo and ex-combatants in Pondores envision their future: as moving forward, by being organized among women and, through this, generating jobs and productive projects which can increase women's independence from their husbands. Reparation and reintegration support has been ineffective so far, as Chapter 4 explained how it tends to focus on providing 'projects for women' without transforming structural gender inequality and gendered norms which keep women attached to caring and household roles. Instead, in addition to more effective and better accompanied support projects, reparation and reintegration support should be more concerned with promoting women's self-esteem, political subjectivity and skills for taking control over their own lives by helping them to formulate their own needs and design strategies to fulfil them. To overcome the passive citizenship practice described in this book, organization among women is crucial, but also engaging men and promoting that they take on an equal part of the time and energy needed for the caring and household tasks which now prevent women from having public agency. TJ and DDR processes could have a stronger impact on the transformation of women's lives and gender inequality if they would replace the 'assistentialist' focus described in the previous chapter by a strategy for promoting organizational and leadership skills, in a broader process of citizenship building. In the Conclusion to this book, I will unpack what this wider process could look like, by bringing together the strands of the argument described across the different chapters, and by connecting them to strategies to promote recognition, redistribution and representation, as outlined in Nancy Fraser's model of trivalent justice.

Conclusion: From Victimhood to Citizenship

I started this book with the question of what the gendered dynamics of current reparation and reintegration laws and policies on the ground are, and whether they effectively transform structural gender inequality, thus enabling communities to move forward. I have analysed this question through a gendered lens, looking at the impacts of conflict on men and particularly women, and how these impacts are addressed in the post-conflict situation to transform gender inequality and establish a more gender-equal peace. I wanted to understand why the increasingly popular gender lens in transitional justice (TJ) and other post-conflict reconstruction mechanisms often does so little to actually transform gender inequality and tends to have such disappointing results in preventing gendered violence in the post-conflict situation. Therefore, rather than looking at sexual violence, often considered as *the* gendered harm produced by conflict which has become a hype in post-conflict reconstruction efforts in and beyond Colombia (Hilhorst and Douma 2018), I looked instead at the everyday gendered experiences in the conflict and post-conflict context, which enable an analysis of the deeper structures of gender inequality. In doing this, I have followed a long tradition in feminist research which looks at everyday experiences of oppression and inequality, since 'the personal is political' (Fonow and Cook 1991). Gender justice is a commonly used but rather vague concept which is understood differently by different actors. Through an intense and long-term process of engaging with women in Colombia, I have tried to identify what it looks like for them. They commonly expressed it in two words: *salir adelante*, or moving forward, which consists of gaining economic independence of their husbands through education and income generation, and becoming more active participants in their communities' public sphere, breaking out of their often suffocating household roles.

I have examined how two crucial peacebuilding and reconciliation mechanisms, reparations and reintegration, fare at promoting this vision. Although reparations address the situation of conflict survivors and reintegration that of former combatants, which can produce tensions between these groups, the two mechanisms share the goals of turning both survivors and ex-combatants into equal citizens and restoring trust in the state and society. Both mechanisms are backward-looking and forward-looking at the same time, as they address past crimes and harms and promote the conditions for healing and equal citizenship. These processes can overlap in practice, when communities are engaged in reintegration and receive support, or when ex-combatants contribute to reparation processes. Finally, both mechanisms, more than other TJ processes, are able to make a tangible change to the lives of those affected by conflict, by providing material and symbolic support which can redefine living conditions and power relationships. They therefore also have potential to address gendered inequality, which tends to have social, economic and political aspects which place women at a disadvantage and in a position of unequal citizenship.

It is important to make this abstract question more concrete. I therefore examined the case of Colombia, a country that has been prominently on the international research and policy radar, for implementing an ambitious reparation and land restitution process, initially during ongoing conflict, and an innovative, collective reintegration process after peace was signed with the FARC guerrillas. I studied these processes through long-term and repeated fieldwork periods on Colombia's Caribbean coast, using participatory, visual and ethnographic methods which foregrounded the words and images of those involved in the processes under study. Analysing the very local, everyday lived experience of these processes, through a gendered lens, has enabled a better understanding of the actual effects that well-meaning gender perspectives can have on people's, and especially women's, lives, and whether these live up to the often high expectations that are created around TJ and disarmament, demobilization and reintegration (DDR). The experiences of the people in these two locations in a single region of Colombia do not necessarily represent the average Colombian experience of reintegration and reparation, also because the experience of conflict-affected people in Colombia's rural areas is very different from those in the cities (Buchely 2015). Nevertheless, other research shows that the gender measures in the peace accords are those whose implementation has made least progress (Echavarría Álvarez et al 2021; Fajardo 2021). Complementing such more quantitative monitoring, my research has allowed a fine-grained view of some of the main obstacles, but also opportunities, for making reparation and reintegration truly gender-transformative. Many of these obstacles, including the tendency to understand gender as women or, even more narrowly, as sexual violence against women, and to add gender along the way instead of integrating a gendered analysis and perspective from the outset of TJ and DDR processes, were confirmed by TJ and DDR stakeholders with a broader experience and understanding of Colombia. They are also apparent in other post-conflict contexts, as is evident from the research by other feminist peacebuilding and TJ scholars cited throughout this book. These combined insights can provide lessons for broader gendered TJ and DDR efforts. It is, however, important to move beyond identifying the obstacles, and, instead, also find solutions. I propose using citizenship as a lens and adopting Nancy Fraser's model of trivalent justice as an approach to devise practical ways of making reparation and reintegration processes more gender-transformative. By connecting TJ theory to citizenship studies, I offer an innovative way to actually recognize and bolster women's agency. In this Conclusion, I outline how I envision this.

Analysing the different aspects of why reparations and reintegration have failed to transform gender inequality in Colombia is important to arrive at solutions which can make these processes more gender-transformative. Gender roles often change during conflict, giving women new roles, especially in terms of generating income, which can produce feelings of emancipation. At the same time, they generate a double burden since women's household and caring tasks are not reduced, even though men's role as breadwinners is often disrupted by conflict. This is less the case for combatants, who tend to experience an everyday practice of gender equality, where women and men – among the rank and file – perform similar tasks and all adopt values of care, solidarity and camaraderie. Nevertheless, these gendered changes generally do not persist in the post-conflict period, as a return to normality comes with the expectation of a return to previous gender roles. This again makes women principally responsible for household and caring tasks, thus largely confining them to the private sphere with few options for economic and political agency. The desire to return to pre-conflict gender roles is especially strong for men, who are eager to re-establish pre-conflict forms of masculinity and its corresponding power, but, to some extent, also for women, whose double burden of productive and reproductive work can produce stress and exhaustion. In spite of their alleged gender perspective, TJ and DDR generally fail to assist women in maintaining the gains they made during conflict, or even in helping men and women to reflect on conflict-era gender role changes, their benefits and challenges and how they could help to ensure a better post-conflict future.

This is the result of the ways in which TJ and DDR mechanisms address conflict experiences, especially their emphasis on certain forms of victimization, in particular, sexual violence. This emphasis means that other gendered experiences, such as the socio-economic effects of conflict, but also experiences of gendered agency and emancipation, are overlooked. This is also true for structural violence, which is often at the root of conflict, for example, because of unequal land possession or the socio-economic marginalization of population groups, as was the case in Colombia. Structural violence also has gendered dynamics, such as gender-based violence, *machismo* and the lack of opportunities for girls to study. It is thus an important factor in explaining why ex-combatants came to join armed groups. Many of them see it as a way to resist structural violence, whereas for women, joining an armed group can offer opportunities to study and thus for emancipation. Structural violence tends to persist after the conflict is over, since peace accords often fail to resolve the deep socio-economic inequalities that gave rise to conflict. Recognizing the importance of structural violence can produce more complex and nuanced understandings of the experiences of both survivors and perpetrators, instead of pushing people into one of these categories, being regarded either as innocent victims or guilty perpetrators. Female ex-combatants are generally only seen as potential victims if they admit to having suffered sexual violence, a crime many of them are reluctant to admit for fear of undermining their self-perception of emancipated women. This victim–perpetrator binary prevents attention to survivors' gendered agency, and to perpetrators' experiences of structural and gendered violence. This keeps intact stereotypes that are unhelpful for creating imaginaries of active citizenship for women. Furthermore, the victim–perpetrator binary fails to identify commonalities in the experiences of survivors and combatants, which are often related to structural violence, even though this in fact could help to promote recognition and solidarity among both groups. Such recognition could not only promote reconciliation but also enable them to learn from each other's experiences of agency. Rather than pushing people into narrow categories of victims and perpetrators, treating them as citizens with common experiences of gendered structural violence but also agency could be more effective at creating a starting point for a different future.

The ways in which reparations and reintegration are implemented are not helpful for transforming gender inequality either. First of all, in Colombia these programmes tend to focus on women rather than on gender and unequal gendered power relations, and they largely disregard men and masculinities. As a result, they understand a gender perspective as 'doing something for women', leading to women-specific trainings and projects which are added on along the way, and often do little to structurally change women's economic position or their active participation in collective public spaces. Instead, the disappointing outcomes of such projects or activities demotivate women from investing their time and energy in them, thus risking the fracturing of women's organization. Eventually, these dynamics weaken women's strength through collective power and agency to make change happen. This collective strength is further weakened by the logic behind the way in which reparations and reintegration support are delivered. They are driven by an 'assistentialist' tendency which is reinforced by the audit culture common to many international, neoliberal state and civil society programmes. This audit culture is translated into a focus on delivering short-term material support or workshops based on the prerequisite of signing an attendance sheet. Even though this enables supporting institutions to show their actions and thus gain legitimacy, they bring about little structural change, while for recipients, it seems like all they have to do is sign the register and wait for support to come. In contrast to a citizenship practice in which individuals actively claim their rights and assume their civil responsibilities, this assistentialist tendency shifts the weight towards the rights and entitlements of citizenship, disregarding the civic duties and responsibilities it also entails. This risks turning people into passive recipients of aid in an otherwise unequal society, an image that contrasts with their previous practices of radical citizenship as peasants and combatants, through land occupations and armed resistance.

This passive attitude makes it hard for women to fulfil their dreams of moving forward (*salir adelante*). The women in Chibolo, for example, explain that "we don't want to stay like this. We want to move forward to have a new future and show our children something new, that we can indeed move forward" (Photovoice booklet 2016). This statement shows the connection of women's idea of moving forward with their role as mothers who want a better future for their children. Motherhood, however, is complex. Although it motivates the desire to move forward, at the same time, it is an obstacle for it. The persisting importance attached to motherhood by many women and, worryingly, also by many very young women is problematic, since the sexual division of household and other work means that motherhood, both for survivors and ex-combatants, severely limits women's options for studying and working. The few women who have been able to consolidate their agency and leadership and who are more autonomous tend to either not have children, or have supporting husbands who take on an equal share in household tasks. This shows the importance of not only making sure that the state provides childcare facilities but also of transforming masculinities to promote gender equality in the long run.

Organizing among women is a crucial means of pushing for changes within families and communities and for demanding basic citizenship rights from the state. Unfortunately, both survivors and ex-combatants struggle to organize themselves effectively and sustainably, and here lies an important avenue for support by reparation and reintegration processes, as well as other post-conflict processes such as the Women, Peace and Security (WPS) Agenda. Organizational, leadership and lobbying skills could help to strengthen women's collective agency, and to demand changes through collective action. Unfortunately, so far, reintegration and reparation support has too often been translated into short-term, superficial projects or workshops that do not sufficiently respond to women's genuine interests and needs. In this way, these two different processes – reparations through the Victims' Law and reintegration through the FARC's collective reincorporation process – show very similar patterns and tendencies which, in spite of their assumed gender and differential focus, prevent them from being effective in transforming gender inequality. Instead, they risk weakening women's agency and citizenship, which are crucial elements for promoting gender equality in the long run.

Gender justice: from theory to practice

As described in the Introduction, a practical approach to think about how gender justice could go beyond 'doing something for women', and instead transform gender inequality is Nancy Fraser's (2008) model of trivalent justice. In this model, for justice to be transformative, it should contain three interconnected elements: recognition, redistribution and representation, which I will discuss in turn to identify ways forward for reparation and reintegration programmes and other TJ mechanisms in and beyond Colombia. They are also crucial insights for policies in the WPS field, including the national action plan (NAP) recommended by the Colombian Commission for the Clarification of Truth, Coexistence and Reconciliation (CEV).

Recognition

Recognition refers to the recognition, valuing and validation of women's experiences. Transforming gender roles requires recognizing women's conflict experiences beyond victimization, also recognizing their agency and potential to contribute in diverse ways to their families, communities and society. This means recognizing their status as equal citizens with the same possibilities as men to develop themselves fully in both the private and public sphere. In terms of addressing the effects of conflict and making use of the potential for change offered by a post-conflict transition, women's – and men's – diverse conflict experiences can be building blocks for the process of citizenship building. Although it is important to also recognize gendered harms, as these, of course, must be addressed, TJ and DDR must abandon their focus on individual victims, on gender as a synonym for women and on sexual violence as the single most important gendered conflict experience. Other gendered harms, including those in the private sphere and after conflict has ended, have too frequently been ignored, even though they are reflective of the continued gendered inequality which facilitated gendered conflict-era violence like sexual violence in the first place.

In addition to a more diverse understanding of gendered harms, women's and men's changed gendered roles and the emancipatory experiences that these often entail for women should receive more attention in order to disrupt stereotypes of women as a vulnerable group in need of support and protection. Instead, showing that women have been crucial social, political and economic actors can help to change social imaginaries about women, to pave the way for greater recognition and acceptance of women's individual and collective agency. Recognition is also needed for the role that structural violence, including gender inequality, plays in conflict. This would help to break down the damaging victim–perpetrator binary that forces people into narrow categories that leave little space for agency. Recognizing the complexity and grey zones in conflict, which can make people victims and perpetrators simultaneously, and make them experience victimization and agency at the same time, creates more openness for looking at the similarities in people's experiences, thus overcoming polarization and instead building a common citizenship identity. A collective identity, rather than polarization between groups, is important both for the collective action which can be part of a practice of active citizenship but also for increasing social cohesion and stability, which is crucial in a post-conflict situation. TJ mechanisms such as truth commissions and historical memory processes can help to uncover such diverse conflict experiences, change ideas about gendered experiences and roles, and build a collective identity. So can forms of art, both at the community level and through films and books aimed at the general population.

A different evaluation of gender roles does not only involve the recognition of women's roles but also of men's roles and of masculinities. Men's roles are affected during and after conflict. Male survivors can feel emasculated when they are unable to perform their role as producers and breadwinners, whereas feelings of emasculation can arise for ex-combatants after conflict when they lose their masculine status as combatant and struggle to provide for their families. In both cases, men try to reassert a pre-conflict, hegemonic model of masculinity by becoming breadwinners and exerting power over women. This presents an obvious obstacle to women's agency and citizenship. To overcome this, the elements which characterize masculinity need to be valued differently. Caring and household tasks, now women's domain and even seen as emasculating for men, need to be recognized as important elements of male citizenship too. A way of doing this is making fatherhood as important to men's experience of masculinity and citizenship as motherhood is for women. Paternity, like work, is in fact already an important aspect of hegemonic models of masculinity (Olavarría 2006). The challenge is to expand the conception of paternity as a mere proof of virility and maintenance of lineage into a caring and supportive conception of fatherhood. Peer groups among (young) men have been successful elsewhere as support mechanisms and safe spaces to discuss and critically reflect upon the harmful effects of masculinity on men's lives (Barker 2005). Discussing wider issues such as the economic well-being of their families, their children's future or the benefit of improved relationships with their partners and children could be a way of engaging men in these longer-term processes of transforming gender relations. This could help them value the importance of taking on a more equal share in their family's reproductive and caring tasks (Connell 2005). Such strategies should be key to gendered reintegration policies, including the processes that may arise when President Petro's 'total peace' policy is successful. Public education and communication campaigns to change social imaginaries which consider caring tasks to be feminine and therefore emasculating for men can also contribute to these change processes. Men should be recognized as important partners for change, whose participation in the private sphere can generate time and space for women to develop their public agency. This shows the important connection between the public and private spheres, which is crucial to address in order to promote women's citizenship (Lister 2003; McEwan 2005; Goetz 2007). For TJ and DDR mechanisms, this means expanding their view of gender to include men and masculinities, and broadening their area of intervention from the public sphere to include the private sphere.

Redistribution

Redistribution refers to the promotion of equitable access to economic and other resources for women and men. As I have described in this book, the lack of basic development services such as running water, electricity, access roads and the like affect the experience of citizenship for both men and women. Both survivors and ex-combatants do not feel the state treats them as equal citizens with access to the basic rights to live a dignified life. Nevertheless, the absence of such services affects women differently, since they make their already intensive household tasks even more straining and physically demanding. This leaves them with little time and energy for activities outside of the household, such as organizing among themselves, which would allow them to implement projects to generate income, or lobby to demand their rights from the government. It is therefore important for states in transition to pay attention to the provision of basic social and infrastructural services, either directly as part of transformative reparations or (community) reintegration support packages, or through separate development programmes targeting conflict-affected and other marginalized areas, such as the territorial rural development plans (PDET) in Colombia, whose implementation is disappointingly slow. Such short-term support is urgent to alleviate people's most urgent needs, and to allow women to move beyond their immediate needs and tasks and reflect on longer-term, more strategic goals.

In terms of the distribution of economic resources and employment opportunities, reparations and reintegration in Colombia mostly focus on men and their economic activities: cattle farming and other agricultural projects, or employment as security guards. Women, in contrast, receive 'women's projects' which are often not as profitable and sustainable and which, moreover, increase women's burden, as they add to their household tasks. This is not specific to Colombia but also common to many DDR programmes around the world, where women have received training on hairdressing or tailoring – traits which are unlikely to make women economically independent (Dietrich Ortega 2009; Jennings 2009; MacKenzie 2012; Vastapuu 2018). These women's projects, moreover, do not offer formal employment opportunities, making for an insecure and instable remuneration, which makes it easy for women to lose interest. This means that women feel they and their economic needs are not adequately and equally considered, and that men have direct access to financial and material resources, whereas women do not. This keeps intact ideas of men as breadwinners, and unequal power relations within families. To overcome this imbalance, from the start of reintegration and reparation programmes, strategies should be designed to ensure women and men have equal and equitable access to productive projects and employment. More efforts could be made to include women in general projects or programmes, such as (cattle) farming or security guard trainings, which are presented as gender-neutral but in fact mostly target men. This could be done by actively engaging both men and women, and integrating a gender perspective in these productive strategies to change social imaginaries about what men's and women's work looks like. If separate projects or strategies are chosen for men and women, a stronger effort should be made to undertake effective (labour) market analyses, to ensure that 'women's projects' have a real potential for being successful, sustainable and profitable, instead of being 'something for women' which only looks nice on paper. Women should also be supported logistically to participate in these projects, for example, by providing childcare facilities. This is, however, unlikely to be a sustainable solution, since most post-conflict and developing states do not offer free or affordable childcare services to their population, and therefore such support will probably cease to exist once TJ or DDR support ends.

To truly make women's economic situation more equal, power and resources should be redistributed beyond the material. The role and task divisions between men and women, in terms of both paid employment but also household and caring tasks, should be redistributed. Women's large share in household and caring tasks, or their 'maternal citizenship' (Lister 2003; Rayas Velasco 2009), leaves them little time to develop their citizenship in the public sphere, in economic or political ways. Men, in contrast, have much more time to develop their public citizenship, thus creating unequal citizenship opportunities which maintains gender inequality in the social, economic and political sphere. In order to transform this inequality, again, it is crucial to engage men more actively in gendered change strategies and in the actual division of household and caring tasks. The recognition of specific work and activities as male or female should be transformed towards an equal distribution of such tasks. In this way, men and women will be able to have more equal access to the important resource of time, which is crucial for citizenship (Lister 2003). More time in turn allows women to develop their agency beyond the household. TJ and DDR processes should therefore design strategies to make such changes in subjectivities and power dynamics, for example, through sensitization processes, including with men on masculinities, as well as psychosocial support.

Representation

Representation refers to the active participation of women and girls in different ways and spaces. Internal representation, in the conception of Williams and Palmer (2016), refers to their participation in peacebuilding processes and TJ, whereas external representation entails their engagement as actors in national, political and economic life. The reparation and reintegration processes described in this book show much room for improvement in terms of women's internal representation. Especially in the case of the Victims' Law, women's participation in the processes to design reparation plans or productive projects is hardly promoted, beyond a formal mention of a gender perspective – the *mujerismo* referred to in Chapter 4. As a result, the process does not correspond to women's needs, and women get offered few opportunities to become active agents in the reparation process, which could in turn lead to a stronger leadership role in their communities. In the case of the FARC, partly thanks to the greater gender equality experienced in the guerrilla movement, women play a more active role in the reintegration process, and they participate more equally in meetings, training and other activities. Nevertheless, here too, it is apparent that decisions about the reincorporation process are generally taken by the leadership of the territorial space for training and reincorporation (ETCR), with a large role for the former male commanders. Although there are a few female leaders who are actively engaged in shaping their own reincorporation process, projects and conditions, most women passively wait and see what their leaders tell them to do. The hierarchy that was present in the FARC as an armed group is still relatively strong, whereas the voicing of critical or dissenting opinions was and is not promoted. This makes it hard to know what women actually need and expect from reintegration.

To overcome this problem, TJ and DDR mechanisms should make a stronger effort to actively engage women in the processes of designing and implementing their programmes from the start onwards, and, furthermore, give women the support needed, either financial, moral or logistical, to enable them to participate in this design process. This means holding meetings at times which are convenient for women, holding not only mixed but also women-only meetings in which women can talk freely and also providing sufficient time and an atmosphere which enables women to actively reflect on their situation, so that the designed strategies and support actually respond to their needs and demands. This is crucial for the new government and its interest in initiating new peace processes, where women should be actively and meaningfully involved from the start onwards. Meaningful participation is also essential to make sure that a potential WPS NAP will respond to women's everyday realities and needs.

For external representation, or women's participation in the public sphere, including politics, women's agency needs to be promoted. Organization among women is an important building block for this, as the ability to share thoughts and experiences creates solidarity which can increase women's self-esteem and make them see themselves as political actors (Lister 2003). Effective organization makes productive projects or small women-led businesses, which can increase women's economic independence, more likely to be successful and sustainable. Finally, it can inspire women to take collective action to demand their citizenship and other rights in their families, communities or from the state, based on a long-term strategic goal they can work towards. This will make women less dependent on the benevolence of the state or accompanying organizations, passively waiting for promises of assistentialist support to materialize, but instead incentivize them to take their fate in their own hands and push for the changes they need to 'move forward'. Although organizational strengthening through organization, lobbying and leadership skills training will require more intensive and continued accompaniment than a few workshops on a specific, demarcated topic, in the long run, this will prove a more sustainable strategy for women and their communities to move forward on the basis of greater agency and citizenship, and thus help them to gain greater equality and autonomy.

Representation should also apply to participation in research on reparation, reintegration and other peacebuilding processes that are meant to transform people's lives. It is impossible to truly understand people's conflict experiences and their needs for the future without using methods that give participants the opportunity and tools to express their opinions in their own words, placing their own emphases, rather than responding to the researcher's specific interests and beliefs. Research must enable women to speak about their own experience, rather than speaking *for* them. This is even more true if the researcher is an outsider, sometimes from a completely different ethnic and class background. Using methods that enable genuine inclusion and participation is even more important when working on topics such as gender, or with women or other groups who tend to be marginalized both from TJ and from research on it. I have experienced that women can find more traditional methods such as interviews intimidating, thus limiting their participation in research, or meaning that the data obtained through such methods is fairly superficial. Therefore, it is essential to choose methods that are able to actively engage women in a way that makes research meaningful and interesting for them. My experience is that visual or other creative research methods can make research participation enjoyable for women, while providing them with tangible research results which can be showed to others, both family members and policy makers.

Furthermore, the visual allows the research to capture aspects of everyday life whose importance otherwise frequently remains unseen or unacknowledged, such as the strain of burdensome household tasks, the inaccessibility of decent bathrooms, women's often unrecognized participation in agricultural activities or the impact of drought on people's livelihoods. The use of such methods not only leads to a better representation of women's views and experiences in the research but can also be part of the process of increasing women's self-esteem, as they perceive a genuine interest in their opinions, start to regard themselves and their experiences as worthy of academic attention and, in the process, can learn to share their opinions publicly with others. In this way, research representation can be one small part of a larger process of increasing women's representation and participation in different arenas, which contributes to building a practice of active citizenship. As for TJ and DDR stakeholders, for researchers this will require a longer-term and perhaps repeated research engagement rather than a one-off field trip to undertake some interviews. Nevertheless, for those researchers interested in making research meaningful for participants and in promoting actual change with their research, creating the trust and providing the tools, space and time needed to enable genuine representation is essential.

Conclusion

The case of Colombia's Caribbean coast demonstrates how reparations and reintegration in Colombia currently fare at transforming gender inequality, and how they could become more effective at promoting gender justice. For the women in Chibolo and Pondores, gender justice means *salir adelante*, or moving forward. This consists in securing a better future for themselves and their children, through education, organization and economic independence by means of productive projects or small businesses. Promoting more active and equal citizenship for women would offer a more sustainable way to achieve this than the often tokenistic and short-term support that is currently provided. For this to become a reality, TJ and DDR processes need to shift gear and redirect their focus. Practitioners working in these areas could help to make this a reality by making sure that the support they deliver can help to promote full and active citizenship for women, based on a transformation of the meaning and content of gendered citizenship. When designing policies, they should ask themselves whether their work helps to:

- *Recognize* women's citizenship: rather than maintaining a victim–perpetrator binary with a focus on women, women – and men – should be regarded as full and equal citizens. This requires not only recognizing women's victimhood but also their agency in and after conflict, based, among others, on the gendered role changes that often proved crucial during the conflict. It also entails changing perceptions of male citizenship, moving away from regarding men as breadwinners only towards a vision of male citizenship which values fatherhood and caring and household tasks. This requires a recognition that gender does not equal women but also involves men, who need to be engaged in processes to transform gender inequality.
- *Redistribute* the resources and roles that sustain women's citizenship: rather than implementing short-term actions to redress specific harms, women's access to the resources and time needed to become active citizens with equal socio-economic opportunities should be guaranteed. This can be done through targeted and well-designed material support projects, based both on women's own interests and needs and effective market analyses, to guarantee that women's economic strategies are indeed successful. Women need time to be able to implement such strategies, and therefore their household tasks need to be alleviated. This can be done through childcare support, but in the long run, caring and household tasks should be distributed more equally among men and women. TJ and DDR support must therefore not only focus on the public sphere but also engage the private sphere and role divisions there.
- *Represent* women in TJ and DDR and, more broadly, in the wider communities and society. To facilitate this, it is not enough to simply monitor the number of women who participate in activities through attendance sheets. Women in patriarchal societies tend to have less experience with participating in public spaces and decision-making processes. They should be supported in acquiring the skills needed for this, for example, through training on political and leadership capacities. In addition, women's organization can help to strengthen their political force to push for changes in the division of resources and roles in their families and communities, even after reparation and reintegration support has ended. To aid this process, technical and financial support to promote their organizational strengthening and the building of a collective identity is needed, preferably on a continuous, longer-term basis. The case of Colombia's Caribbean coast has showed that the absence of such support frequently means that well-intentioned projects die a quiet death, with little structural change for women's lives and positions.

Through a more holistic perspective, which is not aimed only at short-term support or projects for women but combines this with efforts to transform subjectivities and build citizenship practices, women and men will be able to move forward to a future in which they are not simply victims or perpetrators who wait for support, but active citizens who construct their own, more gender-equal futures.

APPENDIX

Checklist for Ethics in Research on Gender and Conflict

Researching issues related to conflict, violence, gendered and other inequalities, especially in places that are not the researcher's home country and which may still not be entirely stable, raises many challenges and questions, in practical but especially ethical terms. How to conduct research in a way that is meaningful, without exposing the participants or the researchers to safety risks or (re)traumatization. How to manage the insecurity and stress of working in an unknown and complex environment. How to work in contexts where working and travelling abroad as a single woman is not culturally expected and might raise questions. Many authors (see, for example, Guillemin and Gillam 2004; Fujii 2012; Theidon 2014; Cronin-Furman and Lake 2018; Schulz 2020; Schmidt 2021) have rightly pointed out that these questions are not frequently discussed in research training or academic publications, while university ethics boards tend to focus more on harms and risks to participants and researchers than on broader ethical research practice. This leaves new researchers to find their own solutions, while they could learn from the experiences that most researchers have had but have not written about.

Fortunately, more and more is being published about the research process and the ethics and practicalities of doing fieldwork, or in fact about why not to do fieldwork, or the need to change the mode of fieldwork (Boesten and Henry 2018; Irgil et al 2021; Krause 2021; Schulz and Kreft 2021; Ginty, Brett and Vogel 2021). This appendix contributes to these emerging debates on the ethics of researching conflict. It deals with some of the silenced parts of research that can produce real doubts, tensions and insecurities for researchers. It combines a practical checklist (Table A.1) that lists the key topics and questions to think about with ethical and methodological reflections based on my own research and suggestions on how to overcome these doubts and tensions. The checklist can thus serve as a tool for students, researchers and practitioners, and as a contribution to debates on methods and fieldwork. After the actual checklist, the appendix describes in more detail

Table A.1: Ethics checklist for research on gender and conflict

Practical ethics	
Basic questions when studying conflict	Risks and benefits of studying a conflict as an insider or outsider - Does my background give me the ability/position to touch upon sensitive issues? - Do I have sufficient contextual knowledge to make sense of the data? - Which conflict to study? - Do I speak the language? - Has the country or region been researched by many others? - How can I gain access to a group/community? Do I have relevant contacts? Can I undertake a pilot visit?
Procedural ethics	Confidentiality, privacy and consent - How can I make sure I can store the data in a confidential way, even without an internet connection? - Do I have access to safe and private locations to undertake interviews? - What are the local norms in terms of privacy? - Is written consent possible or do I need to look for alternatives, such as recorded oral consent? Anonymity - Do participants want to be anonymized? - Do they want their locations to be anonymized? - Are there safety risks involved in not anonymizing?
Visual ethics	Risks inherent in images - Are persons or places identifiable in the images? - Are any illegal acts or harmful stereotypes evident in the images? - What can I do to diminish these risks? (that is, specific training/instructions, cropping or blurring images, metaphoric images)? Consent - Have participants signed copyright forms? - Have they indicated for what purposes they share copyright (that is, publications, presentations, theses)?
Safety	Safety risks for participants - Are there risks to the participants based on what they share with me? - Does my presence produce risks? - What methods/timeframe of research can help to mitigate such risks? Safety risks for the researcher - How do participants/local key contacts consider the risks for an outsider? - Do I have a safety mechanism in place (that is, regular contact with supervisors/friends/colleagues, registration with Embassy)? - Can I implement measures to make me feel safer (that is, wearing a 'wedding ring', specific modes or times of transportation)? - Do I feel stressed, worried or tired? Do I take sufficient breaks?
If things go wrong	Prepare for the unexpected - Be aware that creating rapport and arranging interviews takes time. - Be flexible and prepare for alternative methods and strategies, including remote research.

APPENDIX

Table A.1: Ethics checklist for research on gender and conflict (continued)

Practical ethics	
	- When things do not go according to plan, reflect on why this is the case and use this in your analysis and for future research.
	- Sometimes research is boring – do not worry!

Fundamental ethical questions	
Balancing risks and rewards	What are the risks involved in research, beyond direct safety issues?
	- Is there a risk of re-traumatization and how can this be avoided (for example, don't interview direct victims; don't ask about traumatic experiences)?
	- Is there a risk of research fatigue because of prior long-term or repeated research participation?
	- How can expectations be managed realistically?
	How can research also do something good?
	- Can I use methods that are more engaging or bring the participants something positive?
Power relations	How are the power relations in my project?
	- When do I have power over the participants because of my background, funding and so on?
	- When do the participants have power over me, because of knowledge, willingness to share information and so on?
	- How does my background influence the way I conduct research and analyse the data? Do I recognize this sufficiently?
	- How can I avoid 'speaking for' the participants?
Giving back	How can I give something back to the participants?
	- How can I share my research results in a meaningful way (for example, summaries, translation)?
	- What do the participants expect/desire (research reports, blogs, creative outputs, assistance with lobbying activities)?
	- Can I compensate my participants in material or non-material ways?

Ethics after research	
Writing up	Outlets to write up research
	- Is an academic piece of work the best way to reach a diverse audience/the audience I want to target?
	- What alternative outlets exist (blogs and op-eds, policy papers, news articles)?
	- What do participants and stakeholders prefer?
	Language issues to be mindful of
	- Are the terms I use translatable? How can I make sure they do not lose their original meaning?
	- Do the language and terms I use reproduce stereotypes or inequalities? How can I avoid this?
Relationships after research	How to maintain engagement with the participants
	- Is a return field trip possible, to present, discuss and validate my findings?
	- Is it possible to maintain contact via email/WhatsApp/social media?

its different thematic areas, starting with the practical ethical issues which emerge in research, continuing with more fundamental, underlying ethical questions that researchers deal with, to conclude with ethical challenges which might arise when research is finished.

Practical ethics

How to study a conflict, especially as a foreigner

Studying post-conflict transitions is an interesting experience, but it can also bring many dilemmas. Personally, I have often struggled with why and how to do it. Although there is no doubt that such research is important for policy makers and fellow academics, it may require considerable time and energy from the participants, and sometimes also take an emotional toll on them, whereas its direct benefits may be less clear. I have often wondered whether it is worth doing it at all, especially for PhD or postdoc projects, which tend to have a limited budget and are therefore not able to produce the political or material impacts that larger, more generously funded research projects can achieve. A further dilemma for me was whether it was ethically sound to study a conflict as an outsider. I often felt uncomfortable to research and write about countries that are not my own, and even more so with being described as an 'expert' on Colombia, while there are excellent Colombian researchers who are much more knowledgeable. Those considered 'experts' on conflict are often not actually from the countries and conflicts they write about (Robins and Wilson 2015; Jones 2020). Using participatory and visual research methods helped me to navigate this tension, as I have described throughout this book and will get back to further on in this appendix. Furthermore, I believe that since transitional justice (TJ) and human rights are essentially Western paradigms, there is also a responsibility for Western researchers to critically analyse the political and economic structures of which we are part, and which underpin and maintain global inequalities.

Being an outsider to a country and conflict can also have advantages, for example, the possibility to touch more easily on sensitive issues that might be more delicate to write about by researchers within the country. For instance, in my research with female ex-combatants in Guatemala, I was able to write about the violence that these women experienced from their peers (Weber 2021b), an issue that was considered taboo and which had hardly been discussed publicly. For participants, it can make a difference to know that somebody from far away shows a genuine interest in their situation and experiences. *Genuine* is, however, crucial here, and a real connection to participants generally means that more is needed than a one-off interview. Also, foreign interest tends to be appreciated because of the assumption that it will lead to international attention for participants' situation. This can be problematic, since the direct impact of academic research, or, even more, impact-oriented papers, policy briefs or op-eds, is limited. Explaining this and preventing unrealistic expectations is essential.

This then leads to the question of which conflict or post-conflict situation to study. Having lived and worked in Guatemala for years, this country seemed a logical choice for me. Nevertheless, I felt ready for a change of scenery, preferably outside of Latin America. Yet when I considered this in more practical terms, I quickly realized that language would be a problem. Since I was interested in learning about the experiences of grassroots communities, in most cases, I could not get by with English. Although, of course, it is not impossible to learn a new language, within the short timeframe that UK doctoral funding provides, I was unlikely to acquire good enough skills to have in-depth conversations with people in their own language. I also did not want to work with interpreters, which would have been unpractical with an ethnographic approach which meant I lived in people's communities and houses for long periods of time. So I eventually settled on Colombia, a country which presented an excellent case study location of its recently approved Victims' Law, where I spoke the language and had a basic grasp of the regional cultural context.

Where to do research within Colombia then? Certain communities and regions of Colombia had received many researchers already. So had Bogotá, with its many non-governmental organizations (NGOs) and women's organizations. I feared these locations might have been over-researched (Clark 2008) – more information about this phenomenon will follow. But never having been in a country before makes it hard to know what locations would be best. I was lucky to have the possibility to visit Colombia for an international workshop six months into my doctoral research. I set up a number of meetings with human rights and women's organizations to discuss whether they saw the value and benefit of my research, and to scope whether they worked with communities I might be able to work with. One of these organizations, the Corporación Jurídica Yira Castro (CJYC), a lawyers' organization which accompanied land restitution processes, was indeed interested and suggested two communities in Chibolo where they worked as potential research locations. During the next few months, they confirmed that these communities were indeed interested. In return, I offered to share information with CJYC and write reports or blogs about my research, depending on their interest.

Another six months after my first visit to Colombia, I started my longer-term fieldwork and made my first visit to the communities together with a CJYC employee, in order for her to introduce me, and for me to understand how to actually reach the communities, as this required me to take a bus, a local collective taxi and then one or two motor taxis. The connection with the NGO was crucial to gain access, since unlike the FARC with whom I worked in the following research project, these communities had no public communication channels, and were not easily located on social media. Yet after the introduction through CJYC, I made clear to the communities that I was working independently, and stayed in the communities by myself. Maintaining independence and neutrality is important to avoid becoming part of structures of power that one might not be aware of, which might influence the research process (Hennings 2018). The crucial lesson learned during this experience was the importance of undertaking a pilot field trip before starting long-term fieldwork. I made a similar pilot visit during my next research project, and both trips helped me to set up the conditions for my research and reduce my anxiety about the research considerably. Finding ways to make such a pilot visit, either by budgeting for it, or by looking for conferences or workshops close by that funding can be sought for, is therefore something to consider.

Procedural ethics

Procedural ethics is what Guillemin and Gillam (2004) describe as the ethical issues that are dealt with by university ethics boards. These include things like confidentiality, privacy, anonymity and consent, as well as measures to protect the safety of participants and researchers. These are important issues, but they are by no means the only ones that a thorough ethical assessment should deal with – this is where the more structural, underlying ethical considerations come in. Within procedural ethics, aspects related to confidentiality and privacy are most straightforward. It goes without saying that research data and information about participants should not be shared, that they should be stored safely on a protected server or, if needed, temporarily on an encrypted storage device, and that participants should feel that their information is safe with the researcher. If preferred by participants, a decision can be made not to audio record interviews – an offer that in itself can help to generate trust (Hennings 2018; Irgil et al 2021).

The only real challenge I found here is the expected norm of undertaking interviews in private locations to maintain confidentiality. This was hard in my research locations, where people live in basic conditions, in very small houses. The hot climate means that family and community life mostly takes place in open spaces, whereas the collective culture blurs the public–private distinction even further. I visited people in their houses to undertake interviews. In Chibolo, we generally ended up sitting outside since it was simply too hot inside during the day. This meant that family or community members often passed by for a chat, while interviews would sometimes be interrupted by visitors who women needed to attend to. In terms of the group work, similar challenges existed, as the community meeting areas were open, with just a roof but no walls, or simply took place under a tree. This allowed passers-by – usually male community members – to come and listen, sometimes also giving their opinions about certain issues. The women did not seem to mind, and apart from making clear that the women would take the decisions since this was their space, I felt I had to respect the norms of the collectively oriented culture. Although respecting local spatial geography and cultural norms might fail to comply with the academic prerequisite of providing neutral spaces which guarantee complete confidentiality, it enables the building of trust (Bueno-Hansen 2015). In the territorial space for training and reincorporation (ETCR) in Pondores, I usually managed to interview people inside their houses, but also here, neighbours walked in and out. People here, however, seemed more keen to hold the interviews privately, perhaps because reincorporation was a sensitive issue due to the stigma and safety concerns involved. I therefore sometimes had to interrupt or postpone interviews.

Consent is already a little bit more complicated. Ideally, university ethics boards and journal editors like to see written consent forms in which participants sign to indicate their willingness to participate in the research, with the condition of being able to opt out at any point. Yet there are situations in which written consent can be complicated, for example, with participants who might not read or write well, but also for people for whom signing documents might be a delicate issue, for example, in contexts of displacement like Colombia. I therefore opted for a verbal consent script for my interviews with community participants. Consent was audio recorded after first having explained the participant information sheet, and leaving it with them so that they had my contact details, and could go over the form in their own time or assisted by others.

The most complicated aspect of procedural ethics is, however, anonymity. Anonymity is meant to protect the participants from harm that may arise when their situation becomes publicly known. Nevertheless, it is questionable whether anonymity is actually always in the participants' interest, as there might be valid reasons for them to want their stories to become public. They might hope that publicity generates attention for their cause, which can in turn lead to policy changes or material support. Strict anonymity can thus limit the direct political impact of research and reduce the possibilities for change and actions resulting from it (Ponic and Jategaonkar 2012). It can be perceived as patronizing when in contrast to the participants' explicit desire, their names or the names of their communities or organizations are anonymized. Other authors (Brent 1997; Wood 2006) have also argued that using pseudonyms, though meant to protect participants, can in fact fail to take the participants and their political goals and agency seriously. Anonymization assumes that outside, academic actors are better able to assess and protect participants from harm than they themselves, positioning them as *other* (Ponic and Jategaonkar 2012) and thus undermining the goal of more equal relationships that guided my research. Of course, there is a difference between making public the names of research locations and those of individual participants. In my case, I decided to use the original names of the communities where I undertook research. In Chibolo, I discussed this with community members in focus groups and with some of the community leaders. The participants saw my research as a way of getting their experiences and needs across to a wider audience. In fact, the stories and names of these communities had already been the subject of various reports in printed and online magazines in Colombia. Participants in Pondores also had a keen interest to get their story known publicly, and any help to support their active local communication team was much appreciated. Also here, the ETCR had featured in many news and media reports, whereas the local cooperative had an active social media account, making complete anonymity hard to guarantee in practice. I did, however, use pseudonyms for individual participants, in the hope of preventing community tensions in case confidential opinions given about others became publicly known. In any case, it is important to discuss these issues with the participants themselves, as they are best placed to calculate the risks involved in breaking anonymity (Thomas, Weber and Bradbury-Jones 2020).

Visual ethics

There are additional issues to bear in mind when undertaking visual research. Images and other visual data have obvious risks for anonymity. As I described in Chapter 1, many of the women in Chibolo took the opportunity of having access to a camera to take pictures of their family members, in spite of my requests to the contrary. Many of them also took the task of creating images of their lives quite literally, taking photographs of themselves undertaking their daily chores. There are different ways to go about this. One of them is to spend more time on training processes to make sure participants do not take images of identifiable places or persons, for example, through the use of 'metaphoric' rather than literal images (Ponic and Jategaonkar 2012). This, however, would also have reduced the attraction of the method for the participants, and would have required a longer training process, which I did not consider feasible given the availability and concentration span of the participants. Other researchers have opted for turning photographs into manually or digitally made illustrations, using an artist or software (Vastapuu 2018). I did not have access to the software or budget needed for this. Yet another option is to blur parts of the images to make sure they are no longer identifiable. I did not want to do this either, as I felt it would damage the quality of the pictures and objectify the people on them (Wiles et al 2008). I therefore opted for leaving the pictures as they were in the booklets printed for the women, whereas I removed specific images from my doctoral thesis. For other publications, I only used those images that did not contain identifiable persons, or cropped them, as I did to some images in this book. Furthermore, even though I had recorded verbal consent for the interviews, all photovoice participants signed specific copyright forms in which they decided whether or not to share the copyright over their images and for which purposes. Without this, it is not possible to use images created by others.

There are also other ethical issues related to the visual, including the possibility of images being taken of criminal or illegal acts – fortunately not the case in my research – or to reproduce certain harmful stereotypes. In Chibolo, this was true to some extent, since although some of the images, for example, those included in Chapter 2, showed agency, others presented an image of vulnerability. This was most clearly expressed in a video that two women made of their neighbour and his house, which showed a situation of extreme poverty. They had asked permission to film and the people on the video wanted it to be showed to the president. Yet when we were watching the video in the group, one of the women seemed to realize that the video showed an image of poverty and helplessness, which she seemed uncomfortable with. Photographs or films showing people in a powerless position can reduce people to this powerlessness, or reconfirm stereotypes, for example, of women as vulnerable (Sontag 2003; Lykes and Scheib 2017). This can cause embarrassment and reinforce the feeling of vulnerability and marginalization that people often express (Butler-Kisber 2010; Mitchell 2011). It, moreover, risks pathologizing communities, making them become defined by their being broken and oppressed (Tuck 2009).

For my next research project, I had therefore decided to place a greater emphasis on people's hopes and ideals for the future, hoping to prevent images of vulnerability (Robbins 2013). Nevertheless, as explained in Chapter 1, the FARC participants were less keen on the photovoice process, and in fact many people were reluctant to appear on images and film at all. They were afraid of stigmatization, for being recognized as ex-combatants. They were especially cautious when talking about the negative aspects of the reincorporation process, and did not want such images to be shared inside the country. Therefore, for the video we made, we often audio recorded participants' voices while filming their hands or surroundings, to prevent participants from being identifiable. We made many shots of the surroundings – plants, farm animals and pets – to use as background for people's stories. Furthermore, participants did not speak of any issues they considered particularly sensitive. Some women who initially agreed to be filmed later decided only their voice could be used. Eventually, the video was turned into a podcast, circumventing issues of visual ethics altogether. In addition, I decided to make a short, animated video about my main research results, consulting the short script with the participants. In this way, nobody's identity would become public, while the overarching message of the research could be shared visually with a wider, non-academic audience. Many of the issues to think about in terms of ethics and consent are included in the Statement of Ethical Practice of the Visual Sociology Study Group of the British Sociological Association (2006). For particularly risky research projects, for example, with participants who suffered violence and might be at risk of repercussions, it may be wise to invest time in developing a more rigorous ethics and safety protocol (see Ponic and Jategaonkar 2012), to prevent improvising on the spot. Being flexible and creative, and respecting the opinions of the research participants, should be a principal concern throughout the entire process, whether it is visual or not.

Safety

In post-conflict situations, which may still be politically unstable or where political violence has turned into criminal violence, safety is crucial, both for the participants and the researcher. In my research, safety concerns were most apparent in Pondores. This was unsurprising, since many ex-combatants had been killed by the time my research took place, and their number would only grow. It was therefore crucial to respect participants' decisions surrounding anonymity and the shape which my research would take. I did not, however, consider that my presence or my research increased risks to their safety, as other researchers have described (see, for example, Williams 2018b; Krause 2021). This is an essential question to ask at a regular basis, because research that produces risks for participants, for example, by attracting attention through the presence of a White researcher, or by identifying individuals as perpetrators or survivors of violence, might fail to achieve a balance between risk and reward for participants.

Although I did not feel that participants ran increased risks in Chibolo or Pondores, I did feel I was sometimes exposing myself to risks – not because the context was violent, but because I was working as a lone female researcher in isolated communities who was clearly not local. I sometimes worried whether it was safe to hop on the back of motor taxis whose drivers I did not know. I was aware that this was probably not something the university ethics and safety board would approve of, especially since I had promised to use trusted public transportation, which did not, however, exist. I believed that the alternative of renting a car would make me stand out even more, and could become risky on dirt roads in the rainy season. I therefore opted for the least bad option, in my opinion, and put some basic safety measures in place, like sending messages to research participants, family or friends, to notify them when I would leave and arrive in the fieldwork communities. Also, I asked the participants for their opinions about my safety and whether they knew trusted people who could take me. Local networks are thus crucial for safety in insecure contexts (Malejacq and Mukhopadhyay 2016).

It is, however, also important to maintain a critical view of how safety risks are considered by university safety and ethics committees. When a research project takes place in a post-conflict country, it is almost immediately considered 'high risk'. Parts of those countries – like the Caribbean region in Colombia where I worked – might in fact be quite safe, whereas in parts of Europe and even England, it can be much less safe to undertake research. While I was undertaking research in Chibolo, terrorist attacks took place in Paris and Brussels, taking the lives of dozens of people, while I felt quite safe in the isolated communities. Safety is thus time- and context-specific, and it can change during a research project. It should therefore be assessed on a regular basis, considering the advice of local participants, since they are often best placed to judge safety risks.

I described some of the gendered elements of this, especially in relation to the strong *machismo* in the *Costa*, in Chapter 2. I remember one particularly uncomfortable incident, when I was spied upon when I was washing myself behind a shed – in the absence of a bathroom – by a male family member of the household I was staying with. Even though I caught the spy in the act, he was still bold enough to ask my number when he, as the only one with a motorcycle, was told to bring me to another part of the village. Fortunately, nothing happened. Also, other female researchers have written about unwanted (sexual) attention or even harassment (see, for example, Gifford and Hall-Clifford 2008; Kloß 2017), although this topic is not regularly addressed. Some women decide to make up stories about non-existing husbands, or wear rings to suggest engagement or marriage (Ross 2015). I think these are perfectly valid strategies, and to strangers, I sometimes used them. But I felt that with my research participants, whom I was expecting to tell me about their experiences, I had to be open and honest. To deal with the sometimes uncomfortable situations with men this produced, I maintained constant WhatsApp communication with friends and family in Europe, as far as possible with the bad internet signal, to talk about my challenges and put them in perspective. I also often shared these uncomfortable experiences with female research participants. They, of course, recognized these *machista* attitudes, and sometimes helped me with them. For example, when I attended the annual celebration in one of the communities in Chibolo and was constantly asked to dance or hugged by drunken men, the other women would invite me to sit or dance with them to protect me from unwanted attention. I felt strong female solidarity.

In general, these anecdotes show the importance of putting in place measures of self-care in research. It is not always recognized how emotionally demanding and physically exhausting fieldwork can be, and it is easy to work continuously to try to make the most of your fieldwork period, as travelling back home can mean – but does not need to be – the end of data collection. But to be able to do good research, it is important to be rested and healthy, and therefore breaks and down time are very important. Even though my research was in a remote area of Colombia, every other week or so, I spent some days in a city a few hours away. I had met some people there with whom I could meet for drinks and dinner, and discussions that had nothing to do with TJ or human rights. I also occasionally travelled to Bogotá, for interviews but also to be with friends there, and have a break from the heat. I sometimes felt like losing research time because of those breaks, and I often saw myself inventing excuses for such trips because the participants did not understand why I needed to leave. They instead suggested I should come to Chibolo for a relaxing holiday in the future. Nevertheless, as others have also pointed out (Kloß 2017; Irgil et al 2021), breaks are important to maintain the energy needed to do the research and also to have a critical distance which is needed to know how to respond to unforeseen (gendered) incidents.

What if things go wrong?

Sometimes it can feel like everything goes wrong in research. This is usually not the case – and even if it did, this then provides data in itself, making it an important part of research. More often than not, research simply goes differently than planned. With ethnographic research, it might take a long time before enough rapport is created to start making meaningful connections, making the initial period of research feel like wasted time in which not much happens. This is far from the truth – also early, more superficial conversations can provide important data about the everyday life in your fieldwork location. It is also common for interview requests to stakeholders, like government employees, to take a long time and repeated emails to be responded to. They are often busy people, and academic research is generally not their priority. Sometimes, being in the country, or using other means of communication – for example, WhatsApp instead of email – can help. In general, it is good to realize that field research is not always the exciting event that we prepared for. It often consists of waiting for things to happen, people wanting to talk to you or, in my case, even simply waiting for the rain to stop so that travelling from one village to the next becomes possible. These mundane experiences of waiting and sometimes boredom are a normal part of research and nothing to worry about. In addition to writing field notes, it can be helpful to keep a research diary in which you record these experiences and feelings (Punch 2012; Browne 2019). In this way, you can later assess whether they affected the way you conducted the research or interpreted the data, or whether your feelings can provide meaningful insights about the research location and participants.

At other times, methods do not work as planned. I had, for example, planned to administer surveys with ex-combatants and community members in Pondores, but abandoned this idea after a first field trip in which I discovered strong research fatigue and reluctance to participate in interviews or surveys. As I explained in Chapter 1, the participants in Pondores were not interested in my planned participatory visual methods either. This made me feel quite stressed, as I did not want to limit myself to ethnographic research. With time, however, I found other ways of adding visual methods to my research. This shows the importance of flexibility in research. It is crucial to be prepared for research not going entirely according to plan, and be able to devise alternative approaches which allow you to collect the data you need while doing justice to the needs of the participants. The COVID-19 pandemic is, of course, one of the best examples of how a global event can change everything from one day to the next, and how we sometimes have to rethink the possibility or need for physical research altogether, forcing us to be creative and find other ways. One option might be to offer a broader toolbox of methods, including digital ones, to participants. In my own case, instead of returning to Colombia one year after fieldwork in Pondores as planned, I exchanged and consulted research results through a short written report. Being unable to travel freed up budget for producing animated video. Other researchers too have made the case for reassessing fieldwork-based research, and to consider remote, virtual fieldwork, especially in light of the pandemic (Irgil et al 2021; Rudling 2021). I completely support this, especially from a climate perspective, although it should be recognized that doing research on sensitive topics like violence and traumatic experiences requires a level of trust which might be more challenging to establish through digital methods.

Fundamental ethical considerations

Balancing risks and rewards in research

Although addressing concrete issues like anonymity and confidentiality are, of course, essential, they are not in themselves sufficient for guaranteeing ethical research practice. There are many moments in which ethical considerations come into play which are not addressed in the formal ethics review process. Guillemin and Gillam (2004) call these 'ethically important moments'. For me, one of the most significant and also complex questions is how I can make my research meaningful and beneficial for the participants. Of course, academic research in itself is meaningful, as it can uncover unknown experiences and insights that can help to evaluate and influence policies. Nevertheless, such change processes are very slow and unlikely to directly benefit the people who participate in research. In the meantime, people who are affected by conflict are often in difficult situations, either emotionally, physically or economically, meaning that research is an investment for them in terms of time and energy that they might not be willing to make if it is unclear what is in it for them.

As I described briefly in Chapter 1, research can cause re-traumatization to people affected by conflict and violence, if it makes them remember or relive painful experiences of the past (Sharp 2014; Robins and Wilson 2015). It can also cause safety concerns for them, as explained already. Different authors have reflected on the risks of researching sensitive topics such as conflict violence (see, for example, Lee and Renzetti 1993). They have suggested ways to prevent these, including basing one's work on existing data and testimonies instead of conducting new interviews, focusing on narratives around sensitive issues instead of directly engaging the individuals affected or speaking to civil society stakeholders instead (Boesten 2014; Boesten and Henry 2018; Sanchez Parra 2018; Irgil et al 2021). I have circumvented this problem by not asking participants about their conflict experiences but focusing instead on their current lives and their needs for a better future. As other researchers have also experienced (Walsh 2019), this did not mean that people did not talk about their conflict experiences, since once rapport has been established participants are often glad to find a genuinely interested listener. Nevertheless, it was then their own decision to talk about these experiences.

Although these are excellent strategies to 'do no harm', which is the main goal of procedural ethics (MacKenzie, McDowell and Pittaway 2007), they are not necessarily sufficient. Since even if research avoids re-traumatization, it can still do damage, for example, if participants invest considerable time in research while seeing few tangible effects. This can cause research fatigue, or a feeling of frustration and powerlessness, which can be compounded by a feeling of exploitation when it is clear that the researcher's situation is improved through the research – for example, by completing their PhD or getting a promotion – while the participants remain in the same difficult situation (Clark 2008; Boesten and Henry 2018; Mwambari 2019). This shows that research on social justice topics is not free of power imbalances.

Power in research

Even in feminist approaches to research, which are concerned with reducing power imbalances, there is no denying that power differentials exist. For example, it is generally the researcher who decides where to undertake research, which questions to ask and how to write them up (Wolf 1996; Krystalli 2019). Participants tend to have little control over the research process. This creates a risk of the researchers 'speaking for' the research participants, since differences in ethnic, economic, class and educational background may create an unequal power relationship (Nagy Hesse-Biber 2012). It is needless to say that such inequality is even stronger when researchers come from a country in the so-called Global North and the participants from the Global South, or from more marginalized groups within the researcher's own country. Black and postcolonial feminisms have been crucial in pointing out how feminism itself has often ignored 'other' female voices (hooks 1990; Letherby 2003; Mohanty 2003; Lorde 2007), and how White feminists have taken on neo-colonial roles in 'speaking for' marginalized or 'Third World' participants (Tuhiwai Smith 2012; Tuck and Guishard 2013). Such practices can lead to 'epistemological violence' (Teo 2010), when research reinforces interpretations of inferiority of the 'Other' that can have negative impacts, or 'violence of voicelessness' when participants' voices are appropriated by researchers (Castillejo Cuéllar 2005). This shows that knowledge is power (Gaventa and Cornwall 2008), and means we need to be careful not only with how we undertake research but also with how we write about it. An ongoing practice of reflexivity is therefore crucial, to analyse how our own positionality, as well as our emotions, biases and values, affect the research, and vice versa (Collins 1991; Thornton Dill and Kohlman 2012). Keeping a research diary can be a good tool to reflect on this. In my case, for example, being a woman in a *machista* environment sometimes made me feel vulnerable and powerless, while having the privilege of a White, Western background and education made me aware of my enormously privileged position. I therefore tried to be patient with the frequent questions about the price of travelling to Europe or of my belongings, as well as other sometimes intrusive questions. In the end, studying a post-conflict transition in a country that was not mine, the very least I could do was to be open and transparent about my own life, in an effort to at least somewhat reduce the power inequalities (Castillejo Cuéllar 2005; Nagy Hesse-Biber and Piatelli 2012).

At the same time, it is important to recognize that research participants at times can be in a more powerful position than we are as researchers. For one, they have knowledge that we do not have, and only they decide whether and when they will share it with us. They can exercise agency over researchers as well by sharing contacts, protecting our safety and well-being in a context that they know far better than we do, or in sexualized and gendered ways, especially from male participants towards female researchers (McKenna and Main 2013; Kloß 2017; Schulz 2020). I experienced this, for example, with community leader Josefa, in whose house I often stayed in Chibolo. Although she invested considerable time in showing me her community, she was reluctant to let me explore or visit people by myself, saying I would get lost or something might happen to me. In this way, she tried to manage who I would talk to. Avoiding this control was tricky, because I did not want to antagonize her since she was an important gatekeeper who gave me access to others. Eventually, I managed to stay at other people's houses more often, using Josefa's own argument of the logistical difficulties and safety risks of crossing the village by myself. This example shows that power relations exist between the researcher and the participants, and among participants. By working more closely with certain participants, a researcher can unintentionally reinforce power dynamics, even when using more participatory approaches to research (Turner 1992). It is important to be mindful of such dynamics, and try to balance contacts with different (groups of) participants.

I also sometimes struggled to adapt from my previous position as an international NGO worker to my new position as an academic researcher. During my first fieldwork period, interviews I had arranged with state and civil society stakeholders were frequently cancelled at the last moment, if I was notified at all. The feeling of interviewees exerting power over me was uncomfortable (Krystalli 2021). It took me a while to realize that, in contrast to my previous position, when I was an interesting conversation partner because of the potential funding I brought, this time, there were few incentives for people to talk to me. I needed to be humble, but insistent, and occasionally change my schedule to adapt to my interviewees' agendas.

An issue that is also important to reflect on in conflict research, which can make researchers feel powerless at times (see, for example, Robben 1995; Fujii 2010), is whether we can actually believe what our participants tell us. Some participants might have good reasons not to share the complete truth. This is, for example, the case for perpetrators of violence, like ex-combatants, who might paint an 'excessively cosy view of the past' to prevent incriminating themselves (Broache 2019, 214). This applied to the FARC ex-combatants, who mostly presented themselves as victims of state repression and diminished or denied any involvement in drug trafficking or other crimes. One participant told me that if they had been drug dealers, surely they would not live in poverty but drive nice cars and have Rolex watches. Survivors of violence, in contrast, might regard the research as a way to obtain support, and therefore exaggerate the harshness of their conditions, or present themselves as 'ideal' rather than complex political victims, as I explained in relation to Juana in Chibolo (see Chapter 3). In yet other cases, memories of events which happened decades ago might have faded, and the pre-conflict past might be romanticized because the rupture produced by conflict was so traumatic. All of these things make it difficult to determine the veracity of memories of violence (Hale 1997). Nevertheless, in many cases, it might not necessarily be crucial to verify the exact, factual truth about the past. It is equally significant to understand how people experience the past in the present. The value of data, even if not entirely true, can thus lie in the meaning that the participants attach to their past experiences. Yet even though the exact truth is often not what matters most, it is still important not to take what participants tell you at face value. Trying to triangulate information through interviews with third parties or bibliographic data is a way of doing this.

Giving back

Because of the tricky power relations involved in research, it is important to make sure that research also does some good for the participants, either through practical or political support or on a personal level. As I described in Chapter 1, using participatory and creative research methods to give research participants more control over the content and outputs of the research can be a way to make sure the research not only entails risks but also offers rewards, by raising awareness and creating solidarity among the participants, and by producing tangible research outputs or paving the way for action based on the research.

Outside of participatory research approaches, the idea of 'giving something back' to the participants has also become accepted as a way to reciprocate the time and energy that participants invest in research. There is not one specific way to give back. For many researchers, giving back means to provide participants with copies of their work, for example, articles or theses, sometimes translated (Irgil et al 2021). This is an essential step, as participants in Pondores, for example, complained that most researchers never contacted them after interviewing them, leading to a reluctance to participate in research. How useful sharing academic papers is of course depends on the specific participants, their worldview, educational attainment and the languages they speak. Participants in Chibolo and Pondores were not interested in reading lengthy reports, much less written in academic jargon. In Chibolo, there was more interest in the photovoice booklets that I co-produced with the women, which went from hand to hand. Therefore, using visual research methods and also the simple fact of printing photographs, both those taken as part of the photovoice process and photos I had taken myself, were a good way of giving something back. Some of the images that the women took were used in the community memory reports that the National Centre for Historical Memory produced, thus also contributing to the reparation process. In Pondores, the video and audio-recorded interviews I conducted together with one of the participants remained theirs too, and participants turned them into a podcast. I also produced an animated video here, and, in both locations, I wrote short reports in Spanish to summarize my findings, which the participants could use as they pleased. They were in fact used by CJYC in Chibolo, which included my reports and photovoice booklets in their annual report, as I accidentally found out years later when participants showed me them.

A more sensitive question is whether it is permissible or not to compensate research participants financially or materially. Although this is relatively common in quantitative research, for example, through the handing out of vouchers, it is generally not considered good practice in qualitative research, as it is believed to diminish the objectivity of the data and risks creating dependency on researchers. But not offering anything in return for research participation can feel extractive. Finding out what is appropriate can be difficult, as some participants can be offended by being offered money (Cronin-Furman and Lake 2018; Irgil et al 2021). I always struggled with deciding how much and whom to pay when I stayed at participants' houses. In the communities in Chibolo, with their extremely hospitable culture, it was common practice and even experienced like an honour to host visitors, especially foreigners. I therefore generally brought little gifts if I stayed only one night. For longer stays, I had asked around for a decent price, and generally just left that amount somewhere in the house, only notifying my host about that afterwards, as I knew they would decline if I offered it to them in person. In Pondores, managing payment was easier and we agreed on a price early on with the household where I stayed. Over there, I, moreover, decided to compensate Rebeca, with whom I collaborated to make short videos. To not create jealousy, I also paid a small commission to the gender and tourism committees, whose members featured in the videos. In both Pondores and Chibolo, I donated the cameras that were used for the research, so that the participants could continue to document their experiences after I left.

There are, of course, also non-financial ways of giving back. Many researchers have given English classes or other courses and trainings, especially during longer-term fieldwork. In Chibolo, this was hard because of people's busy schedule. I did, however, support the women's groups here setting up a proper committee with board members. In Pondores, a few weeks into my fieldwork, most people re-initiated their studies as part of the catch-up education programme, after which I was frequently sought to help out with homework and English lessons. I also helped writing news items for the ETCR's Facebook site. It is, however, also important to be critical about some of these well-intended attempts to do something in return. For example, I helped to write a funding proposal for the tourism committee. Although I was quite pleased to have contributed something that the committee was actually needing support with, I was made aware by an Agency for Reincorporation and Normalization (ARN) employee that in fact I had not really helped. I had written the proposal *for* them based on discussions we had, instead of teaching them to write their own proposals. In this way, sometimes we can end up reproducing practices that we criticize in our research. Being mindful and reflective of such experiences helps to prevent them in the future.

Ethics when the field research is finished

While most attention is commonly placed on the ethical considerations of data collection, there are still ethical issues to be aware of when this phase of the research is over. These have to do with how to engage with the participants once fieldwork is over, and with how to write up and publish the findings. Furthermore, it is important to be aware that, although fieldwork might feel like the phase of research that most impacts your life as a researcher, simply because it marks such a stark break from normal life, its impact does not necessarily end when it is over. Some researchers have experienced periods of depression or secondary traumatization when analysing their data safely back home or when being asked about fieldwork and expected to share exciting and exotic stories (Theidon 2014; Irgil et al 2021). Personally, I have found it hard to share what fieldwork was really like with people at home, who had little notion of what living in remote, not always safe conditions was like, and who were often little interested in the nitty-gritty of my research. I also felt frustrated with the political context back in Europe, where Brexit and 'migration crises' were the order of the day; concerns I could not muster sympathy for after having experienced the extreme poverty and yet humour and hospitality of participants in Colombia. It is important to find ways to recognize how research affects the researcher, while re-adapting to your new (old) conditions without too much cynicism. Seeking professional support can help, even just to talk through these changes and feelings, as can the creation of informal support and friendship networks with researchers with similar experiences.

Writing up the research

When writing up the research results, I have frequently struggled to find the right language to describe experiences. First of all, being a Dutch researcher, working in a British university and undertaking research in Colombia has forced me to navigate three languages, which was not always an easy task. Sometimes, I was lost for words in all three languages, whereas some culturally specific terms are challenging to translate accurately. An example is the term 'aha', a constantly used utterance among the community participants, especially in Chibolo. 'Aha' can be used to signify a sense of resignation for not controlling the outcome of events, while it can also denote indignation. Where possible, I do not translate such terms to stay as true as possible to their original meaning, also in an effort to respect participants' own mode of expression as much as possible. This might, however, be more difficult for other languages.

Other issues I struggled with are particular terms which are commonly used in peace and conflict research or gender studies. The term 'empowerment', for example, not only implies the intention to include people and give them opportunities in a context characterized by oppression and economic inequality (McEwan 2005) but also seems to suggest that researchers or practitioners have the capacity to give power to powerless research participants as neo-colonial saviours. Moreover, it ignores how power is not something that can be acquired or shared, but exists in multiple ways in all relations (Foucault 1990). I have therefore tried to use other terms which have similar meanings but have less unequal connotations, such as emancipation. I am also uncomfortable with describing my participants as 'vulnerable'. Like Butler (2006), I believe that it is our global system, characterized by economic, political and gendered – among other – power inequalities, which actively excludes or marginalizes groups of people, placing them at greater risk of vulnerability. I therefore prefer to speak of 'exclusion' or 'marginalization', in order to emphasize the process and system that produces inequality. As described in the Introduction, I had similar reflections on whether to use the term victim or survivor, and opted to speak about participants instead of informants, whereas others have pointed out the unequal power relations implied in the term beneficiaries or recipients of aid and support (Autesserre 2014). These examples show how language can unintentionally reproduce power dynamics or stereotypes. Although it can make writing a complicated process, and I am sure there are still many questionable expressions in my own writing, it is important to critically reflect upon them.

When writing up the research, it is also important to consider which audiences we write for, and how we can address diverse audiences. Although there is often an expected academic output at the end of a research project, either a PhD thesis, monograph or academic articles, these are not always meaningful or impactful for the participants. Personally, I have sometimes found it demotivating to spend weeks working on academic articles that are unlikely to reach a massive audience. We should therefore think in advance about ways to make research as accessible as possible to other audiences. Asking the participants in what other ways our research can help them is a first step. Blog posts are an easy way to turn academic research into something more accessible to non-academic audiences or those without an in-depth understanding about the particular academic theories. Blogs are easier to translate into other languages than academic articles, and could potentially be written together with participants, making the publication process more equal. Policy briefs are another potential outlet. Universities often have policy or communication teams that can help draft and disseminate these. Other options, like animated videos, cartoons or other creative 'translations' of research, might require additional budget, but this can sometimes be obtained through universities, or from international development cooperation. All of this requires time, so it is best to start exploring potential funding avenues early on.

A final consideration is whether what we publish can have negative impacts on 'the field', for example, by providing information that can have political effects (Knott 2019). In case of doubt, it is best to consult the participants or other stakeholders who can judge the political or safety implications of publishing certain information. In this way, ethical procedures become a long-term, iterative and collaborative process (Kostovicova and Knott 2020).

Engaging with participants after research

It can be challenging to know how to relate to research participants once fieldwork or a research project is finished. As a ground rule, I believe it is important to maintain contact, especially during the first period after fieldwork is over, in order to clarify potential issues in the data, and to be able to find ways, either physically or digitally, to share initial analyses to validate and complement the research results. Ideally, this entails a return trip to present the results and discuss them, especially as sharing reports and receiving written feedback might be hard with participants who are not used to reading research reports. I travelled back a year after my first long fieldwork period in Chibolo with a short, colourful printed leaflet which combined the key insights of my research with images. Although some participants were disappointed that this was all I was bringing instead of material support, others said that they agreed with the statements in the leaflet, and we had a community discussion about it. As described in Chapter 1, giving back my research results to the FARC ex-combatants was more complicated due to the COVID-19 pandemic, although I have tried to do this via digital means. In general, it can be challenging to present research findings, especially if you fear that some of them might not be well received by the participants, for example, when they contain criticism. I worried about that in relation to the FARC, and also to some extent in Chibolo, as I was clearly discussing gender inequality in the communities. I tried to frame my criticisms in a constructive way, formulating them as obstacles to overcome to achieve a better situation. I did not receive any strong objections – except suggestions from some FARC ex-combatants who countered my criticism of the lack of gender equality in the FARC's top ranks. This shows that, albeit difficult, sharing research results is not only the most transparent and ethically correct thing to do but can also offer insights into the data analysis (Fruehling Springwood and King 2001).

In terms of longer-term engagement, my personal experience is that participants are often keen to maintain contact after a long period of fieldwork. Nowadays, many people have smartphones, making it easier to send WhatsApp messages or follow each other on social media. Although I initially tried to avoid it, once one participant had found my profile on Facebook, many of the people in Chibolo connected with me. I felt unable to decline their friendship requests, after they had shared their houses and experiences with me. Connecting in this way also offered me a means to stay up to date about general developments in the communities, reach out to the participants when I was planning to publish something I wanted to share or ask permission for and to announce further visits. This was even easier with the FARC, as they are savvy social media users. I also experienced maintaining contact as a positive experience myself, as it felt like a less drastic break from the field. Maintaining contact can also pave the way for longer-term research engagements, which can provide interesting insights into changing situations over several years. Unfortunately, as time went by without being able to visit Pondores and Chibolo because of the pandemic, and participants themselves being enmeshed in their daily struggles, contact has become less frequent. But the basis laid with intense fieldwork and online communication will hopefully prove robust enough to enable further visits, sharing experiences and *telenovela* watching when life gets back a bit more to the old normal.

References

Aguirre, Daniel, and Irene Pietropaoli. 2008. 'Gender Equality, Development and Transitional Justice: The Case of Nepal'. *International Journal of Transitional Justice* 2 (3): 356–77.

Albarracín, Juan, and Sarah Zukerman Daly. 2019. 'Determinants of State Strength and Capacity: Understanding Citizen Allegiance'. In *As War Ends: What Colombia Can Tell Us about the Sustainability of Peace and Transitional Justice*, edited by James Meernik, Jacqueline H.R. DeMeritt and Mauricio Uribe-López, 91–112. Cambridge: Cambridge University Press.

Alison, Miranda. 2004. 'Women as Agents of Political Violence: Gendering Security.' *Security Dialogue* 35 (4): 447–63.

Amnistía Internacional. 2014. *Un Título de Propiedad No Basta: Por Una Restitución Sostenible de Tierras En Colombia*. Madrid: Amnistía Internacional.

Anthias, Floya, and Nira Yuval-Davis. 1992. *Racialized Boundaries: Race, Nation, Gender, Colour and Class and the Anti-Racist Struggle*. London: Routledge.

Arias Ortíz, Gerson Iván, and Carlos Andrés Prieto Herrera. 2020. *Lecciones Del Fin Del Conflicto En Colombia: Dejación de Armas y Tránsito a La Legalidad de Las Farc*. Barcelona: Fondo de Capital Humano para la Transición Colombiana, Instituto para las Transiciones Integrales (IFIT).

Asociación Freytter Elkartea. 2021. Mujeres de La Región Caribe: Pilar de La Reincorporación y La Lucha Por La Paz En Colombia. www.youtube.com/watch?v=mju_xcHH-AU

Autesserre, Séverine. 2014. *Peaceland: Conflict Resolution and the Everyday Politics of International Intervention*. Cambridge: Cambridge University Press.

Avoine, Priscyll Anctil, and Rachel Tillman. 2015. 'Demobilized Women in Colombia: Embodiment, Performativity and Social Reconciliation'. In *Female Combatants in Conflict and Peace: Challenging Gender in Violence and Post-Conflict Reintegration*, edited by Seema Shekhawat, 216–31. Basingstoke: Palgrave Macmillan.

Baaz, Maria Eriksson, and Maria Stern. 2012. 'Fearless Fighters and Submissive Wives: Negotiating Identity among Women Soldiers in the Congo (DRC)'. *Armed Forces & Society* 39 (4): 711–39.

Baines, Erin. 2009. 'Complex Political Perpetrators: Reflections on Dominic Ongwen'. *Journal of Modern African Studies* 47 (2): 163–91.

Baines, Erin. 2015. '"Today, I Want to Speak Out the Truth": Victim Agency, Responsibility, and Transitional Justice'. *International Political Sociology* 9 (4): 316–32.

Baines, Erin. 2017. *Buried in the Heart: Women, Complex Victimhood and the War in Northern Uganda*. Cambridge: Cambridge University Press.

Baird, Adam. 2015. 'Duros and Gangland Girlfriends: Male Identity, Gang Socialization, and Rape in Medellín'. In *Violence at the Urban Margins*, edited by Javier Auyero, Philippe Bourgois and Nancy Scheper-Hughes, 112–32. New York: Oxford University Press.

Ball, Nicole, and Luc Van de Goor. 2006. *Disarmament, Demobilization and Reintegration: Mapping Issues, Dilemmas and Guiding Principles*. The Hague: Clingendael.

Bar-Tal, Daniel, Lily Chernyak-Hai, Noa Schori and Ayelet Gundar. 2009. 'A Sense of Self-Perceived Collective Victimhood in Intractable Conflicts'. *International Review of the Red Cross* 91 (874): 229–58.

Bareiro, Line. 1997. 'Construcción Femenina de Ciudadanía'. In *Ciudadanas. Una Memoria Inconstante*, edited by Line Bareiro and Clyde Soto, 1–15. Caracas: Nueva Sociedad.

Barker, Gary. 2005. *Dying to Be Men: Youth, Masculinity and Social Exclusion*. Abingdon: Routledge.

Barker, Gary. 2006. 'Men's Participation as Fathers in Latin America and the Caribbean: Critical Literature Review and Policy Options'. In *The Other Half of Gender: Men's Issues in Development*, edited by Ian Bannon and Maria C. Correia, 43–72. Washington: The World Bank.

Barrios Sabogal, Laura Camila, and Solveig Richter. 2019. 'Las Farianas: Reintegration of Former Female FARC Fighters as a Driver for Peace in Colombia'. *Cuadernos de Economía* 38 (78): 753–84.

Bernal, Victoria. 2001. 'From Warriors to Wives: Contradictions of Liberation and Development in Eritrea'. *Northeast African Studies* 8 (3): 129–54.

Bernath, Julie. 2016. '"Complex Political Victims" in the Aftermath of Mass Atrocity: Reflections on the Khmer Rouge Tribunal in Cambodia'. *International Journal of Transitional Justice* 10 (1): 46–66.

Berry, Marie E. 2018. *War, Women, and Power: From Violence to Mobilization in Rwanda and Bosnia-Herzegovina*. Cambridge: Cambridge University Press.

Björkdahl, Annika, and Johanna Mannergren Selimovic. 2015. 'Gendering Agency in Transitional Justice'. *Security Dialogue* 46 (2): 165–82.

Boesten, Jelke. 2010. 'Analyzing Rape Regimes at the Interface of War and Peace in Peru'. *International Journal of Transitional Justice* 4 (1): 110–29.

Boesten, Jelke. 2014. *Sexual Violence during War and Peace: Gender, Power, and Post-Conflict Justice in Peru*. New York: Palgrave Macmillan.

Boesten, Jelke, and Marsha Henry. 2018. 'Between Fatigue and Silence: The Challenges of Conducting Research on Sexual Violence in Conflict'. *Social Politics* 25 (4): 568–88.

Bop, Codou. 2001. 'Women in Conflicts, Their Gains and Their Losses'. In *The Aftermath: Women in Post-Conflict Transformation*, edited by Sheila Meintjes, Anu Pillay and Meredith Turshen, 19–34. London: Zed Books.

Borer, Tristan Anne. 2003. 'A Taxonomy of Victims and Perpetrators: Human Rights and Reconciliation in South Africa'. *Human Rights Quarterly* 25 (4): 1088–116.

Bouris, Erica. 2007. *Complex Political Victims*. Bloomfield: Kumarian Press.

Bowd, Richard, and Alpaslan Özerdem. 2013. 'How to Assess Social Reintegration of Ex-Combatants'. *Journal of Intervention and Statebuilding* 7 (4): 453–75.

Brandes, Stanley. 2003. 'Drink, Abstinence, and Male Identity in Mexico City'. In *Changing Men and Masculinities in Latin America*, edited by Mathew C. Gutmann, 153–76. Durham: Duke University Press.

Brent, Jeremy. 1997. 'Community without Unity'. In *Contested Communities: Experiences, Struggles, Policies*, edited by Paul Hoggett, 68–83. Bristol: Policy Press.

Broache, Michael. 2019. 'Abetting Atrocities? Reporting the Perspectives of Perpetrators in Research on Violence'. In *Experiences in Researching Conflict and Violence: Fieldwork Interrupted*, edited by Althea-Maria Rivas and Brendan Ciarán Browne, 205–20. Bristol: Policy Press.

Browne, Brendan Ciarán. 2019. 'Writing the Wrongs: Keeping Diaries and Reflective Practice'. In *Experiences in Researching Conflict and Violence: Fieldwork Interrupted*, edited by Althea-Maria Rivas and Brendan Ciarán Browne, 187–203. Bristol: Policy Press.

Brydon, Lynne. 1989. 'Gender, Households and Rural Communities'. In *Women in the Third World: Gender Issues in Rural and Urban Areas*, edited by Lynne Brydon and Sylvia Chant, 47–68. Aldershot: Edward Elgar Publishing.

Buchely, Lina. 2015. 'The Conflict of the Indicators: A Case Study on the Implementation of the Victims' and Land Restitution Law in Cali, Valle Del Cauca, Colombia'. *International Organizations Law Review* 12 (1): 19–49.

Buchely, Lina. 2018. 'The Affective State and Precarious Citizenship: Conflict, Historical Memory, and Forgiveness in Bojayá, Colombia'. *Contemporary Readings in Law and Social Justice* 10 (1): 7–34.

Buckley-Zistel, Susanne, and Magdalena Zolkos. 2012. 'Introduction: Gender in Transitional Justice'. In *Gender in Transitional Justice*, edited by Susanne Buckley-Zistel and Ruth Stanley, 1–33. Basingstoke: Palgrave Macmillan.

Bueno-Hansen, Pascha. 2015. *Feminist and Human Rights Struggles in Peru: Decolonizing Transitional Justice*. Urbana: University of Illinois Press.

Bueno-Hansen, Pascha. 2018. 'The Emerging LGBTI Rights Challenge to Transitional Justice in Latin America'. *International Journal of Transitional Justice* 12 (1): 126–45.

Bulmer, Sarah, and Maya Eichler. 2017. 'Unmaking Militarized Masculinity: Veterans and the Project of Military-to-Civilian Transition'. *Critical Military Studies* 3 (2): 161–81.

Burnyeat, Gwen, and Andrei Gómez-Suárez. 2022. 'Petro's First 100 Days: Peace Takes Priority'. Canning House Blog.

Butler, Judith. 2006. *Precarious Life: The Powers of Mourning and Violence*. London: Verso.

Butler-Kisber, Lynn. 2010. *Qualitative Inquiry: Thematic, Narrative and Arts-Informed Perspectives*. Los Angeles: Sage Publications.

Cairo, Heriberto, Ulrich Oslender, Carlo Emilio Piazzini Suárez, Jerónimo Ríos, Sara Koopman, Vladimir Montoya Arango, Flavio Bladimir Rodríguez Muñoz and Liliana Zambrano Quintero. 2018. '"Territorial Peace": The Emergence of a Concept in Colombia's Peace Negotiations'. *Geopolitics* 23 (2): 464–88.

Calderón, Valentina, Margarita Gafaro and Ana María Ibáñez. 2011. 'Forced Migration, Female Labor Force Participation, and Intra-Household Bargaining: Does Conflict Empower Women?' MicroCon Research Working Paper 56.

Callahan, William S. 2020. *Sensible Politics: Visualizing International Relations*. New York: Oxford University Press.

Cárdenas, Javier, and Nadia Stefania Pérez. 2019. 'Dilemas En La Implementación de Un Acuerdo de Paz: Power-Sharing En El Proceso de Reincorporación de Las FARC-EP'. In *Excombatientes y Acuerdo de Paz Con Las FARC-EP En Colombia: Balance de La Etapa Temprana*, edited by Erin McFee and Angelika Rettberg, 69–89. Bogotá: Ediciones Uniandes.

Cardoza, Sanchez, German Antonio, Claudia Marcela Castellanos Acosta, Sandra Gonzalez Sanabria, Jovita Castellanos Puertas, Eliecer Gerardo Morales Polanco and Jhenifer Mojica Florez. 2022. 'La Paz Será Con Las Mujeres Rurales o No Será: Vigencia Del Acuerdo de Paz, Políticas Públicas Prioritarias, Perspectivas de Implementación e Incidencia Desde Las Organizaciones de Mujeres Campesinas'. Oxfam and PRODETER. https://oi-files-cng-prod.s3.amazonaws.com/lac.oxfam.org/s3fs-public/Informe_La%20Paz%20ser%C3%A1%20con%20las%20muejres%20o%20no%20ser%C3%A1_2021.pdf

Carlin, Ryan E., Jennifer L. McCoy and Jelena Subotic. 2019. 'Leading the Public to Peace: Trust in Elites, the Legitimacy of Negotiated Peace, and Support for Transitional Justice.' In *As War Ends: What Colombia Can Tell Us about the Sustainability of Peace and Transitional Justice*, edited by James Meernik, Jacqueline H.R. DeMeritt and Mauricio Uribe-López, 283–304. Cambridge: Cambridge University Press.

Carranza-Franco, Francy. 2019. *Demobilisation and Reintegration in Colombia: Building State and Citizenship*. London: Routledge.

Carrillo González, Lorena. 2017. 'Cotidianidades Desarmadas, El Reto Invisible de Las Transiciones Territoriales: La Ventana Abierta de La Zonas Veredales Transitorias de Normalización En El Proceso de Paz Con Las FARC-EP'. *Agora U.S.B.* 17 (2): 462.

Castillejo Cuéllar, Alejandro. 2005. 'Unraveling Silence: Violence, Memory and the Limits of Anthropology's Craft'. *Dialectical Anthropology* 29 (2): 159–80.

Castrillón Palacio, Elisa. 2022. 'Los Avances de La Comisión de La Verdad En El Capítulo de Género'. La Silla Vacía.

Centro de Memoria Histórica. 2012. *Justicia y Paz: Tierras y Territorios En Las Versiones Libres de Los Paramilitares.* Bogotá: Centro de Memoria Histórica.

Centro Nacional de Memoria Histórica. 2014. *Guerrilla y Población Civil: Trayectoria de Las FARC 1949-2013.* Centro Nacional de Memoria Histórica. Bogotá: Centro Nacional de Memoria Histórica.

Centro Nacional de Memoria Histórica. 2017. *La Guerra Inscrita En El Cuerpo: Informe Nacional de Violencia Sexual En El Conflicto Armado.* Bogotá: Centro Nacional de Memoria Histórica.

Céspedes-Báez, Lina María. 2018. 'Creole Radical Feminist Transitional Justice: An Exploration of Colombian Feminism in the Context of Armed Conflict'. In *Truth, Justice and Reconciliation in Colombia: Transitioning from Violence*, edited by Fabio Andrés Díaz Pabón, 102–18. Abingdon: Routledge.

Céspedes-Báez, Lina María. 2019. 'A (Feminist) Farewell to Arms: The Impact of the Peace Process with the FARC-EP on Colombian Feminism'. *Cornell International Law Journal* 52 (1): 39–64.

Céspedes-Báez, Lina María. 2020. 'Problems and Inconsistencies in the Protection of Women in the Colombian Land Restitution Process'. In *Just Memories: Remembrance and Restoration in the Aftermath of Political Violece*, edited by Camila De Gamboa Tapias and Bert Van Roermund, 191–220. Cambridge: Intersentia.

Chant, Sylvia. 2003. 'Introduction: Gender in a Changing Continent'. In *Gender in Latin America*, edited by Sylvia Chant and Nikki Craske, 1–18. New Brunswick: Rutgers University Press.

Chaparro Moreno, Liliana. 2009. 'Ley de Justicia y Paz. Se Perpetúa La Impunidad de Los Crímenes Sexuales y de Género Cometidos Contra Las Mujeres'. In *¿Justicia Desigual? Género y Derechos de Las Víctimas En Colombia?*, edited by UNIFEM, 85–116. Bogotá. www.dejusticia.org/wp-content/uploads/2017/04/fi_name_recurso_177.pdf

Charlesworth, Hillary, and Christine Chinkin. 2000. *The Boundaries of International Law: A Feminist Analysis.* Manchester: Manchester University Press.

Cheng, Christine. 2018. *Extralegal Groups in Post-Conflict Liberia: How Trade Makes the State the State.* Oxford: Oxford University Press.

Chernick, Marc W. 2003. 'Colombia: Does Injustice Cause Violence?' In *What Justice? Whose Justice? Fighting for Fairness in Latin America*, edited by Susan Eva Eckstein and Timothy P. Wickham-Crowley, 185–214. Berkeley: Cambridge University Press.

Civico, Aldo. 2016. *The Para-State: An Ethnography of Colombia's Death Squad*. Oakland: University of California Press.

Clark, Janine Natalya. 2014. 'A Crime of Identity: Rape and Its Neglected Victims'. *Journal of Human Rights* 13 (2): 146–69.

Clark, Phil. 2014. 'Bringing Them All Back Home: The Challenges of DDR and Transitional Justice in Contexts of Displacement in Rwanda and Uganda'. *Journal of Refugee Studies* 27 (2): 234–59.

Clark, Tom. 2008. '"We're Over-Researched Here!": Exploring Accounts of Research Fatigue within Qualitative Research Engagements'. *Sociology* 42 (5): 953–70.

Cleaver, Frances. 2002. 'Men and Masculinities: New Directions in Gender and Development'. In *Masculinities Matter! Men, Gender and Development*, edited by Frances Cleaver, 1–18. London: Zed Books.

Cockburn, Cynthia. 2001. 'The Gendered Dynamics of Armed Conflict and Political Violence'. In *Victims, Perpetrators or Actors? Gender, Armed Conflict, and Political Violence*, edited by Caroline O.N. Moser and Fiona Clark, 13–29. London: Zed Books.

Cockburn, Cynthia. 2007. *From Where We Stand: War, Women's Activism and Feminist Analysis*. London: Zed Books.

Coffey, Amanda. 1999. *The Ethnographic Self: Fieldwork and the Representation of Identity*. London: Sage Publications.

Cohen, Dara Kay. 2013. 'Female Combatants and the Perpetration of Violence: Wartime Rape in the Sierra Leone Civil War'. *World Politics* 65 (3): 383–415.

Cohen, Elizabeth F. 2009. *Semi-Citizenship in Democratic Politics*. Cambridge: Cambridge University Press.

Collins, Patricia Hill. 1991. 'Learning from the Outsider Within: The Sociological Significance of Black Feminist Thought'. In *Beyond Methodology: Feminist Scholarship as Lived Research*, edited by Mary Margaret Fonow and Judith A. Cook, 35–59. Bloomington: Indiana University Press.

Collins, Patricia Hill. 2019. *Intersectionality as Critical Social Theory*. Durham: Duke University Press.

Comisión Nacional de Mujer Género y Diversidad – FARC, and Victoria Sandino Simanca Herrera. 2018. 'Feminismo Insurgente: Una Apuesta Fariana de Paz'. Bogotá.

Comisión de la Verdad. 2022a. *Mi Cuerpo Es La Verdad: Experiencias de Mujeres y Personas LGBTIQ+ En El Conflicto Armado. Hay Futuro Si Hay Verdad*. Bogotá: Comisión para el Esclarecimiento de la Verdad la Convivencia y la No Repetición.

Comisión de la Verdad. 2022b. *No Hay Futuro Si No Hay Verdad: Informe Final*. Bogotá: Comisión para el Esclarecimiento de la Verdad la Convivencia y la No Repetición. www.ptonline.com/articles/how-to-get-better-mfi-results

Connell, R.W. 2001. 'The Social Organization of Masculinity'. In *The Masculinities* Reader, edited by Stephen M. Whithead and Frank J. Barrett, 30–50. Cambridge: Polity.

Connell, R.W. 2005. 'Change among the Gatekeepers: Men, Masculinities, and Gender Equality in the Global Arena'. *Signs* 30 (3): 1801–25.

Consejo Nacional de Política Económica y Social. 2018. 'Documento CONPES 3931. Política Nacional Para La Reincorporación Social y Económica de Exientegrantes de Las FARC-EP'. Bogotá.

Cornwall, Andrea. 2000. 'Beneficiary, Consumer, Citizen: Perspectives on Participation for Poverty Reduction'. *Sida Studies* 2: 1–92.

Cornwall, Andrea. 2004. 'Spaces for Transformation? Reflections on Issues of Power and Difference in Participation in Development." In *Participation: From Tyranny to Transformation? Exploring New Approaches to Participation in Development*, edited by Samuel Hickey and Giles Mohan, 75–91. London: Zed Books.

Cornwall, Andrea, and Rachel Jewkes. 1995. 'What Is Participatory Research?' *Social Science & Medicine* 41 (12): 1667–76.

Corporación Humanas. 2015. 'Aportes de Las Sentencias de Justicia y Paz a Los Derechos de Las Mujeres: Estudio de Caso'. Bogotá.

Corredor, Elizabeth S. 2021. 'On the Strategic Uses of Women's Rights: Backlash, Rights-Based Framing, and Anti-Gender Campaigns in Colombia's 2016 Peace Agreement'. *Latin American Politics and Society* 63 (3): 46–68.

Corredor, Elizabeth S. 2022. 'Feminist Action at the Negotiation Table: An Exploration Inside the 2010–2016 Colombian Peace Talks'. *International Negotiation*. https://doi.org/10.1163/15718069-bja10063

Coulter, Chris. 2009. *Bush Wives and Girl Soldiers: Women's Lives through War and Peace in Sierra Leone*. Ithaca: Cornell University Press.

Crenshaw, Kimberlé. 1989. 'Demarginalizing the Intersection of Race and Sex: A Black Feminist Critique of Antidiscrimination Doctrine, Feminist Theory and Antiracist Policies'. *The University of Chicago Legal Forum* 139 (1): 139–67.

Cronin-Furman, Kate, and Milli Lake. 2018. 'Ethics Abroad: Fieldwork in Fragile and Violent Contexts'. *PS – Political Science and Politics* 51 (3): 607–14.

Crosby, Alison, and M. Brinton Lykes. 2011. 'Mayan Women Survivors Speak: The Gendered Relations of Truth Telling in Postwar Guatemala'. *International Journal of Transitional Justice* 5 (3): 456–76.

Crosby, Alison, M. Brinton Lykes and Brisna Caxaj. 2016. 'Carrying a Heavy Load: Mayan Women's Understandings of Reparation in the Aftermath of Genocide'. *Journal of Genocide Research* 18 (2–3): 265–83.

Denov, Myriam, and Alexandra Ricard-Guay. 2013. 'Girl Soldiers: Towards a Gendered Understanding of Wartime Recruitment, Participation, and Demobilisation'. *Gender and Development* 21 (3): 473–88.

Destrooper, Tine, and Stephan Parmentier. 2018. 'Gender-Aware and Place-Based Transitional Justice in Guatemala: Altering the Opportunity Structures for Post-Conflict Women's Mobilization'. *Social and Legal Studies* 27 (3): 323–44.

Dietrich Ortega, Luisa Maria. 2009. 'Transitional Justice and Female Ex-Combatants: Lessons Learned from International Experience'. In *Disarming the Past: Transitional Justice and Ex-Combatants*, edited by Ana Cutter Patel, Pablo De Greiff and Lars Waldorf, 158–88. New York: Social Science Research Council.

Dietrich Ortega, Luisa Maria. 2012. 'Looking Beyond Violent Militarized Masculinities: Guerrilla Gender Regimes in Latin America'. *International Feminist Journal of Politics* 14 (4): 489–507.

Dietz, Mary G. 1987. 'Context Is All: Feminism and Theories of Citizenship'. *Daedalus* 116 (4): 1–24.

Dixon, Peter, and Pamina Firchow. 2022. 'Collective Justice: Ex-Combatants and Community Reparations in Colombia'. *Journal of Human Rights Practice* 14 (2): 434–53.

Domingo, Pilar. 2009. 'Ciudadanía, Derechos y Justicia En América Latina: Ciudadanización-Judicialización de La Política'. *Revista CIDOB d'Afers Internacionals* 85–86: 33–52.

Drumond, Paula, and Tamya Rebelo. 2020. 'Global Pathways or Local Spins? National Action Plans in South America'. *International Feminist Journal of Politics* 22 (4): 462–84.

Durbach, Andrea, and Louise Chappell. 2014. 'Leaving Behind the Age of Impunity: Victims of Gender Violence and the Promise of Reparations'. *International Feminist Journal of Politics* 16 (4): 543–62.

Duriesmith, David. 2014. 'Is Manhood a Causal Factor in the Shifting Nature of War?' *International Feminist Journal of Politics* 16 (2): 236–54.

Eastmond, Marita, and Johanna Mannergren Selimovic. 2012. 'Silence as Possibility in Postwar Everyday Life'. *International Journal of Transitional Justice* 6 (3): 502–24.

Eaton, Kent. 2006. 'The Downside of Decentralization: Armed Clientelism in Colombia'. *Security Studies* 15 (4): 533–62.

Echavarría Álvarez, Josefina, Mateo Gómez Vásquez, Brenda Forero Linares, Mariana Balen Giancola, Miyerlandy Cabanzo Valencia, Elise Ditta, Enrique Gutiérrez Pulido et al 2021. *Cinco Años Después de La Firma Del Acuerdo Final: Reflexiones Desde El Monitoreo a La Implementación*. Notre Dame, IN: Kroc Institute for International Peace Studies/Keough School of Global Affairs.

Eggert, Jennifer Philippa. 2018. 'Female Fighters and Militants during the Lebanese Civil War: Individual Profiles, Pathways, and Motivations'. *Studies in Conflict & Terrorism*. DOI: 10.1080/1057610X.2018.1529353

El-Bushra, Judy, and Judith Gardner. 2016. 'The Impact of War on Somali Men: Feminist Analysis of Masculinities and Gender Relations in a Fragile Context'. *Gender and Development* 24 (3): 443–58.

Ellerby, Kara. 2017. *No Shortcut for Change: An Unlikely Path to a More Gender-Equitable World*. New York: New York University Press.

Elliott, Karla. 2016. 'Caring Masculinities: Theorizing an Emerging Concept'. *Men and Masculinities* 19 (3): 240–59.

Enloe, Cynthia. 2000. *Maneuvers: The International Politics of Militarizing Women's Lives*. Berkely: University of California Press.

Enloe, Cynthia. 2002. 'Demilitarization – or More of the Same? Feminist Questions to Ask in the Postwar Moment'. In *The Postwar Moment: Militaries, Masculinities and International Peacekeeping*, edited by Cynthia Cockburn and Dubravka Žarkov, 22–32. London: Lawrence & Wishart.

Evans, Matthew. 2016. 'Structural Violence, Socioeconomic Rights, and Transformative Justice'. *Journal of Human Rights* 15 (1): 1–20.

Fajardo, July Samira. 2021. 'La Paz Avanza Con Las Mujeres: III Informe de Observaciones Sobre Los Avances En La Implementación Del Enfoque de Género Del Acuerdo de Paz'. Grupo de Género en la Paz – GPAZ. https://generoypaz.co/informes/gpaz_informe_2021.pdf

Fals-Borda, Orlando. 1987. 'The Application of Participatory Action-Research in Latin America'. *International Sociology* 2 (4): 329–47.

Farah Quijano, María A. 2009. 'Social Policy for Poor Rural People in Colombia: Reinforcing Traditional Gender Roles and Identities?' *Social Policy and Administration* 43 (4): 397–408.

FARC. 2020. 'Estrategia Integral Para La Reincorporación de Las Mujeres de Las FARC'. Bogotá.

Farmer, Paul. 1996. 'On Suffering and Structural Violence: A View from Below'. *Daedalus* 125 (1): 261–83.

Farmer, Paul. 2004. 'An Anthropology of Structural Violence'. *Current Anthropology* 45 (3): 305–25.

Fattal, Alexander L. 2018. *Guerrilla Marketing: Counterinsurgency and Capitalism in Colombia*. Chicago: University of Chicago Press.

Federici, Silvia. 2012. *Revolution at Point Zero: Housework, Reproduction, and Feminist Struggle*. Oakland: PM Press.

Firchow, Pamina. 2018. *Reclaiming Everyday Peace: Local Voices in Measurement and Evaluation after War*. Cambridge: Cambridge University Press.

Fiscalía General de la Nación. 2021. 'Sentencias Ley 975 de 2005'. www.fiscalia.gov.co/colombia/sentencias-ley-975-de-2005

Flisi, Isabella. 2016. 'The Reintegration of Former Combatants in Colombia: Addressing Violent Masculinities in a Fragile Context'. *Gender and Development* 24 (3): 391–407.

Florez-Morris, Mauricio. 2007. 'Joining Guerrilla Groups in Colombia: Individual Motivations and Processes for Entering a Violent Organization'. *Studies in Conflict and Terrorism* 30 (7): 615–34.

Fonow, Mary Margaret, and Judith A. Cook. 1991. 'Back to the Future: A Look at the Second Wave of Feminist Epistemology and Methodology'. In *Beyond Methodology: Feminist Scholarship as Lived Research*, edited by Mary Margaret Fonow and Judith A. Cook, 1–15. Bloomington: Indiana University Press.

Foucault, Michel. 1990. *The Will to Knowledge: The History of Sexuality Volume I*. London: Penguin Books.

Franke, Katherine M. 2006. 'Gendered Subjects of Transitional Justice'. *Columbia Journal of Gender and Law* 15 (3): 813–28.

Fraser, Nancy. 2008. *Scales of Justice: Reimagining Political Space in a Globalizing World*. Cambridge: Polity Press.

Freire, Paulo. 1996. *Pedagogy of the Oppressed*. 2nd edn. London: Penguin Books.

Friedman, Rebekka. 2018. 'Remnants of a Checkered Past: Female LTTE and Social Reintegration in Post-War Sri Lanka'. *International Studies Quarterly* 62: 632–42.

Fruehling Springwood, Charles, and C. Richard King. 2001. 'Unsettling Engagements: On the Ends of Rapport in Critical Ethnography'. *Qualitative Inquiry* 7 (4): 403–17.

Fujii, Lee Ann. 2010. 'Shades of Truth and Lies: Interpreting Testimonies of War and Violence'. *Journal of Peace Research* 47 (2): 231–41.

Fujii, Lee Ann. 2012. 'Research Ethics 101: Dilemmas and Responsibilities'. *PS – Political Science and Politics* 45 (4): 717–23.

Galtung, J. 1969. 'Violence, Peace, and Peace Research'. *Journal of Peace Research* 6 (3): 167–91.

Gamboa, Tapias, Camila De and Fabio Andrés Díaz Pabón. 2018. 'The Transitional Justice Framework Agreed between the Colombian Government and the FARC-EP'. In *Truth, Justice and Reconciliation in Colombia: Transitioning from Violence*, edited by Fabio Andrés Díaz Pabón, 66–84. Abingdon: Routledge.

García-Godos, Jemima. 2013. 'Colombia: Accountability and DDR in the Pursuit of Peace?' In *Transitional Justice and Peacebuilding on the Ground: Victims and Ex-Combatants*, edited by Chandra Lekha Sriram, Jemima García-Godos, Johanna Herman and Olga Martin-Ortega, 219–37. Abingdon: Routledge.

Gaventa, John, and Andrea Cornwall. 2008. 'Power and Knowledge'. In *The SAGE Handbook of Action Research: Participative Inquiry and Practice*, edited by Peter Reason and Hilary Bradbury, 2nd edn, 172–89. London: Sage Publications.

Geertz, Clifford. 1975. 'Thick Description: Toward an Interpretive Theory of Culture'. In *The Interpretation of Culture: Selected Essays*, edited by Clifford Geertz, 3–30. London: Hutchinson.

Gibney, Matthew J. 2006. 'Who Should Be Included? Non-Citizens, Conflict and the Constitution of the Citizenry'. CRISE Working Paper, no. 17: 1–14.

Giddens, Anthony. 1984. *The Constitution of Society: Outline of the Theory of Structuration*. Cambridge: Polity Press.

Gifford, Lindsay, and Rachel Hall-Clifford. 2008. 'From Catcalls to Kidnapping Playing by the Rules'. *Knowledge Exchange* September: 26–7.

Ginty, Roger Mac, Roddy Brett and Birte Vogel, eds. 2021. *The Companion to Peace and Conflict Fieldwork*. Cham: Palgrave Macmillan.

Giraldo-Gartner, Vanesa. 2020. 'Victims, Revolutionaries, or Heroic Mothers? The Debate of Reproductive Politics in the FARC'. PoLAR Online Emergent Conversation, no. 10. https://polarjournal.org/2020/11/24/victims-revolutionaries-or-heroic-mothers-the-debate-of-reproductive-politics-in-the-farc/

Goetz, Anne Marie. 2007. 'Gender Justice, Citizenship and Entitelements: Core Concepts, Central Debates and New Directions for Research'. In *Gender Justice, Citizenship, and Development*, edited by Maitrayee Mukhopadhyay and Navsharan Singh, 15–57. New Delhi: Zubaan and International Development Research Centre.

Goldstein, Joshua S. 2001. *War and Gender: How Gender Shapes the War System and Vice Versa*. Cambridge: Cambridge University Press.

Gómez-Suárez, Andrei. 2016. *El Triunfo Del No: La Paradoja Emocional Detrás Del Plebiscito*. Bogotá: Icono.

González González, Fernán E. 2014. *Poder y Violencia En Colombia*. Bogotá: Odecofi-Cinep.

Gonzales Vaillant, Gabriela, Michael Kimmel, Farshad Malekahmadi and Juhi Tyagi. 2012. 'The Gender of Resistance: A Case Study Approach to Thinking about Gender in Violent Resistance Movements'. In *Gender, Agency and Political Violence*, edited by Laura J. Shepherd and Linda Åhäll, 55–78. Basingstoke: Palgrave Macmillan.

Govier, Trudy, and Wilhelm Verwoerd. 2004. 'How Not to Polarize "Victims" and "Perpetrators"'. *Peace Review* 16 (3): 371–77.

Gready, Paul, Jelke Boesten, Gordon Crawford and Polly Wilding. 2010. 'Transformative Justice – a Concept Note'. www.wun.ac.uk/files/transformative_justice_-_concept_note_web_version.pdf

Gready, Paul, and Simon Robins. 2014. 'From Transitional to Transformative Justice: A New Agenda for Practice'. *International Journal of Transitional Justice* 8 (3): 339–61.

Gready, Paul, and Simon Robins. 2017. 'Rethinking Civil Society and Transitional Justice: Lessons from Social Movements and "New" Civil Society'. *International Journal of Human Rights* 21 (7): 956–75.

Green, Duncan. 2012. *From Poverty to Power: How Active Citizens and Effective States Can Change the World*. 2nd edn. Rugby: Practical Action Publishing.

Greenberg, Marcia E., and Elaine Zuckerman. 2009. 'The Gender Dimensions of Post-Conflict Reconstruction: The Challenges in Development'. In *Making Peace Work: The Challenges of Social and Economic Reconstruction*, edited by Tony Addison and Tilman Brück, 101–35. New York: Palgrave MacMillan, UNU-WIDER.

Greiff, Pablo De. 2009. 'Articulating the Links between Transitional Justice and Development: Justice and Social Integration'. In *Transitional Justice and Development: Making Connections*, edited by Pablo De Greiff and Roger Duthie, 28–75. New York: Social Science Research Council.

Grupo de Memoria Histórica. 2010. *La Tierra En Disputa: Memorias de Despojo y Resistencias Campesinas En La Costa Caribe 1960–2010*. Bogotá: Centro Nacional de Memoria Histórica.

Grupo de Memoria Histórica. 2013. *Basta Ya! Colombia: Memoria de Guerra y Dignidad*. Bogotá: Centro Nacional de Memoria Histórica.

Guardiola Rivera, Óscar. 2014. *Cómo Construir Sociedades: Diez Cosas Que Nunca Nos Dicen Sobre La Paz y La Guerra*. Bogotá: Editorial Pontificia Universidad Javeriana.

Guembe, María José, and Helena Olea. 2006. 'No Justice, No Peace: Discussion of the Legal Framework Regarding Demobilization of Non-State Groups in Colombia'. In *Transitional Justice in the New Millennium: Beyond Truth versus Justice*, edited by Naomi Roht-Arriaza and Javier Mariezcurrena, 120–42. Cambridge: Cambridge University Press.

Guillemin, Marilys, and Lynn Gillam. 2004. 'Ethics, Reflexivity, and "Ethically Important Moments" in Research'. *Qualitative Inquiry* 10 (2): 261–80.

Gutiérrez Bonilla, Martha Lucía, Donny Meertens, July Samira Fajardo Farfán, Eliana Pinto Velásquez, María Cristina Ocampo de Herrán and Anna Balaguer Soriano. 2015. 'El Conflicto Armado y Su Impacto En Los Proyectos de Vida de Las Mujeres Indígenas y Campesinas En Busca de Justicia, Departamento Del Cesar / Colombia'. In *El Camino Por La Justicia: Victimización y Resistencia de Mujeres Indígenas y Campesinas En Guatemala y Colombia*, edited by Patricia Ramírez Parra, 101–217. Medellín: Imprenta Universidad de Antioquia.

Gutierrez, Esther, Luzdaris Diaz, Liliana Valencia, Ledys Madarriaga, Mariluis Garcia, Maricela Conde and Yeslie Hernandez. 2020. *Enfoque Etnico*. Video, Fonseca.

Gutiérrez, Francisco, and Mauricio Barón. 2005. 'Estado, Control Territorial Paramilitar y Orden Político En Colombia: Notas Para Una Economía Política Del Paramilitarismo, 1978–2008'. In *Nuestra Guerra Sin Nombre: Transformaciones Del Conflicto En Colombia*, edited by Francisco Gutiérrez, María Emma Wills and Gonzalo Sánchez Gómez, 152–76. Bogotá: Grupo Editorial Norma.

Gutiérrez, José A, and Emma Murphy. 2022. 'The Unspoken Red-Line in Colombia: Gender Reordering of Women Ex-Combatants and the Transformative Peace Agenda'. *Cooperation and Conflict*. https://doi.org/10.1177/00108367221099085

Gutiérrez Sanín, Francisco. 2019. 'Lo Bueno, Lo Malo y Lo Feo de La Restitución de Tierras En Colombia: Una Lectura Política e Institucional'. In *La Tierra Prometida: Balance de La Política de Restitución de Tierras En Colombia*, edited by Francisco Gutiérrez Sanín, Rocío del Pilar Peña Huertas and María Mónica Parada Hernández, 9–37. Bogotá: Editorial Universidad del Rosario.

Gutiérrez Sanín, Francisco, and Francy Carranza-Franco. 2017. 'Organizing Women for Combat: The Experience of the FARC in the Colombian War'. *Journal of Agrarian Change* 17 (4): 770–78.

Gutmann, Mathew C. 2003. 'Introduction: Discarding Manly Dichotomies in Latin America'. In *Changing Men and Masculinities in Latin America*, edited by Mathew C. Gutmann, 1–26. Durham: Duke University Press.

Hagen, Jamie J. 2016. 'Queering Women, Peace and Security'. *International Affairs* 92 (2): 313–32.

Haji, Reeshma, Shelley McKeown and Neil Ferguson. 2016. 'Social Identity and Peace Psychology: An Introduction'. In *Understanding Peace and Conflict through Social Identity Theory: Contemporary Global Perspectives*, edited by Shelley McKeown, Reeshma Haji and Neil Ferguson, xv–xx. Cham: Springer.

Hale, Charles R. 1997. 'Consciousness, Violence, and the Politics of Memory in Guatemala'. *Current Anthropology* 38 (5): 817–38.

Hamber, Brandon, and Richard A. Wilson. 2002. 'Symbolic Closure through Memory, Reparation and Revenge in Post-Conflict Societies'. *Journal of Human Rights* 1 (1): 35–53.

Harper, Douglas. 2010. 'Talking about Pictures: A Case for Photo Elicitation'. *Visual Studies* 17 (1): 13–26.

Hauge, Wenche Iren. 2020. 'Gender Dimensions of DDR – Beyond Victimization and Dehumanization: Tracking the Thematic'. *International Feminist Journal of Politics* 22 (2): 206–26.

Hawkesworth, Mary. 2012. 'Truth and Truths in Feminist Knowledge Production'. In *The Handbook of Feminist Research*, edited by Sharlene Nagy Hesse-Biber, 92–118. Los Angeles: Sage Publications.

Hayner, Priscilla B. 2001. *Unspeakable Truths: Confronting State Terror and Atrocity*. New York: Routledge.

Hayward, Clarissa Rile. 2017. 'Responsibility and Ignorance: On Dismantling Structural Injustice'. *The Journal of Politics* 79 (2): 396–408.

Hearn, Jeff, and Alp Biricik. 2016. 'Gender and Citizenship'. In *Handbook on Gender in World Politics*, edited by Jill Steans and Daniela Tepe, 85–93. Cheltenham: Edward Elgar Publishing.

Helms, Elissa. 2013. *Innocence and Victimhood: Gender, Nation and Women's Activism in Postwar Bosnia-Herzegovina*. Madison: University of Wisconsin Press.

Hennings, Anne. 2018. 'With Soymilk to the Khmer Rouge: Challenges of Researching Ex-Combatants in Post-War Contexts'. *International Peacekeeping* 25 (5): 630–52.

Henshaw, Alexis Leanna. 2016. 'Where Women Rebel'. *International Feminist Journal of Politics* 18 (1): 39–60.

Herrera, Natalia, and Douglas Porch. 2008. '"Like Going to a Fiesta": The Role of Female Fighters in Colombia's FARC-EP'. *Small Wars & Insurgencies* 19 (4): 609–34.

Hilhorst, Dorothea, and Nynke Douma. 2018. 'Beyond the Hype? The Response to Sexual Violence in the Democratic Republic of the Congo in 2011 and 2014'. *Disasters* 42 (1): S79–98.

Hogg, Michael A. 2016. 'Social Identity Theory'. In *Understanding Peace and Conflict through Social Identity Theory: Contemporary Global Perspectives*, edited by Shelley McKeown, Reeshma Haji and Neil Ferguson, 3–17. Cham: Springer.

Hogg, Michael A., and Deborah I. Terry. 2000. 'Social Identity and Self-Categorization Processes in Organizational Contexts'. *Academy of Management Review* 25 (1): 121–40.

hooks, bell. 1990. *Yearning: Race, Gender, and Cultural Politics*. Boston: South End Press.

Hsiung, Ping-Chun. 1996. 'Between Bosses and Workers: The Dilemma of a Keen Observer and a Vocal Feminist'. In *Feminist Dilemmas in Fieldwork*, edited by Diane L. Wolf, 122–37. Boulder: Westview Press.

Hume, Mo. 2007. 'Unpicking the Threads: Emotion as Central to the Theory and Practice of Researching Violence'. *Women's Studies International Forum* 30 (2): 147–57.

Hume, Mo. 2009. 'Researching the Gendered Silences of Violence in El Salvador'. *IDS Bulletin* 40 (3): 78–85.

Hume, Mo, and Polly Wilding. 2019. 'Beyond Agency and Passivity: Situating a Gendered Articulation of Urban Violence in Brazil and El Salvador'. *Urban Studies* 42 (1): 512–25.

Humphreys, MacArtan, and Jeremy M. Weinstein. 2007. 'Demobilization and Reintegration'. *Journal of Conflict Resolution* 51 (4): 531–67.

Hylton, Forrest. 2006. *Evil Hour in Colombia*. London: Verso.

Ibáñez, Ana Cristina. 2001. 'El Salvador: Women and Untold Stories – Women Guerrillas – Ana Cristina'. In *Victims, Perpetrators or Actors? Gender, Armed Conflict, and Political Violence*, edited by Caroline O.N. Moser and Fiona C. Clark, 117–30. London: Zed Books.

Irgil, Ezgi, Anne-Kathrin Kreft, Myunghee Lee, Charmaine N Willis and Kelebogile Zvobgo. 2021. 'Field Research: A Graduate Student's Guide'. *International Studies Review* 23 (4): 1495–517.

Janetsky, Megan. 2021. '"Baby Boom" among Colombian Rebels Was a Sign of Hope. Now the Families Face Uncertainty'. *National Geographic*. www.nationalgeographic.com/culture/article/rebel-baby-boom-was-a-sign-of-hope-now-it-represents-uncertainty

Jelin, Elizabeth. 1994. 'Las Familias En América Latina'. *ISIS Internacional – Ediciones de Las Mujeres* 20: 1–24.

Jelin, Elizabeth. 1996. 'Citizenship Revisited: Solidarity, Responsibility, and Rights'. In *Constructing Democracy: Human Rights, Citizenship and Society in Latin America*, edited by Elizabeth Jelin and Eric Hershberg, 101–20. Boulder: Westview Press.

Jennings, Kathleen M. 2009. 'The Political Economy of DDR in Liberia: A Gendered Critique'. *Conflict, Security & Development* 9 (4): 475–94.

Jiménez Ocampo, Sandro, Martha Nubia Bello, Donny Meertens, Flor Edilma Osorio and Rocío Venegas Luque. 2009. *Internally Displaced People in Colombia, Victims in Permanent Transition: Ethical and Political Dilemmas of Reparative Justice in the Midst of Internal Armed Conflict*. Bogotá: Ediciones Ántropos.

Jones, Adam. 2006. 'Straight as a Rule: Heteronormativity, Gendercide, and the Noncombatant Male'. *Men and Masculinities* 8 (4): 451–69.

Jones, Briony. 2015. 'Stories of "Success": Narrative, Expertise, and Claims to Knowledge'. *Canadian Journal of Law and Society / Revue Canadienne Droit et Société* 30 (2): 293–308.

Jones, Briony. 2020. 'The Performance and Persistence of Transitional Justice and Its Ways of Knowing Atrocity'. *Cooperation and Conflict* 56 (2): 163–80.

Kabachnik, Peter, Magdalena Grabowska, Joanna Regulska, Beth Mitchneck and Olga V. Mayorova. 2012. 'Traumatic Masculinities: The Gendered Geographies of Georgian IDPs from Abkhazia'. *Gender, Place & Culture* 20 (6): 773–93.

Kabeer, Naila. 2012. 'Empowerment, Citizenship and Gender Justice: A Contribution to Locally Grounded Theories of Change in Women's Lives'. *Ethics and Social Welfare* 6 (3): 216–32.

Kaplan, Oliver, and Enzo Nussio. 2018. 'Community Counts: The Social Reintegration of Ex-Combatants in Colombia'. *Conflict Management and Peace Science* 35 (2): 132–53.

Kapur, Ratna. 2002. 'The Tragedy of Victimization Rhetoric: Resurrecting the "Native" Subject in International/Post-Colonial Feminist Legal Politics'. *Harvard Human Rights Journal* 15 (1): 1–38.

Kaufman, Michael. 1987. 'The Construction of Masculinity and the Triad of Men's Violence'. In *Beyond Patriarchy: Essays by Men on Pleasure, Power, and Change*, edited by Michael Kaufman. Toronto: Oxford University Press.

Kent, Lia. 2014. 'Narratives of Suffering and Endurance: Coercive Sexual Relationships, Truth Commissions and Possibilities for Gender Justice in Timor-Leste'. *International Journal of Transitional Justice* 8 (2): 289–313.

Kent, Lia. 2016. 'After the Truth Commission: Gender and Citizenship in Timor-Leste'. *Human Rights Review* 17 (1): 51–70.

Ketola, Hanna. 2020. 'Withdrawing from Politics? Gender, Agency and Women Ex-Fighters in Nepal'. *Security Dialogue* 51 (6): 519–36.

Kloß, Sinah Theres. 2017. 'Sexual(ized) Harassment and Ethnographic Fieldwork: A Silenced Aspect of Social Research'. *Ethnography* 18 (3): 396–414.

Knight, Mark, and Alpaslan Özerdem. 2004. 'Guns, Camps and Cash: Disarmament, Demobilization and Reinsertion of Former Combatants in Transitions from War to Peace'. *Journal of Peace Research* 41 (4): 499–516.

Knott, Eleanor. 2019. 'Beyond the Field: Ethics after Fieldwork in Politically Dynamic Contexts'. *Perspectives on Politics* 17 (1): 140–53.

Koopman, Sara. 2020. 'Building an Inclusive Peace Is an Uneven Socio-Spatial Process: Colombia's Differential Approach'. *Political Geography* 83 (102252): 1–11.

Kostovicova, Denisa, and Eleanor Knott. 2020. 'Harm, Change and Unpredictability: The Ethics of Interviews in Conflict'. *Qualitative Research* 22 (1): 56–73.

Krause, Jana. 2021. 'The Ethics of Ethnographic Methods in Conflict Zones'. *Journal of Peace Research* 58 (3): 329–41.

Kreft, Anne-Kathrin, and Philipp Schulz. 2022. 'Political Agency, Victimhood, and Gender in Contexts of Armed Conflict: Moving beyond Dichotomies'. *International Studies Quarterly* 66 (2).

Krystalli, Roxani. 2019. 'Narrating Violence: Feminist Dilemmas and Approaches'. In *Handbook on Gender and Violence*, edited by Laura J. Shepherd, 173–88. Cheltenham: Edward Elgar.

Krystalli, Roxani. 2020a. 'Attendance Sheets and Bureaucracies of Victimhood in Colombia'. PoLAR Online Emergent Conversation, no. 10. https://polarjournal.org/2020/11/24/attendance-sheets-and-bureaucracies-of-victimhood-in-colombia

Krystalli, Roxani. 2020b. 'Women, Peace, and Victimhood'. Global Observatory.

Krystalli, Roxani. 2021. 'Narrating Victimhood: Dilemmas and (In)Dignities'. *International Feminist Journal of Politics* 23 (1): 125–46.

Lagarde y de los Ríos, Marcela. 2014. *Los Cautiverios de Las Mujeres: Madresposas, Monjas, Putas, Presas y Locas*. México, DF: Siglo xxi Editores.

Lambourne, Wendy. 2009. 'Transitional Justice and Peacebuilding after Mass Violence'. *International Journal of Transitional Justice* 3 (1): 28–48.

Laplante, Lisa J. 2015. 'Just Repair'. *Cornell International Law Journal* 48 (3): 513.

Laplante, Lisa J., and Kimberly Theidon. 2006. 'Transitional Justice in Times of Conflict: Colombia's Ley de Justicia y Paz'. *Michigan Journal of International Law* 28 (1): 49–108.

Lawther, Cheryl. 2020. '"Let Me Tell You": Transitional Justice, Victimhood and Dealing with a Contested Past'. *Social and Legal Studies* 30 (6): 890–912.

Lazar, Sian. 2013a. 'Education for Credit: Development as Citizenship Project in Bolivia, 2004'. In *The Anthropology of Citizenship: A Reader*, edited by Sian Lazar, 107–19. Chichester: Wiley Blackwell.

Lazar, Sian. 2013b. 'Introduction'. In *The Anthropology of Citizenship: A Reader*, edited by Sian Lazar, 1–22. Chichester: Wiley Blackwell.

Lee, Raymond M., and Claire M. Renzetti. 1993. 'The Problems of Researching Sensitive Topics: An Overview and Introduction'. In *Researching Sensitive Topics*, edited by Raymond M. Lee and Claire M. Renzetti, 3–13. Newbury Park: Sage Publications.

Lemaitre, Julieta. 2016. 'After the War: Displaced Women, Ordinary Ethics, and Grassroots Reconstruction in Colombia'. *Social & Legal Studies* 25 (5): 545–65.

Lemaitre, Julieta, and Kristin Bergtora Sandvik. 2014. 'Beyond Sexual Violence in Transitional Justice: Political Insecurity as a Gendered Harm'. *Feminist Legal Studies* 22 (3): 243–61.

Lemaitre, Julieta, and Kristin Bergtora Sandvik. 2016. 'Structural Remedies and the One Million Pesos: On the Limits of Court-Ordered Social Change for Internally Displaced Women in Colombia'. In *The Public Law of Gender: From the Local to the Global*, edited by Kim Rubenstein and Katharine G. Young, 99–119. Cambridge: Cambridge University Press.

León, Magdalena. 2011. 'La Desigualdad de Género En La Propiedad de La Tierra En América Latina'. In *Du Grain à Moudre. Genre, Développement Rural et Alimentation*, edited by C. Verschuur, 189–207. Berne: Commission Nationale Suisse pour l'UNESCO.

Letherby, Gayle. 2003. *Feminist Research in Theory and Practice*. Buckingham: Open University Press.

Levi, Primo. 2013. *The Drowned and the Saved*. London: Abacus.

Lister, Ruth. 1997. 'Dialectics of Citizenship'. *Hypatia* 12 (4): 6–26.

Lister, Ruth. 2003. *Citizenship: Feminist Perspectives*. Basingstoke: Palgrave Macmillan.

Lloyd-Sherlock, Peter. 2008. 'Doing a Bit More for the Poor? Social Assistance in Latin America'. *Journal of Social Policy* 37 (4): 621–39.

Lomeli, Jafte Dilean Robles, and Joanne Rappaport. 2018. 'Imagining Latin American Social Science from the Global South: Orlando Fals Borda and Participatory Action Research'. *Latin American Research Review* 53 (3): 597–612.

Londoño Fernández, Luz María, and Yoana Fernanda Nieto Valdivieso. 2007. *Mujeres No Contadas: Procesos de Desmovilización y Retorno a La Vida Civil de Mujeres Excombatientes En Colombia 1990–2003*. Medellín: La Carreta Editores E.U.

Lorde, Audre. 2007. 'The Master's Tools Will Never Dismantle the Master's House'. In *Sister Outsider: Essays and Speeches*, 110–14. Berkeley: Crossing Press.

Lykes, M. Brinton. 2010. 'Silence(ing), Voice(s) and Gross Violations of Human Rights: Constituting and Performing Subjectivities through PhotoPAR'. *Visual Studies* 25 (3): 238–54.

Lykes, M. Brinton, and Alison Crosby. 2015. 'Creative Methodologies as a Resource for Mayan Women's Protagonism'. In *Psychosocial Perspectives on Peacebuilding*, edited by Brandon Hamber and Elizabeth Gallagher, 147–86. Cham: Springer International Publishing.

Lykes, M. Brinton, and Holly Scheib. 2017. 'The Artistry of Emancipatory Practice: Photovoice, Creative Techniques, and Feminist Anti-Racist Participatory Action Research'. In *The SAGE Handbook of Action Research*, edited by Hilary Bradbury, 3rd edn, 130–41. London: Sage Publications.

Maanen, John Van. 1988. *Tales of the Field: On Writing Ethnography*. Chicago: University of Chicago Press.

MacKenzie, Catriona, Christopher McDowell and Eileen Pittaway. 2007. 'Beyond "Do No Harm": The Challenge of Constructing Ethical Relationships in Refugee Research'. *Journal of Refugee Studies* 20 (2): 299–319.

MacKenzie, Megan. 2009. 'Securitization and Desecuritization: Female Soldiers and the Reconstruction of Women in Post-Conflict Sierra Leone'. *Security Studies* 18 (2): 241–61.

MacKenzie, Megan. 2012. *Female Soldiers in Sierra Leone: Sex, Security and Post-Conflict Development*. New York: New York University Press.

MacKenzie, Megan, and Alana Foster. 2017. 'Masculinity Nostalgia: How War and Occupation Inspire a Yearning for Gender Order'. *Security Dialogue* 48 (3): 206–23.

Madlingozi, Tshepo. 2007. 'Good Victim, Bad Victim: Apartheid's Beneficiaries, Victims and the Struggle for Social Justice'. In *Law, Memory and the Legacy of Apartheid: Ten Years after AZAPO v President of South Africa*, edited by Wessel Le Roux and Karin Van Marle, 107–26. Pretoria: Pretoria University Law Press.

Malejacq, Romain, and Dipali Mukhopadhyay. 2016. 'The "Tribal Politics" of Field Research: A Reflection on Power and Partiality in 21st-Century Warzones'. *Perspectives on Politics* 14 (4): 1011–28.

Mani, Rama. 2002. *Beyond Retribution: Seeking Justice in the Shadows of War*. Cambridge: Polity Press.

Mantilla, Silvia. 2011. 'Conflicto y Paz En Colombia En Tiempos de Globalización'. In *Paz Paso a Paso: Una Mirada Desde Los Estudios de Paz a Los Conflictos Colombianos*, edited by Adam Baird and José Fernando Serrano, 217–40. Bogotá: Editorial Pontificia Universidad Javeriana.

Manz, Beatriz. 1995. 'Reflections on Antropología Comprometida: Conversations with Ricardo Falla'. In *Fieldwork under Fire: Contemporary Studies of Violence and Survival*, edited by Antonius C.G.M. Robben and Carolyn Nordstrom, 261–75. Berkeley: University of California Press.

Martín-Baró, Ignacio. 1994. *Writings for a Liberation Psychology*, edited by Adrianne Aron and Shawn Corne. Cambridge: Harvard University Press.

McEvoy, Kieran, and Kirsten McConnachie. 2013. 'Victims and Transitional Justice: Voice, Agency and Blame'. *Social & Legal Studies* 22 (4): 489–513.

McEwan, Cheryl. 2005. 'New Spaces of Citizenship? Rethinking Gendered Participation and Empowerment in South Africa'. *Political Geography* 24 (8): 969–91.

McFee, Erin. 2016. 'The Double Bind of "Playing Double": Passing and Identity among Ex-Combatants in Colombia'. *Peace and Conflict* 22 (1): 52–9.

McFee, Erin, and Angelika Rettberg. 2019. 'Contexto de Los Desafíos de La Implementación Temprana En Colombia'. In *Excombatientes y Acuerdo de Paz Con Las FARC-EP En Colombia: Balance de La Etapa Temprana*, edited by Erin McFee and Angelika Rettberg, 1–17. Bogotá: Ediciones Uniandes.

McKenna, Stacey A., and Deborah S. Main. 2013. 'The Role and Influence of Key Informants in Community-Engaged Research: A Critical Perspective'. *Action Research* 11 (2): 113–24.

McMullin, Jaremey R. 2013. 'Integration or Separation? The Stigmatisation of Ex-Combatants after War'. *Review of International Studies* 39: 385–414.

Meertens, Donny. 2010. 'Forced Displacement and Women's Security in Colombia'. *Disasters* 34 (2): 147–64.

Meertens, Donny. 2015. 'Discursive Frictions: The Transitional Justice Paradigm, Land Restitution and Gender in Colombia'. *Papel Político* 20 (2): 353–81.

Meertens, Donny. 2019. *Elusive Justice: Women, Land Rights, and Colombia's Transition to Peace*. Madison: University of Wisconsin Press.

Meger, Sara. 2016. 'The Fetishization of Sexual Violence in International Security'. *International Studies Quarterly* 60 (1): 149–59.

Mertus, Julie. 2004. 'Shouting from the Bottom of the Well: The Impact of International Trials for Wartime Rape on Women's Agency'. *International Feminist Journal of Politics* 6 (1): 110–28.

Mies, Maria. 1991. 'Women's Research or Feminist Research? The Debate Surrounding Feminist Science and Methodology'. In *Beyond Methodology: Feminist Scholarship as Lived Research*, edited by Mary Margaret Fonow and Judith A. Cook, 60–84. Bloomington: Indiana University Press.

Mies, Maria. 1998. *Patriarchy & Accumulation on a World Scale: Women in the International Division of Labour*. London: Zed Books.

Millán Cruz, Fernando. 2019. *Con Ojos de Mujer: Relatos En Medio de La Guerra*. Bogotá: Penguin Random House Grupo Editorial.

Miller, Zinaida. 2008. 'Effects of Invisibility: In Search of the "Economic" in Transitional Justice'. *International Journal of Transitional Justice* 2 (3): 266–91.

Mitchell, Claudia. 2011. *Doing Visual Research*. London: Sage Publications.

Moffett, Luke. 2016. 'Reparations for "Guilty Victims": Navigating Complex Identities of Victim-Perpetrators in Reparation Mechanisms'. *International Journal of Transitional Justice* 10 (1): 146–67.

Mohanty, Chandra Talpade. 2003. *Feminism without Borders: Decolonizing Theory, Practicing Solidarity*. Durham: Duke University Press.

Molyneux, Maxine. 2007. 'Refiguring Citizenship: Research Perspectives on Gender Justice in the Latin American and Caribbean Region'. In *Gender Justice, Citizenship, and Development*, edited by Maitrayee Mukhopadhyay and Navsharan Singh, 58–115. New Delhi: Zubaan and International Development Research Centre.

Molyneux, Maxine. 2010. 'Justicia de Género, Ciudadanía y Diferencia En América Latina'. *Studia Histórica. Historia Contemporánea* 28: 181–211.

Moon, Claire. 2012. '"Who'll Pay Reparations on My Soul?": Compensation, Social Control and Social Suffering'. *Social & Legal Studies* 21 (2): 187–99.

Moosa, Zohra, Maryam Rahmani and Lee Webster. 2013. 'From the Private to the Public Sphere: New Research on Women's Participation in Peace-Building'. *Gender and Development* 21 (3): 453–72.

Moreno Camacho, Manuel Alejandro and María Elena Díaz Rico. 2016. 'Posturas En La Atención Psicosocial a Víctimas Del Conflicto Armado En Colombia'. *Agora U.S.B.* 16 (1): 193.

Mouffe, Chantal. 1992. 'Democratic Citizenship and the Political Community'. In *Dimensions of Radical Democracy: Pluralism, Citizenship, Community*, edited by Chantal Mouffe, 225–39. London: Verso.

Mueller-Hirth, Natascha. 2017. 'Temporalities of Victimhood: Time in the Study of Postconflict Societies'. *Sociological Forum* 32 (1): 186–206.

Muggah, Robert. 2010. 'Innovations in Disarmament, Demobilization and Reintegration Policy and Research: Reflections on the Last Decade'. NUPI Working Paper, Oslo.

Muggah, Robert, and Chris O'Donnell. 2015. 'Next Generation Disarmament, Demobilization and Reintegration'. *Stability: International Journal of Security & Development* 4 (1): 1–12.

Murthy, Dhiraj. 2008. 'Digital Ethnography: An Examination of the Use of New Technologies for Social Research'. *Sociology* 42 (5): 837–55.

Mwambari, David. 2019. 'Local Positionality in the Production of Knowledge in Northern Uganda'. *International Journal of Qualitative Methods* 18: 1–12.

Myrttinen, Henri. 2003. 'Disarming Masculinities'. *Disarmament Forum* 4: 37–46.

Myrttinen, Henri, Lana Khattab and Jana Naujoks. 2017. 'Re-Thinking Hegemonic Masculinities in Conflict-Affected Contexts'. *Critical Military Studies* 3 (2): 103–19.

Nagy Hesse-Biber, Sharlene. 2012. 'Feminist Research: Exploring, Interrogating, and Transforming the Interconnections of Epistemology, Methodology and Method'. In *The Handbook of Feminist Research*, edited by Sharlene Nagy Hesse-Biber, 2nd edn, 2–26. Los Angeles: Sage Publications.

Nagy Hesse-Biber, Sharlene, and Deborah Piatelli. 2012. 'The Synergistic Practice of Theory and Method'. In *Handbook of Feminist Research: Theory and Practice*, edited by Sharlene Nagy Hesse-Biber, 176–86. Thousand Oaks: Sage Publications.

Nasi, Carlo. 2018. 'The Peace Process with the FARC-EP'. In *Truth, Justice and Reconciliation in Colombia: Transitioning from Violence*, edited by Fabio Andrés Díaz Pabón, 34–49. Abingdon: Routledge.

Neocosmos, Michael. 2006. 'Can a Human Rights Culture Enable Emancipation? Clearing Some Theoretical Ground for the Renewal of a Critical Sociology'. *South African Review of Sociology* 37 (2): 356–79.

Nguyen, Viet Than. 2016. *Nothing Ever Dies: Vietnam and the Memory of War*. Cambridge: Harvard University Press.

Ní Aoláin, Fionnuala. 2006. 'Political Violence and Gender during Times of Transition'. *Columbia Journal of Gender and Law* 15 (3): 829–49.

Ní Aoláin, Fionnuala, Dina Francesca Haynes and Naomi Cahn. 2011. 'Disarmament, Demobilization, and Reintegration (DDR) Programs'. In *On the Frontlines: Gender, War, and the Post-Conflict Process*, edited by Fionnuala Ní Aoláin, Dina Francesca Haynes and Naomi Cahn, 131–51. Oxford: Oxford University Press.

Nieto-Valdivieso, Yoana Fernanda. 2017. 'The Joy of the Militancy: Happiness and the Pursuit of Revolutionary Struggle'. *Journal of Gender Studies* 26 (1): 78–90.

Nodo de Saberes Populares Orinoco-Magdalena. 2018. *Guerrilleras: Testimonios de Cinco Combatientes de Las FARC*. Bogotá: NC Producciones.

Nordstrom, Carolyn. 1997. *A Different Kind of War Story*. Philadelphia: University of Pennsylvania Press.

Nwogu, N.V. 2010. 'When and Why It Started: Deconstructing Victim-Centered Truth Commissions in the Context of Ethnicity-Based Conflict'. *International Journal of Transitional Justice* 4 (2): 275–89.

O'Reilly, Maria. 2017. *Gendered Agency in War and Peace: Gender Justice and Women's Activism in Post-Conflict Bosnia-Herzegovina*. London: Palgrave Macmillan.

O'Rourke, Catherine. 2013. *Gender Politics in Transitional Justice*. Abingdon: Routledge.

Ocampo, Myriam, Pilar Baracaldo, Lorena Arboleda and Angélica Escobar. 2014. 'Relatos de Vida de Mujeres Desmovilizadas: Análisis de Sus Perspectivas de Vida'. *Informes Psicológicos* 14 (1): 109–28.

Olavarría, José. 2006. 'Men's Gender Relations, Identity, Work–Family Balance in Latin America'. In *The Other Half of Gender: Men's Issues in Development*, edited by Ian Bannon and Maria C. Correia, 29–42. Washington: World Bank.

Oliveira, Elsa. 2019. 'The Personal Is Political: A Feminist Reflection on a Journey into Participatory Arts-Based Research with Sex Worker Migrants in South Africa'. *Gender and Development* 27 (3): 523–40.

Olujic, Maria B. 1995. 'The Croatian War Experience'. In *Fieldwork under Fire: Contemporary Studies of Violence and Survival*, edited by Antonius C.G.M. Robben and Carolyn Nordstrom, 186–205. Berkeley: University of California Press.

Orozco, Iván. 2003. 'La Posguerra Colombiana: Divagaciones Sobre La Venganza, La Justicia y La Reconciliación' Working Paper. *Kellogg Institute for International Studies* 306: 1–75.

Otto, Dianne. 2010. 'Power and Danger: Feminist Engagement with International Law through the UN Security Council'. *The Australian Feminist Law Journal* 32: 97–121.

Paarlberg-Kvam, Kate. 2019. 'What's to Come Is More Complicated: Feminist Visions of Peace in Colombia'. *International Feminist Journal of Politics* 21 (2): 194–223.

Pailey, Robtel Neajai. 2016. 'Birthplace, Bloodline and Beyond: How "Liberian Citizenship" Is Currently Constructed in Liberia and Abroad'. *Citizenship Studies* 20 (6–7): 811–29.

Pankhurst, Donna. 2008. 'Post-War Backlash Violence against Women: What Can "Masculinity" Explain?' In *Gendered Peace: Women's Struggles for Post-War Justice and Reconciliation*, edited by Donna Pankhurst, 293–320. New York: Routledge.

Pateman, Carole. 1988. *The Sexual Contract*. Cambridge: Polity Press.

Pearce, Jenny. 1990. *Colombia: Inside the Labyrinth*. London: Latin America Bureau Research and Action.

Peláez Grisales, Holmedo. 2015. 'Una Mirada Al Problema de Los Sujetos y Grupos Desaventajados de Especial Protección En Colombia y La Apuesta Por Una Necesaria Fundamentación Teórica Desde Las Teorías Contemporáneas de La Justicia'. *Estudios Socio-Jurídicos* 17 (1): 125–68.

Peñaranda Currie, Isabel. 2020. 'Failure, Politics, and Regional Development: What Developmentalism and Infrastructure Reveal about Present "Post-Conflict" Programs'. PoLAR Online Emergent Conversation, no. 10. https://polarjournal.org/2020/11/24/failure-politics-and-regional-development-what-developmentalism-and-infrastructure-reveal-about-present-post-conflict-programs

Pieke, Frank N. 1995. 'Witnessing the 1989 Chinese People's Movement'. In *Fieldwork under Fire: Contemporary Studies of Violence and Survival*, edited by Antonius C.G.M. Robben and Carolyn Nordstrom, 62–80. Berkeley: University of California Press.

Pillow, Wanda S., and Chris Mayo. 2012. 'Feminist Ethnography: Histories, Challenges, and Possibilities'. In *The Handbook of Feminist Research*, edited by Sharlene Nagy Hesse-Biber, 187–205. Los Angeles: Sage Publications.

Pink, Sarah. 2007. *Doing Visual Ethnography*. 2nd edn. London: Sage Publications.

Planeta Paz. 2012. *La Cuestión Agraria En Colombia: Tierras Desarrollo y Paz*. Bogotá.

Ponic, Pamela, and Natasha Jategaonkar. 2012. 'Balancing Safety and Action: Ethical Protocols for Photovoice Research with Women Who Have Experienced Violence'. *Arts and Health* 4 (3): 189–202.

Portilla Benavides, Ana Cristina, and Cristián Correa. 2015. 'Estudio Sobre La Implementación Del Programa de Reparación Individual En Colombia'. Bogotá/New York: Centro Internacional para la Justicia Transicional.

Punch, Samantha. 2012. 'Hidden Struggles of Fieldwork: Exploring the Role and Use of Field Diaries'. *Emotion, Space and Society* 5 (2): 86–93.

Purdeková, Andrea. 2015. *Making Ubumwe: Power, State and Camps in Rwanda's Unity-Building Project*. New York: Berghahn Books.

Ramazanoglu, Caroline, and Janet Holland. 2002. *Feminist Methodology: Challenges and Choices*. London: Sage Publications.

Rayas Velasco, Lucía. 2009. *Un Análisis de Género Desde El Cuerpo de Las Mujeres Combatientes*. Mexico, DF: El Colegio de México.

Rettberg, Angelika. 2013. 'Victims of the Colombian Armed Conflict: The Birth of a Political Actor'. http://dx.doi.org/10.2139/ssrn.2317270

Reyes Posada, Alejandro. 1987. 'La Violencia y El Problema Agrario En Colombia'. *Análisis Político* 2: 30–46.

Richani, Nazih. 2002. *Systems of Violence: The Political Economy of War and Peace in Colombia*. Albany: State University of New York Press.

Robben, Antonius C.G.M. 1995. 'The Politics of Truth and Emotion among Victims and Perpetrators of Violence'. In *Fieldwork under Fire: Contemporary Studies of Violence and Survival*, edited by Antonius C.G.M. Robben and Carolyn Nordstrom, 81–104. Berkeley: University of California Press.

Robben, Antonius C.G.M., and Carolyn Nordstrom. 1995. 'The Anthropology and Ethnography of Violence and Sociopolitical Conflict'. In *Fieldwork under Fire: Contemporary Studies of Violence and Survival*, edited by Antonius C.G.M. Robben and Carolyn Nordstrom, 1–24. Berkeley: University of California Press.

Robbins, Joel. 2013. 'Beyond the Suffering Subject: Toward an Anthropology of the Good'. *Journal of the Royal Anthropological Institute* 19: 447–62.

Robins, Simon. 2012. 'Transitional Justice as an Elite Discourse'. *Critical Asian Studies* 44 (1): 3–30.

Robins, Simon, and Eric Wilson. 2015. 'Participatory Methodologies with Victims: An Emancipatory Approach to Transitional Justice Research'. *Canadian Journal of Law and Society/Revue Canadienne Droit et Société* 30 (2): 219–36.

Rodríguez López, Maivel, Eleni Andreouli and Caroline Howarth. 2015. 'From Ex-Combatants to Citizens: Connecting Everyday Citizenship and Social Reintegration in Colombia'. *Journal of Social and Political Psychology* 3 (2): 171–91.

Roht-Arriaza, Naomi, and Katharine Orlovsky. 2009. 'A Complementary Relationship: Reparations and Development'. In *Transitional Justice and Development: Making Connections*, edited by Pablo De Greiff and Roger Duthie, 170–213. New York: Social Science Research Council.

Rosaldo, Renato. 2013. 'Cultural Citizenship in San Jose, California, 1994'. In *The Anthropology of Citizenship: A Reader*, edited by Sian Lazar, 75–8. Chichester: Wiley Blackwell.

Rose, Gillian. 2013. 'On the Relation Between "Visual Research Methods" and Contemporary Visual Culture'. *The Sociological Review* 61: 709–27.

Ross, Karen. 2015. '"No Sir, She Was Not a Fool in the Field": Gendered Risks and Sexual Violence in Immersed Cross-Cultural Fieldwork'. *Professional Geographer* 67 (2): 180–6.

Rubio-Marín, Ruth. 2012. 'Reparations for Conflict-Related Sexual and Reproductive Violence: A Decalogue'. *William & Mary Journal of Women and the Law* 19 (1): 69–104.

Rubio-Marín, Ruth, and Clara Sandoval. 2011. 'Engendering the Reparations Jurisprudence of the Inter-American Court of Human Rights: The Promise of the Cotton Field Judgment'. *Human Rights Quarterly* 33 (4): 1062–91.

Rudling, Adriana. 2019. '"I'm Not That Chained-Up Little Person": Four Paragons of Victimhood in Transitional Justice Discourse'. *Human Rights Quarterly* 41 (2): 421–40.

Rudling, Adriana. 2021. 'Now Is the Time to Reassess Fieldwork-Based Research'. Nature Human Behaviour 5: 967.

Ruiz González, Luis Enrique, María Mónica Parada Hernández and Rocío del Pilar Peña Huertas. 2019. 'Ciegos y Cojos Por Decisión Propia: Poder Infraestructural y Restitución En Colombia'. In *La Tierra Prometida: Balance de La Política de Restitución de Tierras En Colombia*, edited by Francisco Gutiérrez Sanín, Rocío del Pilar Peña Huertas and María Mónica Parada Hernández, 117–38. Bogotá: Editorial Universidad del Rosario.

Saeed, Huma. 2016. 'Victims and Victimhood: Individuals of Inaction or Active Agents of Change? Reflections on Fieldwork in Afghanistan'. *International Journal of Transitional Justice* 10 (1): 168–78.

Salcedo López, Diana. 2013. 'Género, Derechos de Las Víctimas y Justicia Transicional: Retos En Colombia'. *Revista Paz y Conflictos* 6: 124–51.

Sanchez Parra, Tatiana. 2018. 'The Hollow Shell: Children Born of War and the Realities of the Armed Conflict in Colombia'. *International Journal of Transitional Justice* 12 (1): 45–63.

Sánchez Salcedo, José Fernando, and Bernt Schnettler. 2022. 'Reconfiguring Spaces in FARC's Demobilisation Camps: The Cases of Tierra Grata and Pondores, Colombia'. *Visual Studies*. https://doi.org/10.1080/1472586X.2022.2059555

Sandoval, Clara, Hobeth Martínez-Carrillo and Michael Cruz-Rodríguez. 2022. 'The Challenges of Implementing Special Sanctions (Sanciones Propias) in Colombia and Providing Retribution, Reparation, Participation and Reincorporation'. *Journal of Human Rights Practice* 14 (2): 478–501.

Sandvik, Kristin Bergtora, and Julieta Lemaitre. 2015. 'From IDPs to Victims in Colombia: A Bottom-Up Reading of Law in Post-Conflict Transitions'. In *International Law and Post-Conflict Reconstruction Policy*, edited by Matthew Saul and James A. Sweeney, 251–71. London: Routledge.

Santamaría, Ángela, and Fallon Hernández. 2020. 'Fostering Solidarity for Gender/Ethnic Reincorporation: The Experience of Female Indigenous Ex-Combatants in Tierra Grata, Cesar'. *Journal of Gender Studies* 29 (2): 117–29.

Schmidt, Rachel. 2021. 'When Fieldwork Ends: Navigating Ongoing Contact with Former Insurgents'. *Terrorism and Political Violence* 33 (2): 312–23.

Schulz, Philipp. 2019. '"To Me, Justice Means to Be in a Group": Survivors' Groups as a Pathway to Justice in Northern Uganda'. *Journal of Human Rights Practice* 11 (1): 171–89.

Schulz, Philipp. 2020. 'Recognizing Research Participants' Fluid Positionalities in (Post-)Conflict Zones'. *Qualitative Research* 21 (4): 550–67.

Schulz, Philipp, and Anne-Kathrin Kreft. 2021. 'Researching Conflict-Related Sexual Violence: A Conversation between Early-Career Researchers'. *International Feminist Journal of Politics* 23 (3): 496–504.

Secretaría Técnica del Componente Internacional de Verificación CINEP/PPP-CERAC. 2020. 'Cuarto Informe de Verificación de La Implementación Del Enfoque de Género En El Acuerdo Final de Paz En Colombia'. Bogotá.

Sharp, Joanne. 2014. 'The Violences of Remembering'. *Area* 46 (4): 357–58.

Shnabel, Nurit, Samer Halabi and Masi Noor. 2013. 'Overcoming Competitive Victimhood and Facilitating Forgiveness through Re-Categorization into a Common Victim or Perpetrator Identity'. *Journal of Experimental Social Psychology* 49 (5): 867–77.

Shore, Cris, and Susan Wright. 2015. 'Audit Culture Revisited: Rankings, Ratings, and the Reassembling of Society'. *Current Anthropology* 56 (3): 421–44.

Sikkink, Kathryn, Phuong N. Pham, Douglas A. Johnson, Peter Dixon, Bridget Marchesi, Patrick Vinck, Ana María Rivera, Francisco Osuna and Keri Culber. 2015. 'Evaluación de Medidas Para Reparaciones Integrales En Colombia: Logros y Desafíos'. Cambridge: Harvard Kennedy School Carr Center for Human Rights Policy and Harvard Humanitarian Initiative.

Simić, Olivera. 2015. 'Wartime Rape and Its Shunned Victims'. In Amy E. Randall (ed) *Genocide and Gender in the Twentieth Century: A Comparative Survey*, 237–57. London: Bloomsbury.

Sjoberg, Laura. 2016. *Women as Wartime Rapists: Beyond Sensation and Stereotyping*. New York: New York University Press.

Sjoberg, Laura, and Caron E. Gentry. 2007. *Mothers, Monsters, Whores: Women's Violence in Global Politics*. London: Zed Books.

Sontag, Susan. 2003. *Regarding the Pain of Others*. New York: Picador.

Sontag, Susan. 2008. *On Photography*. London: Penguin Books.

Specht, Irma. 2013. 'Gender, Disarmament, Demobilization and Reintegration and Violent Masculinities'. In *Gender Violence in Armed Conflicts. IDN Cadernos No. 11*, 61–90. Lissabon: Instituto da Defensa Nacional.

Specht, Irma, and Larry Attree. 2006. 'The Reintegration of Teenage Girls and Young Women'. *Intervention* 4 (3): 219–28.

Sriram, Chandra Lekha, and Johanna Herman. 2009. 'DDR and Transitional Justice: Bridging the Divide?' *Conflict, Security & Development* 9 (4): 455–74.

Stanley, Liz, and Sue Wise. 1993. *Breaking Out Again: Feminist Ontology and Epistemology*. 2nd edn. London: Routledge.

Steele, Abbey. 2017. *Democracy and Displacement in Colombia's Civil War*. Ithaca: Cornell University Press.

Sultana, Farhana. 2007. 'Reflexivity, Positionality and Participatory Ethics: Negotiating Fieldwork Dilemmas in International Research'. *ACME: An International E-Journal for Critical Geographies* 6 (3): 374–85.

Swaine, Aisling. 2018. *Conflict-Related Violence against Women: Transforming Transition*. Cambridge: Cambridge University Press.

Tabak, Shana. 2011. 'False Dichotomies of Transitional Justice: Gender, Conflict and Combatants in Colombia'. *International Law and Politics* 44: 103–63.

Tajfel, Henri. 1974. 'Social Identity and Intergroup Behaviour'. *Social Science Information* 13 (2): 65–93.

Tate, Winifred. 2007. *Counting the Dead: The Culture and Politics of Human Rights Activism in Colombia*. Berkeley: University of California Press.

Tate, Winifred. 2018. 'Paramilitary Politics and Corruption Talk in Colombia'. *Culture, Theory and Critique* 59 (4): 419–41.

Tate, Winifred. 2020. 'Anthropology of Policy: Tensions, Temporalities, Possibilities'. *Annual Review of Anthropology* 49: 83–99.

Taussig, Michael. 2003. *Law in a Lawless Land: Diary of a Limpieza in Colombia*. Chicago: University of Chicago Press.

Taylor, Lucy. 2004. 'Client-Ship and Citizenship in Latin America'. *Bulletin of Latin American Research* 23 (2): 213–27.

Teitel, Ruti G. 2001. *Transitional Justice*. Oxford: Oxford University Press.

Teitel, Ruti G. 2003. 'Transitional Justice Genealogy'. *Harvard Human Rights Journal* 16 (69): 69–94.

Teo, Thomas. 2010. 'What Is Epistemological Violence in the Empirical Social Sciences?' *Social and Personality Psychology Compass* 4/5: 295–303.

Theidon, Kimberly. 2003. 'Disarming the Subject: Remembering War and Imagining Citizenship in Peru'. *Cultural Critique* 54: 67–87.

Theidon, Kimberly. 2007a. 'Gender in Transition: Common Sense, Women and War'. *Journal of Human Rights* 6 (4): 453–78.

Theidon, Kimberly. 2007b. 'Transitional Subjects: The Disarmament, Demobilization and Reintegration of Former Combatants in Colombia'. *International Journal of Transitional Justice* 1 (1): 66–90.

Theidon, Kimberly. 2009. 'Reconstructing Masculinities: The Disarmament, Demobilization, and Reintegration of Former Combatants in Colombia'. *Human Rights Quarterly* 31 (1): 1–34.

Theidon, Kimberly. 2013. *Intimate Enemies: Violence and Reconciliation in Peru*. Philadelphia: University of Pennsylvania Press.

Theidon, Kimberly. 2014. '"How Was Your Trip?" Self-Care for Researchers and Writers Working on Violence'. *Social Science Research Council – Working Papers* 2: 1–17.

Thomas, Siân Natasha, Sanne Weber and Caroline Bradbury-Jones. 2020. 'Using Participatory and Creative Methods to Research Gender-Based Violence in the Global South and with Indigenous Communities: Findings from a Scoping Review'. *Trauma, Violence, and Abuse* 23 (2): 342–55.

Thomson, Marilyn. 2002. 'Boys Will Be Boys: Addressing the Social Construction of Gender'. In *Masculinities Matter! Men, Gender and Development*, edited by Frances Cleaver, 166–85. London: Zed Books.

Thornton Dill, Bonnie, and Marla H. Kohlman. 2012. 'Intersectionality: A Transformative Paradigm in Feminist Theory and Social Justice'. In *The Handbook of Feminist Research*, edited by Sharlene Nagy Hesse-Biber, 2nd edn, 154–74. Los Angeles: Sage Publications.

Thylin, Theresia. 2018. 'Leaving War and the Closet? Exploring the Varied Experiences of LGBT Ex-Combatants in Colombia'. *Women, Gender & Research* 2–3: 97–109.

Touquet, Heleen, and Philipp Schulz. 2020. 'Navigating Vulnerabilities and Masculinities: How Gendered Contexts Shape the Agency of Male Sexual Violence Survivors'. *Security Dialogue* 52 (3): 213–30.

Tuck, Eve. 2009. 'Suspending Damage: A Letter to Communities'. *Harvard Educational Review* 79 (3): 409–28.

Tuck, Eve, and Monique Guishard. 2013. 'Uncollapsing Ethics: Racialized Sciencism, Settler Coloniality and an Ethical Framework of Decolonial Participatory Action Research'. In *Challenging Status Quo Retrenchment: New Directions in Critical Research*, edited by Tricia M. Kress, Curry Malott and Bradley J. Porfilio, 3–28. Charlotte: Information Age Publishing.

Tuhiwai Smith, Linda. 2012. *Decolonizing Methodologies*. 2nd edn. London: Zed Books.

Turner, Joe. 2016. '(En)Gendering the Political: Citizenship from Marginal Spaces'. *Citizenship Studies* 20 (2): 141–55.

Turner, Terence. 1992. 'Defiant Images: The Kayapo Appropriation of Video'. *Anthropology Today* 8 (6): 5–16.

Ugarriza, Juan Esteban, and Rafael Camilo Quishpe. 2019. 'Guerrilla Sin Armas: La Reintegración Política de La FARC Como Transformación de Los Comunistas Revolucionarios En Colombia'. In *Excombatientes y Acuerdo de Paz Con Las FARC-EP En Colombia: Balance de La Etapa Temprana*, edited by Erin McFee and Angelika Rettberg, 135–62. Bogotá: Ediciones Uniandes.

Unidad de Restitución de Tierras. 2021. 'Avances de Restitución. Corte 31 Mayo 2021'. www.restituciondetierras.gov.co/inicio

United Nations General Assembly. 2005. 'Basic Principles and Guidelines on the Right to a Remedy and Reparation'. General Assembly Resolution 60/147 of 16 December 2005.

United Nations Inter-Agency Working Group on Disarmament Demobilization and Reintegration. 2006. 'Module 5.10: Women, Gender and DDR'. *Integrated Disarmament, Demobilisation and Reintegration Standards* (IDDRS). www.unddr.org/uploads/documents/IDDRS 5.10 Women, Gender and DDR.pdf

Uprimny Yepes, Rodrigo. 2009. 'Transformative Reparations of Massive Gross Human Rights Violations: Between Corrective and Distributive Justice'. *Netherlands Quarterly of Human Rights* 27 (4): 625–47.

Vastapuu, Leena, illustrated by Emmi Nieminen. 2018. *Liberia's Women Veterans: War, Roles and Reintegration*. London: Zed Books.

Vázquez, Norma. 1997. 'Motherhood and Sexuality in Times of War: The Case of Women Militants of the FMLN in El Salvador'. *Reproductive Health Matters* 5 (9): 139–46.

Vegh Weis, Valeria. 2017. 'The Relevance of Victims' Organizations in the Transitional Justice Process: The Case of the Grandmothers of Plaza de Mayo in Argentina'. *Intercultural Human Rights Law Review* 60: 1–70.

Vergel Tovar, Carolina. 2011. 'El Concepto de Justicia de Género: Teorías y Modos de Uso'. *Revista de Derecho Privado* 21: 119–46.

Viaene, Lieselotte. 2011. 'Dealing with the Legacy of Gross Human Rights Violations in Guatemala: Grasping the Mismatch between Macro Level Policies and Micro Level Processes'. *The International Journal of Human Rights* 15 (7): 1160–81.

Visual Sociology Study Group of the British Sociological Association. 2006. 'Statement of Ethical Practice for the British Sociological Association – Visual Sociology Group'. Durham: British Sociological Association.

Viveros Vigoya, Mara. 2003. 'Contemporary Latin American Perspectives on Masculinity'. In *Changing Men and Masculinities in Latin America*, edited by Mathew C. Gutmann, 27–57. Durham: Duke University Press.

Waardt, Mijke De. 2013. 'Are Peruvian Victims Being Mocked?: Politicization of Victimhood and Victims' Motivations for Reparations'. *Human Rights Quarterly* 35 (4): 830–49.

Waardt, Mijke De. 2016. 'Naming and Shaming Victims: The Semantics of Victimhood'. *International Journal of Transitional Justice* 10 (3): 1–19.

Waardt, Mijke De, and Sanne Weber. 2019. 'Beyond Victims' Mere Presence: An Empirical Analysis of Victim Participation in Transitional Justice in Colombia'. *Journal of Human Rights Practice* 11 (1): 209–28.

Waardt, Mijke De, and Eva Willems. 2022. 'Recipients versus Participants: Politics of Aid and Victim Representation in Transitional Justice Practices in Peru'. *Human Rights Quarterly* 44 (2): 339–63.

Waldorf, Lars. 2009. 'Linking DDR and Transitional Justice'. In *Disarming the Past: Transitional Justice and Ex-Combatants*, edited by Ana Cutter Patel, Pablo De Greiff and Lars Waldorf, 14–34. New York: Social Science Research Council.

Waldorf, Lars. 2012. 'Anticipating the Past: Transitional Justice and Socio-Economic Wrongs'. *Social & Legal Studies* 21 (2): 171–86.

Walsh, Sinéad. 2019. 'Empathy as a Critical Methodological Tool for Peace Research'. In *Experiences in Researching Conflict and Violence: Fieldwork Interrupted*, edited by Althea-Maria Rivas and Brendan Ciarán Browne, 221–37. Bristol: Policy Press.

Wang, Caroline, and Mary Ann Burris. 1997. 'Photovoice: Concept, Methodology, and Use for Participatory Needs Assessment'. *Health Education & Behavior* 24 (3): 369–87.

Wang, Caroline, Jennifer L. Cash and Lisa S. Powers. 2000. 'Who Knows the Streets as Well as the Homeless? Promoting Personal and Community Action Through Photovoice'. *Health Promotion Practice* 1 (1): 81–9.

Weber, Sanne. 2018. 'From Victims and Mothers to Citizens: Gender-Just Transformative Reparations and the Need for Public and Private Transitions'. *International Journal of Transitional Justice* 12 (1): 88–107.

Weber, Sanne. 2021a. 'Defying the Victim–Perpetrator Binary: Female Ex-Combatants in Colombia and Guatemala as Complex Political Perpetrators'. *International Journal of Transitional Justice* 15 (2): 264–83.

Weber, Sanne. 2021b. 'From Gender-Blind to Gender-Transformative Reintegration: Women's Experiences with Social Reintegration in Guatemala'. *International Feminist Journal of Politics* 23 (3): 396–417.

Weber, Sanne. 2021c. 'The Personal and Socio-Economic Dynamics of Resilience and Transitional Justice in Colombia'. In *Resilience, Adaptive Peacebuilding and Transitional Justice: How Societies Recover after Collective Violence*, edited by Janine Natalya Clark and Michael Ungar, 187–209. Cambridge: Cambridge University Press.

Welsh, Alexandra. 2015. 'Women of the Jungle: Guerrilleras on the Front Lines of the FARC-EP'. *Glendon Journal of International Studies* 8 (1): 1–14.

Werbner, Pnina, and Nira Yuval-Davis. 1999. 'Introduction: Women and the New Discourse of Citizenship'. In *Women, Citizenship and Difference*, edited by N. Yuval-Davis and Pnina Werbner, 1–38. London: Zed Books.

Wessels, Michael G. 2016. 'Reintegration of Child Soldiers: The Role of Social Identity in the Recruitment and Reintegration of Child Soldiers'. In *Understanding Peace and Conflict through Social Identity Theory: Contemporary Global Perspectives*, edited by Shelley McKeown, Reeshma Haji and Neil Ferguson, 105–20. Cham: Springer.

Wiegink, Nikkie, Ralph Sprenkels and Birgitte Refslund Sørensen. 2019. 'Introduction: War Veterans and the Construction of Citizenship Categories'. *Conflict and Society* 5 (1): 72–8.

Wiles, Rose, Jon Prosser, Anna Bagnoli, Andrew Clark, Katherine Davies, Sally Holland and Emma Renold. 2008. 'Visual Ethics: Ethical Issues in Visual Research'. ESRC National Centre for Research Methods Review Paper. http://orca.cf.ac.uk/25561/

Willems, Rens, and Mathijs Van Leeuwen. 2014. 'Reconciling Reintegration: The Complexity of Economic and Social Reintegration of Ex-Combatants in Burundi'. *Disasters* 39 (2): 316–38.

Williams, Sarah, and Emma Palmer. 2016. 'Transformative Reparations for Women and Girls at the Extraordinary Chambers in the Courts of Cambodia'. *International Journal of Transitional Justice* 10 (2): 311–31.

Williams, Timothy. 2018a. 'Agency, Responsibility, and Culpability: The Complexity of Roles and Self-Representations of Perpetrators'. *Journal of Perpetrator Research* 2 (1): 39–64.

Williams, Timothy. 2018b. 'Visiting the Tiger Zone – Methodological, Conceptual and Ethical Challenges of Ethnographic Research on Perpetrators'. *International Peacekeeping* 25 (5): 610–29.

Wilson, Kalpana. 2008. 'Reclaiming "Agency", Reasserting Resistance'. *IDS Bulletin* 39 (6): 83–91.

Wilson, Kalpana. 2010. 'Picturing Gender and Poverty: From Victimhood to Agency'. In *The International Handbook of Gender and Poverty*, edited by Sylvia Chant, 301–6. Cheltenham: Edward Elgar Publishing.

Wittman, Hannah. 2013. 'Reframing Agrarian Citizenship: Land, Life and Power in Brazil, 2009'. In *The Anthropology of Citizenship: A Reader*, edited by Sian Lazar, 149–62. Chichester: Wiley Blackwell.

Wolf, Diane L. 1996. 'Situating Feminist Dilemmas in Fieldwork'. In *Feminist Dilemmas in Fieldwork*, edited by Diane L. Wolf, 1–55. Boulder: Westview Press.

Wood, Elisabeth Jean. 2006. 'The Ethical Challenges of Field Research in Conflict Zones'. *Qualitative Sociology* 29 (3): 373–86.

Wright, Hannah. 2020. '"Masculinities Perspectives": Advancing a Radical Women, Peace and Security Agenda?' *International Feminist Journal of Politics* 22 (5): 652–74.

Yuval-Davis, Nira. 1997. 'Women, Citizenship and Difference'. *Feminist Review* 57 (1): 4–27.

Zambrano Quintero, Liliana. 2019. 'La Reincorporación Colectiva de Las FARC-EP: Una Apuesta Estratégica En Un Entorno Adverso'. *Revista CIDOB d'Afers Internacionals* 121: 45–66.

Žarkov, Dubravka. 2006. 'Towards a New Theorizing of Women, Gender, and War'. In *Handbook of Gender and Women's Studies*, edited by Kathy Davis, Mary Evans and Judith Lorber, 214–33. London: Sage Publications.

Žarkov, Dubravka. 2007. *The Body of War: Media, Ethnicity and Gender in the Break-Up of Yugoslavia*. Durham: Duke University Press.

Zuluaga-Sánchez, Gloria-Patricia, and Carolina Arango-Vargas. 2013. 'Mujeres Campesinas: Resistencia, Organización y Agroecología En Medio Del Conflicto Armado'. *Cuadernos de Desarrollo Rural* 10 (72): 159–80.

Zulver, Julia Margaret. 2021. 'The Endurance of Women's Mobilization during "Patriarchal Backlash": A Case from Colombia's Reconfiguring Armed Conflict'. *International Feminist Journal of Politics* 23 (3): 440–62.

Zulver, Julia, and Sanne Weber. 2020. 'Colombian Court Recognises Victims of Sexual Violence within Ranks of the FARC'. Open Democracy. www.opendemocracy.net/en/democraciaabierta/corte-colombiana-reconoce-a-víctimas-de-violencia-sexual-dentro-de-las-filas-de-las-farc-en

Index

References to figures appear in *italic* type; those in **bold** type refer to tables.

A

Active Citizens project 121, 139
active citizenship 4, 8, 14–16, 75, 99
 and clientelism 136
 and differential perspective 113, 118
 and gradations 129, 132–4, 138, 144
 and motherhood 157–8
 into passive citizenship 134
 and post-conflict gender equality 146, 154, 156, 160
 in practice 160–1
 transition, from passive citizenship 163
 and victimhood 168, 171, 176–8
 see also citizenship
agency 13–14, 55, 74, 133, 187
 and citizenship 14, 75
 collective, of women 158
 and innocent victimhood as narrative capital 85
 lack of 138
 as limited 161
 political *see* political agency
 recognition of 75
 silence as 83–4, 88
 and structural violence and poverty 139
 and victimization, as mutually exclusive 91
 and vulnerability 103
Agency for Reincorporation and Normalization (ARN) 26, 69, 94, 104–6, 121, 123–5, 131, 152
alcohol consumption 12, 67–8, 70, 88, 111
amnesties 7, 20, 21–2
anti-gender discourse 28
Arhuaco cultural tradition 56
armed clientelism 136
Asociación Nacional de Usuarios Campesinos (National Association of Tenant Farmers (ANUC)) 31, 64, 107
assistentalism 136–8, 168
audit culture
 overview 168–9
 and transitional justice 141–4, 155

Autodefensas Unidas de Colombia (United Self-Defence Forces of Colombia (AUC)) 19, 21

B

baby boom 16, 108, 156
Baines, Erin 79
basic services, need for 33, 63, 65, 147, *147*, **148**
Berry, Marie E 120
blogs, significance of 198
Bloque Norte 33, 83
Bogotá 122, 133, 140, 160
Buchely, Lina 96
Butler, Judith 198

C

Camino Diferencial de Vida programme 80
Caribbean coast, research on 31–7
 participatory visual approach 41–7
 research methods 37–41
Cartagena 133
cattle farming 31, 33, 59, 108, 109, *110*, 120, 133, 172–3
chicken projects 111, 118–19, 122, 138, *150*
cinco claves campaign 80
citizenship 132–6
 and agency 14, 75
 agrarian 132, 133
 clientelism and assistentalism as obstacles to 136–8
 experiences of 130–2
 gendered 2–3, 99, 125, 162, 177
 precarious 96
 and reparation and reintegration bureaucracies 138–44
 significance of 7–8, 129
 status and practice, differences between 8
 time as crucial to 162
 undermining of practices of 123
 see also active citizenship; post-conflict gender equality; radical citizenship

232

INDEX

clientelist system 129, 135, 136–8, 146
CODHES 118
collective action 123, 133, 169, 175
  and collective identity 171
  and post-conflict gender equality 146, 158, 163
  and social cohesion 92
collective agency
  political 134
  of women 158, 169, 171
collective identity 96, 171, 177
collective reincorporation 2, 26, 44, 65, 131, 132, 169
  see also reincorporation process
collective reintegration 166
  see also reintegration process
collective reparation 1, 4, 83, 133
  and differential perspective 102–3, 114–15, 118
  and reconciliation 23, 24, 26, 27, 34, 43
  see also reparation process
Colombian Commission for the Clarification of Truth, Coexistence and Reconciliation (CEV) 20, 25, 30, 81, 86, 95, 117, 170
Common Alternative Revolutionary Force 26
complex political perpetrators 79, 95–7
complex political victims 78–9, 95–7
Comprehensive System of Truth, Justice, Reparation and Non-Repetition 25
Conejo 93, 98, 124–6, 140
Connell, R.W. 52
Conpes 3784 policy 102
Conpes 3931 policy 104
Constitutional Court 29, 80, 81
Corporacion Juridica Yira Castro (CJYC) 183, 195
La Costa 31, 34, 47
  clientelism in 136
  culture of 51–2
'Cotton Field' decision 5
COVID-19 pandemic, impact of 46, 47, 62, 97, 191, 199, 200
cross-categorization 93, 95

D

demobilization 5, 20, 33, 59, 61, 90
  of AUC 21–2
  consequences of 12, 17, 35
  of FARC 26, 44, 111
  see also disarmament, demobilization and reintegration (DDR) process
differential perspectives 101–6, 113, 115, 127
direct violence 4–5, 78, 84
disarmament, demobilization and reintegration (DDR) process 1–2, 5–6, 12, 20, 49, 77, 96, 103, 142, 155, 166–7, 174, 177
  and development 26

and FARC *see Fuerzas Armadas Revolucionarias de Colombia* (Revolutionary Armed Forces of Colombia) (FARC)
gender perspectives in 10–11, 12, 100, 103–4, 127–8, 162, 172
goals of 6
and Justice and Peace Law 21
participation monitoring 142
productivity projects 122
staff, treatment of 126
supporting organizations in 155, 173
and transitional justice 3–8, 14–15, 26, 93
and understanding of local dynamics 125
displacement 1, 59, 103, 130, 133, 185
  forced 20, 46
  and gender roles during conflict 53–5
  gendered impacts of 81
  and gendered victim–perpetrator dichotomy 79–83, 90, 91, 93–4
  and hegemonic masculinity 55
  and reconciliation 19, 20, 22, 23, 29, 33, 42, 44
  and vulnerability 103
  see also internally displaced persons (IDPs)
disruptive politics 158
drug trade, and guerrilla movements 18–19, 33, 35
drug trafficking 19, 21–2, 24, 194
Duque, Iván 24, 31

E

education, importance of 147, 149, 151–2
Ejército de Liberación Nacional (National Liberation Army) (ELN) 18, 25, 30
El Salvador 156
Entrelazando programme 106
'entrepreneurial mum' initiative 61
epistemological violence 193
ETCR *see* territorial space for training and reincorporation (ETCR)
ethics
  checklist, for gender and conflict research 179–82, **180–1**
  and field research as finished 196–200
  fundamental considerations in 191–6
  practical 182–91
  procedural 184–6
  and safety 188–90
  visual 186–8
ethnography, importance of 39, 41, 45, 47
ex-combatants
  of FARC 34–6, 41, 44–5, 85–7, 93, 107, 111, 116, 139
  female 44–6, 81, 85–8, 107, 113, 114, 124–5, 134, 151, 155
  LGBTQ rights 114
  male 11–12, 86, 87
  portrayal, as victims 89–90
  reincorporation process for 131

F

farianas 90, 91, 107–8, 124, 125
farming 31, 33, 35, 59, 109–12, *110*, 120, 132–3, 140, 150, 152, 173–4
fatherhood, significance of 55, 108, 157–8, 171, 177
femininities 57, 106–14, 127
  see also motherhood
Finca Nueva Colombia 111
Fonseca, map of *34*
forced displacement 20, 46
Fraser, Nancy 13, 108, 119, 122, 127, 158, 167, 170
Fuerzas Armadas Revolucionarias de Colombia (Revolutionary Armed Forces of Colombia) (FARC) 1, 2, 18, 174
  abortions in 86
  active citizenship in 134
  and baby boom 108, 156
  and drug trafficking 19
  Gender Commission 160, 161
  and gender perspective 104
  and homosexuality 113
  as notorious 19
  peace negotiations with 20–1, 24–7
  reincorporation process/zone of 34–7, 44, 73, 74, 86, 87, 98
  and sexual violence 86, 87, 89–91
  victimhood narrative of 82
  and victim–perpetrator dichotomy 85
  women in 56–9, 71, 107–8, 114

G

Galtung, J. 4
gender, in practice 114–18
  and good intentions having intended consequences 122–7
  as women's projects 118–22
gender equality 2, 125, 128, 134
  and *machismo* and motherhood 56–8, 71
  post-conflict 15, 16, 146–64
  and victimhood and citizenship 165, 167, 169, 170, 174, 178
  and violence and reconciliation 30, 41, 45
gender justice 16, 50, 108, 122, 127, 162, 165
  and recognition 170–2, 177
  and redistribution 172–4, 177
  and representation 174–6, 177
  theory and practice of 170–6
  transformative 12–15, 69
  see also citizenship
Gender Subcommission 27–8, 104
Gender Table 105
gendered changes 49–50
  conflict-related 50–9
  and *machismo* and violence 67–71
  and organization and decision-making 64–7

and positive changes 71–5
and post-conflict situation 59–64
and roles, during conflict 52–9
Gibney, Matthew J. 130
Gillam, Lynn 184, 191
grey zone, of people 78, 80
La Guajira 2, 27, 34, 105, 121–2, 140, 144, 155
Guatemala 151, 156, 182, 183
guerrilla movements 1, 10, 135, 151, 156, 174
  and drug boom 18–19
  formation and establishment of 18–21
  and gender equality 57–8
  government's peace negotiation initiatives 20–1, 24–7, 30
  and *machismo* and motherhood 56–60, 66, 73
  professionalization of 18–19
  and reconciliation 23, 25, 30, 44
  and victim–perpetrator dichotomy 84, 87, 96
  see also Fuerzas Armadas Revolucionarias de Colombia (Revolutionary Armed Forces of Colombia) (FARC)
Guillemin, Marilys 184, 191

H

hegemonic masculinity 12, 52, 69, 70, 86, 158
  and displacement 55
  and heteronormativity 114
  and paternity 171
High Council for Reintegration (ACR) 26, 104
High-Level Agency for Gender 105
historical memory 34, 74, 115, 171
  and agency 96
  collective 43
Hogg, Michael A. 93
homologation of knowledge 151–2
homophobia 114
human rights 138, 182, 183, 190
  and active citizenship 134
  processes, women in 103
  violations 3–4, 19, 22, 25, 79, 80
Humanas 80

I

ideal victims 78, 84
Indigenous people 23, 35, 39, 50, 56, 81, 87
innocent victimhood 84–5
insurgent feminism 74
insurgent masculinities 57, 73, 106, 113, 157, 158
Integrated Disarmament Demobilization and Reintegration Standards (IDDRS) 11
Inter-American Court of Human Rights 5
internally displaced persons (IDPs) 1, 6, 15, 16, 23, 24, 27, 44, 49, 79, 82, 96, 130, 138
  see also displacement

INDEX

intersubjectivity, idea of 71
intra-family violence 20, 81, 88–90

J

Justice and Peace Law (JPL) 21–2, 100

L

Land Fund 27
land occupation 31, 52, 134, 169
  as radical citizenship 132
  women's role in 132–3
land restitution process 1, 20, 23–4, 33–4, 72, 143, 166, 183
  and differential perspective 101, 102, 108, 109
  and victim–perpetrator dichotomy 80, 82, 83, 94
Land Restitution Unit (LRU) 23, 101, 102, 114, 118, 126
LGBTQ persons 27–30, 86, 113, 114, 115, 127
Liberia 11

M

machismo 49, 52, 67–71, 74, 84, 116, 133, 167, 189
  see also masculinities; patriarchy
MacKenzie, Megan 7
Magdalena 33, 105, 126
Márquez, Francia 30
masculinities 30, 75, 104, 127, 139, 163
  caring 61, 157, 162
  crisis of 11–12
  and gendered changes across war and peace 45, 49, 68
  hegemonic 12, 52, 55, 69, 70, 86, 114, 158, 171
  insurgent 57, 73, 106, 113, 157, 158
  militarized, transforming 11, 12, 22
  new 72, 73, 112–14
  nostalgia 55
  and reparation, reintegration, and transformation 2, 8, 15, 16
  representation of 106–14
  and victimhood 167–9, 172, 174
  see also machismo; patriarchy
material reparations 24, 130
McEwan, Cheryl 132
memory 83, 194
  community 195
  historical 34, 43, 74, 96, 115, 171
  and innocent victimhood 85
  painful 55
  social 75
  visual 44
miscommunications, in women's projects 123–5
motherhood 16, 50, 51, 106–8, 144, 154
  as complex 169

and *farianas* 107
feeling of failing in roles of 54
and guerrilla membership 58–9
and *salir adelante* 155–6
teenage 156–7
mujerismo (womanism) 116, 174

N

national action plan (NAP), WPS Agenda 30, 117, 125, 170, 175
National Centre for Historical Memory (NCHM) 23, 43, 126, 195
National Protection Unit (NPU) 61, 112
National Reincorporation Commission 105
National Summit of Women for Peace 27
negative peace 4–5
new masculinities 72–3, 112–14
Nwogu, N.V. 92

P

PAIPI programme 137
La Palizua 31, 33, 71–2, 109, 115, 137
  homosexuality in 114
  house in 37
  land occupation in 132
  women's projects and outcomes in 118–20
Palmer, Emma 174
paramilitary groups 1, 60, 103–5, 133
  and reconciliation 19–23, 25, 33, 35
  and victim–perpetrator dichotomy 80, 82–4, 91, 93–4
parapolítica scandal 19, 22
participatory research 41–7
passive citizenship 134, 144, 145, 158, 164
passivity 13, 77, 96, 132, 138, 169
Pateman, Carole 50
paternalist welfare programmes 137
paternity, significance of 69, 171
patriarchy 2, 9–10, 12, 108, 177
  and *machismo* and motherhood 50–2, 61, 65, 70–1
  and reconciliation 23, 39, 42
  and victim–perpetrator dichotomy 84, 87, 90
  see also machismo; masculinities
PDETs *see* territorial rural development plans (PDETs)
peace and conflict, gendering 8–10
  and post-conflict situations 10–12
  and sexual violence 9–10
  and transformative gender justice 12–14
peacemakers, women as 106–8
peasants 18–20, 31, 50, 52, 55, 64, 72, 82, 96, 109, 111, 122, 126, 132, 169
perpetrators
  complex political 79, 95–7
  as victims, possibility of 78, 85–91
  see also victim–perpetrator dichotomies
Petro, Gustavo 30

235

photovoice process 42–4, 46, 54–5, 60, 71, 195
physical harm and violence, against
  women 68
La Pola 31, 33, 64, 67, 72, 115, 150
  audit culture in 143–4
  house in 36
  land occupation in 132
  women's projects and outcomes in 118–20, 122–3
political agency 9, 12, 167
  autonomous 136
  collective 134
  weakening of 137
post-conflict formula 7
post-conflict gender equality 146, 182
  and gendered dreams for future and reality 146–58
  and participation, organization, and collective political agency 158–63
post-conflict programme crisis 10–12
poverty 12, 14, 81, 90, 91, 120, 151, 153
  and displacement 20
  extreme 46, 93, 187, 197
  overcoming 138, 147, 149, 154
  and passivity 138
  and structural violence 138, 139
precarious citizenship 96
Presidential Office for Women 104
Pupo, Rodrigo Tovar 33
Purdeková, Andrea 31

R

radical citizenship 16, 132–4, 138, 145, 169
  see also citizenship
recognition 13, 81, 83, 93, 95, 104, 109, 150, 162, 163, 164, 170–2, 177
reconciliation policies 95–6
  and Caribbean coast 31–7
  and gendering of peace and justice 27–30
  and Justice and Peace Law 21–2
  and participatory visual research 41–7
  and peace with FARC 24–7
  and research methods 37–41
  significance of 17–21
  and Victims' Law 23–4
redistribution 5, 13, 16, 119, 122, 157, 162–3, 164, 172–4, 177
reincorporation process 134, 141, 151–3, 174, 185, 187
  collective 2, 26, 44, 65, 131, 132, 169
  and differential perspective 100, 108, 111–15, 117, 121, 127
  ethnic perspective of 87
  and gender 103–6
  and *machismo* and motherhood 61, 62, 69, 71, 73, 74
  rural 26, 65
  victim–perpetrator dichotomy 86–9, 93–4, 98

and violence, gender, and reconciliation 28, 29, 34, 35, 44–7
reinsertion support 5–6
reintegration process 2–7, 11, 12, 14, 16, 49, 76
  and citizenship gradations 129, 131, 136, 138–45
  and differential perspective 101–6, 116, 118
  and post-conflict gender equality 146, 151, 163, 164
  and reconciliation 21, 26, 29, 31, 35
  and victimhood and citizenship 165–70, 172–6
  see also reincorporation process; reparation process
reparation process 7, 100
  differential perspective of 101–6
  and gender in practice 114–27
  and masculinity and femininity representations 106–14
  see also collective reparation; reincorporation process; reintegration process
representation 13, 16, 18, 96, 99, 106, 128, 158, 164, 174–6, 177
re-traumatization, possibility of 192
Rosa Blanca 86
Rwanda 117

S

salir adelante (moving forward) principle 2–4, 14, 77, 127, 129, 146, 154–6, 165, 169, 175, 176
Sandino, Victoria 88
Santos, Juan Manuel 1, 21, 24, 25, 31, 42
security guards job 61, 112, 144, 172, 173
self-esteem, importance of 147, 149, 152, 158, 175, 176
sexual violence 13, 15, 20, 22, 28–30, 41, 68, 165–8, 170
  against ex-combatants 85–6
  and FARC 86, 87, 89–91
  fetishization of 29
  and gendered victim hierarchy 79–80
  hypes 9, 29, 41, 80–1, 83, 165
  as key gendered victimizing experience 81
  male 11–12
  prioritization of 9
  survivors of 102, 103, 168
  victims of 80–1, 88, 90, 101
shared experiences 93–7
silence, and agency 83–4, 88
Sisma Mujer 80
social cohesion 92, 123, 171
social identity 15, 79, 91–2, 93–7
social memory, gap in 75
social reintegration, significance of 6
  see also reintegration process
South African Truth and Reconciliation Commission (TRC) 7

Special Jurisdiction for Peace (JEP) 25–6, 30
Sri Lanka 11
staff, treatment of 126–7
Statement of Ethical Practice of the Visual Sociology Study Group of the British Sociological Association 188
structural inequalities 3, 5, 31, 43, 49, 61–4, 101, 134, 138
structural violence 83, 89, 90–5, 99, 102, 142
 absence of 5
 and gendered dynamics 167–8
 importance of 167–8
 and poverty 138, 139
 recognition of 94–5, 168, 171
 understanding of 93
stunted citizens 130
Subcommission on Gender 80
Subcommission on the End of the Conflict 28, 104
survivors 2, 4, 17, 31, 79, 83, 121, 133, 165–6, 194
 challenges 46
 and ex-combatants 93–4, 168, 169
 and JEP 25–6
 LGBTQ rights 114
 male 11, 171
 recognition of 93–4
 reintegration of *see* reintegration process
 reparations for *see* reparation process
 representation of 82, 99
 representatives of 23
 rights, lack of 21
 of sexual violence 9, 22, 102, 103
 state's commitment with 130, 142
 and TJ *see* transitional justice (TJ)
 victimhood 85, 91, 94–5
symbolic reparations 24, 80, 130

T

tailoring projects 11, 35, 61, 118, 139, 140–1, 150–3, *151*, 173
territorial rural development plans (PDETs) 27, 29, 131, 172
territorial space for training and reincorporation (ETCR) 34–5, 58, 61–2, 65–6, 98, 108, 111, 152, 185
 and agency 161–2
 and gender 115–16
 junta de acción comunal (community action board) 116
 positive changes for women in 73
 and reincorporation process 131
three Rs model *see* trivalent justice
Timochenko 1
total peace law 30
tourism projects 35, 45, 61, 66, 73, 87, 135, 139, 160, 161
transformative justice 5, 13, 119, 158

transitional justice (TJ) 2, 3–5, 77, 103, 118, 182
 and audit culture 141–4
 critique of 4–5
 and disarmament, demobilization and reintegration (DDR) process 3–8, 14–15, 26, 93
 and gender 12–14, 69
 gendered attention in 9
 and gendered gains 74–5
 participation monitoring 142
 and self-identity 96
 staff, treatment of 126
 supporting organizations in 155
 victim-centred 114
 victim–perpetrator hierarchies in 77–9
trivalent justice 13, 16, 74–5, 164, 167, 170
 see also recognition; redistribution; representation
truth commissions 4, 20, 25, 30, 81, 86, 95, 117, 170, 171
truth telling 4, 7, 21

U

Unión Patriótica (Patriotic Union) (UP) 20
Unit for the Search of Disappeared Persons 25
United Nations
 Development Programme (UNDP) 121
 Food and Agriculture Organization (UNFAO) 119–20, 123, 140
 Monitoring Mission 162
 Security Council Resolution 1325 11
Uribe, Alvaro 21, 25

V

veterinarians, women as 71, 72
victim participation, invited spaces for 133
victimhood 4, 5, 106
 gendered 82–5, 99
 and IDPs 82
 innocent 84–5
 and passivity 81, 134
 portrayal 92, 96, 97
 and radical citizenship 133
 as temporal identity 96
 transition to citizenship 165–78
victim–perpetrator dichotomies 77, 168
 ethics of researching 97–9
 and gendered victim categories in Colombia 80–91
 and hierarchies, in transitional justice 77–9
 and social identity 91–7
Victims' Law 1, 4, 23–4, 82, 92
 differential perspective of 101–3, 113, 115
 and gendered gains 75
 and land restitution 23–4, 109
 and participatory research 42
 and reconciliation 22, 29, 31, 36

reparation measures of 24
victim category in 80
Victims' Registry 81, 82
Victims' Unit (VU) 23, 24, 118
　Reparations Area 102–3
　and victimhood 82, 83
　Women's and Gender Group 80, 102, 103
vulnerability 10–12, 23, 46, 50, 170, 187, 193
　and agency 14
　-based understandings 103
　and differential perspective 101
　risk of 198

sexualized 9, 20, 81
and victim–perpetrator dichotomy 77, 82, 96

W

whataboutery, concept of 90
Williams, Sarah 174
Women, Peace and Security (WPS) Agenda 8, 9, 30, 117, 125, 169, 170, 175
Women and Land Programme 101–2
Women's Link Worldwide 90–1
wood-making workshops 35

www.ingramcontent.com/pod-product-compliance
Lightning Source LLC
Chambersburg PA
CBHW051537020426
42333CB00016B/1970